Book Reviews

Finally, a comprehensive exploration of our most exceptional learners that fills a critical twenty-year gap in the literature. This groundbreaking book masterfully weaves together rigorous research with authentic parent and practitioner voices and multicultural perspectives, creating a holistic portrait of highly to profoundly gifted children that extends far beyond IQ scores. Through compelling case studies and integration of Dabrowski's Theory of Positive Disintegration and asynchronous development, Els De Wit and Vanessa Wood illuminate the complex needs of these remarkable yet often invisible learners. Essential reading for teachers, counselors, psychologists, and parents—this book gives voice and visibility to a population that has been overlooked and misunderstood for far too long and transforms how we understand and support these extraordinary young minds.

—Keri M. Guilbault, Ed.D., Associate Professor and Director, Study for Exceptional Talent, Johns Hopkins University, School of Education and Center for Talented Youth (CTY)

This book provides a truly holistic view of highly–profoundly gifted individuals, emphasizing not only their cognitive abilities but also their social-emotional needs, intercultural contexts, and lived experiences. It highlights how being different from the average is simply another way of being human, and it brings this to life with vivid examples and powerful testimonials from experts and parents. The chapter on "philosophizing" stands out as an important contribution, offering a refreshing and supportive perspective on metacognition. As one of the few comprehensive works on this under-researched population, it is both insightful and inspiring—a valuable resource for educators, researchers, and families.

—Szilvia Fodor, Ph.D., Psychologist, Associate Professor, Eötvös Loránd University, Budapest, Hungary; Vice President, European Council for High Ability (ECHA)

A timely book that combines both truths with a call to give profoundly gifted children the peers, mentors, and opportunities they need to truly thrive. As a neuropsychologist working with gifted children and adults, I found Highly–Profoundly Gifted *both refreshing and courageous in its honesty. One of the most compelling themes is the historical context: how, across different eras, societies have resisted creating specialized education for the highly gifted—often out of fear of elitism, the perception of inequity, or concern that such children might disrupt the status quo. This reluctance persists despite the reality acknowledged in the book. From my professional perspective, I was particularly struck by how the book captures a critical truth: the human brain—and especially the gifted brain—has a profound drive to grow. When that need is unmet, it can become destructive, leading to mental health challenges. Too often, giftedness is missed entirely due to misdiagnosis, resulting in inadequate support and missed opportunities for development. Beyond its powerful message, the book serves as an accessible yet comprehensive guide—a small encyclopedia on the highly–profoundly gifted, including personal stories from parents. For many parents, these narratives will be invaluable in promoting insight, solutions, and a sense of belonging.*

—Iseult Beets, Ph.D., Neuropsychologist

Vanessa R. Wood, Els De Wit, and their contributors not only give readers a clear and concise explanation of profound giftedness but also offer a comprehensive and equitable framework for identifying giftedness and highly–profoundly gifted individuals. The richness and beauty of this book provide readers with a wide perspective of giftedness—from a theoretical perspective based on Dabrowski's Theory of Positive Disintegration, to a historical and sociocultural perspective, and an exploration into the lives of highly and profoundly gifted individuals across time and culture. I highly recommend this book to parents and educators who wish to recognize the signs of profound giftedness in their children and learn how to activate complex development to richer and higher levels.

—Krystyna Laycraft, Ph.D.,
The Center for C.H.A.O.S. Studies; Dabrowski Scholar

I highly recommend this book for those who want to learn and read more about giftedness. Even though the focus is on highly–profoundly gifted individuals, I see it as very rewarding for those interested in giftedness in general. Personally, I would like to use the first two parts as course material in a course on giftedness. These parts provide understanding and knowledge, well-founded in research, about the gifted individual. In part two, the reader also gets an understanding of the historical development of how the concept of giftedness has been used and influenced by political opinions. Testimonies from and about gifted individuals themselves make the theories and research come alive.

—Elizabet Mellroth, Ph.D., Senior Lecturer,
Karlstad University, Sweden; President, International Group for
Mathematical Creativity and Giftedness

Highly–Profoundly Gifted

Universal Understandings and Holistic Approaches

Els De Wit, MA and Vanessa R. Wood, Psy.D.

Gifted Unlimited, LLC

Edited by: Frances Irene Regan
Interior design: The Printed Page
Cover design: The Printed Page

Published by
Gifted Unlimited, LLC
12340 U.S. Highway 42, No. 453
Goshen, KY 40026
www.giftedunlimitedllc.com

ISBN: 978-1-953360-47-2

Printed and bound in the United States of America.

Dedication

Highly–Profoundly gifted children, adolescents, young adults, and families across the globe.

The International Gifted Consortium (IGC), Research Center for Highly–Profoundly Gifted.

The IGC is a 501c3, nonprofit organization engaging better understanding, identification, and support through open-access research, education-outreach, professional development, and educational programs designed to meet the distinctly unique social, emotional, physical, cognitive, and altruistic development of highly–profoundly gifted children, adolescents, young adults, and families. GiftedConsortium.org

Contents

Preface

You can find books and articles about guiding a gifted child and with a deep dive search you can find a handful of research articles specific to highly–profoundly gifted children. However, no books have been dedicated to exploring giftedness through the unique developmental paths and lived experiences of the highly–profoundly gifted. This resource addressed that significant void. Parents, teachers, and psychologists—those on the front lines—must be able to recognize, understand, support, and advocate for the highly and profoundly gifted children and adolescents in their care.

For years, I have counseled highly and profoundly gifted children and have consistently observed the same issue: the serious lack of accurate information and proper recognition. In 2020, I wrote the first book in Dutch on highly–profoundly gifted children. A book that purposefully stepped away from the prototype genius child, defined by cognitive ability alone. It was my aim to provide information to those who were unfamiliar with the holistic concept of giftedness and to ensure that the most pertinent questions are asked when inquiring with a counselor, therapist, or teacher. It was also my aim to ensure that you ask the right questions of yourself.

Parents were given a voice and once again, parents shared their stories. I am grateful to each one of them. The mountain to climb is not only a lonely walk for the child, the teenager, and the gifted adult, but also the entire entourage. Parents, teachers, counselors, and family members all embark on the search for support. It is often told that it is hard to find meaningful connection and camaraderie. Highly–profoundly gifted individuals experience distinct developmental differences and unique lived realities that are unfamiliar to most.

No matter what country you live in, when you are the parent of a gifted child, your worries are the same: how can I help my child? What will become of them? No matter what era you live in, when you are the teacher of a gifted child, your worries are the same: how can I recognize a gifted child and what do they need? No matter what the age of the gifted individual, they likely wonder, why don't I fit in?

Public perception of highly and profoundly gifted individuals is starkly different than the authentic reality of the highly–profoundly gifted individual. Words such as genius, mastermind, prodigy, whiz-kid are often used. This narrow and unrevealing view is portrayed throughout history and comes with preconceived notions. The lives of highly–profoundly gifted individuals are often misconceived as a continuous, upward trajectory. We typically only remember the ones that succeed; the other geniuses and whiz-kids disappear into oblivion. Yet, there are important questions to ask and lessons to uncover. Why didn't some become as successful as others? Did something go wrong? And, most importantly, what were *their* intended goals in life? In our society, it is rarely considered that a ground-breaking career in the spotlight may not be *their* desire or career choice.

This book aims to explore the lives of highly and profoundly gifted individuals across time and cultures, offering a more accurate portrayal of giftedness and what it truly means to be highly–profoundly gifted. We sought out experts who approach the topic with a holistic perspective, free from cultural bias. We purposely examine giftedness in specific cultures to provide different perspectives on the topic.

This book is meant to be kept by your bedside. Some chapters are very accessible and are easy to read. Other chapters are meant for those who want more, in-depth information. As you explore the uniqueness of the highly and profoundly gifted, turn to the chapters that best meet your needs along the way. Re-reading chapters throughout the process may also help you gather new insights and allow you to see things in a new light.

We begin with an exploration of Dabrowski's theory of positive disintegration—a holistic and affirming perspective on giftedness and human development. I follow with an explanation of Dabrowski's theory with *the minimal theory,* a theory I composed to break down the barriers to understanding. The theory aims to clarify the minimum you should know beyond cognitive ability. I strongly advise you to read this chapter multiple times, because Dabrowski's theory is known for its complexity and many layers.

There are a lot of lessons to be learned from history. How have people guided gifted children in the past and where did the children end up? As the first chapter reveals, many brilliant children were overlooked for their contributions and instead mischaracterized, sometimes even posthumously. A phenomenon we can still see today, but why is that? In the second chapter, we will discuss the gaps between highly–profoundly gifted people and society. How can highly–profoundly gifted individuals thrive in a society that is so different? The book concludes with an exploration of the needs and educational options for highly–profoundly gifted children, blending theory with practical insight. What children need in life, in school, and at home.

I firmly believe that we can learn a lot from each other. Instead of re-inventing the wheel, we can save a lot of effort by looking across borders and considering what happens there. In this book, we cross the globe to examine how different countries perceive giftedness and the highly–profoundly gifted population. With scholarly experts, we explore the solutions—or lack thereof—offered to support these individuals through schooling, holistic development, personal purpose, and future careers. Finally, we end with testimonials from parents. We listen to parents who get the challenges, struggles, and blisses of having one or more highly–profoundly gifted child. It provides a unique and comforting look at raising highly–profoundly gifted children. The perfect child at school who has an emotional meltdown once he opens the front door. The happy kid at parties who comes home exhausted from all the noise and "childish" games. And the child who was able to pull through because of that one teacher who really got them. The challenges and life lessons shared by these parents will help guide you through your own journey, offering both recognition and support along the way.

Els De Wit

Acknowledgment

We wish to thank the contributors from all over the world for sharing their experiences. You immediately stepped in and were as delighted as we were to write this book. We are grateful for your enthusiasm throughout the process. Thank you for your advice, for thinking alongside us, and for providing resources.

Thank you to the gifted adults and all the parents for finding the courage—and time to share your personal experiences. We are convinced that readers will find your words and experiences strengthening in their own journey. We thank Gifted Unlimited, LLC who immediately supported the concept of this book. Our sincere gratefulness goes out to those who found the time to read the manuscript and provide insightful advice on how to make the experience for the reader even better.

Special thanks to:

- All the children and teenagers who share the journey and who have shared their authentic lived experiences with us.
- Nadine Van den Eynden-Morpeth, who unselfishly read through the manuscript and gave expert advice and continued mentorship.
- The International Gifted Consortium (IGC) for supporting this book from the very start.

Introduction

What is giftedness? And why is it essential that we, as a society, continue to seek understanding? First and foremost, giftedness is not a new development. The research literature spans over one hundred years. Psychologists, clinicians, educators, parents, and researchers have described tendencies, behaviors, and developmental patterns in gifted individuals that are different from their chronological aged peers. In the highly–profoundly gifted, these differences are *distinctly different* and are often marked by greater-than-typical sensitivities, intensities, and awareness referred to as *excitability*. Psychologist and psychiatrist, Dr. Kazimierz Dabrowski helped us identify these greater-than-typical responses of the nervous system through the term *overexcitability*. His human development theory explains the development, developmental potential, and influence of overexcitabilities—and the marked developmental difference in the combination of multiple overexcitabilities.

This theory was instrumental in combining research and knowledge into explainable understanding based on human development. We must use this foundational understanding to further explore the depths of human development and experience. Anne Beneventi, Director of the Annemarie Roeper Method of Qualitative Assessment, reminds us, "the only instrument complex enough to understand a human being is another human being."

Together, we explore the perceptions of giftedness and human experience across cultures and across time. We visit the United States of America, Belgium, Germany, Sweden, South Korea, France, Finland,

Ireland, Turkey, and Slovenia. Through our travels, across the globe, we challenge you to not only seek the differences, but to also recognize the similarities. Many of which are disheartening. We need to do better for our developing children, adolescents, and young adults. We have the knowledge; we have the understanding. We need to pursue even greater understanding, but more importantly, we need to embrace and implement into practice our existing understandings—now. The development, developmental potential, and most importantly, the well-being of our highly–profoundly gifted children, adolescents, young adults, and future contributors are at stake.

Dr. Vanessa R. Wood

Part 1
A Holistic View of Giftedness and Highly–Profoundly Gifted Individuals

Chapter 1

The Term Highly–Profoundly Gifted

Vanessa R. Wood, Psy.D. and Els De Wit, M.A.

How important is the level of giftedness? And why are there so many gifted terms? These are excellent questions. The level of giftedness can be very important, especially for the developing child and their educational needs. We must first ask ourselves, what is the goal of identification? How will identification benefit the well-being of my child, my student, or the adolescent in my professional care? Prior to 1997—the levels of giftedness were separated by IQ score and included: mildly gifted, moderately gifted, highly gifted, exceptionally gifted, and profoundly gifted.[1]

In 2000, The Davidson Institute, began serving profoundly gifted young people, identified with an IQ score of 145 or greater.[2] Today, the term *highly–profoundly gifted* refers to individuals at the highest levels of giftedness, typically scoring in the 99.6–99.99th percentile—less than 1% of the population. In this context, highly–profoundly gifted applies to children and adolescents with similar IQ percentile scores, as well as the most similar educational and developmental needs.[3]

To assess the appropriateness of the term *highly–profoundly gifted* in identifying and supporting these children's educational and developmental needs, one must first understand the inherent complexities of profound giftedness. In 2020, The International Gifted Consortium (IGC), Research Center for Highly–Profoundly Gifted defined *profound giftedness* through a historical literature review spanning nearly a century.[3] This definition integrated the works of Terman (1925), Hollingworth (1942), Dabrowski and Piechowski (1977), the Columbus Group (1991), Clark (1997), Gross (2004), and Webb et al. (2016).[4-10]

Profound giftedness is significant advanced cognitive abilities and development, as compared to those of peers in the chronological age group, experienced through heightened sensitivity, intensity, and awareness identifiable through social, emotional, physical, cognitive and/or altruistic behaviors, developmental milestones, and life experiences across the lifespan. This intuitive and often asynchronous, human development is at high risk of misunderstanding, misidentification, and misdiagnosis (the 3Ms), and requires support and scaffolding from like-minded peers, mentors, and practitioners to meet the profoundly gifted individual's exceptionally unique educational and developmental needs, and to provide fitting opportunities for positive growth and well-being.[3]

Human Development is Naturally Asynchronous

Giftedness can be understood within the framework of human development.[3] For the most inclusive identification of profound giftedness, both individual developmental potential and cognitive abilities must be considered. Development is often nonlinear and can occur at varying rates depending on the individual.[11,12] This unique developmental trajectory creates distinct strengths as well as relative weaknesses in comparison to those strengths. In profoundly gifted children, cognitive abilities and other areas of strength are exceptionally advanced—hence the term *profoundly gifted*.[3]

For a comprehensive assessment of profound human development, a qualitative assessment of a child's social, emotional, physical, cognitive, and altruistic-moral development must be included.[3] Qualitative assessment is valuable both independently and in conjunction with quantitative measures such as cognitive ability and achievement tests.[13] Anne Beneventi, Director of the Annemarie Roeper Method of Qualitative Assessment, stated, *"The only instrument complex enough to understand a human being is another human being."*[14] Qualitative assessment considers a child's tendencies, developmental milestones, life experiences, and developmental potential, offering a more holistic understanding of their unique growth trajectory.[3]

Developmental potential, as identified by psychologist and psychiatrist Kazimierz Dabrowski, is a crucial consideration alongside documented development and achievement. The assessment of developmental potential can help identify discrepancies in quantitative measurements.[3] According to Dabrowski, developmental potential encompasses family history, social and environmental influences, autonomous forces (such as strong independence and self-direction), overexcitabilities, and an individual's special abilities and talents.[10,11]

Current Gold Standard—Wechsler Intelligence Scale for Children, Fifth Edition (WISC-V)

Quantitatively, individuals who score in the 99.9th percentile on measures of cognitive ability are considered profoundly gifted.[2] The Stanford-Binet was once regarded as the gold standard for measuring cognitive ability.[4] Its higher subtest ceiling scores resulted in full-scale IQs that exceeded those possible on today's most widely accepted assessments.

Currently, the Wechsler Intelligence Scale for Children, Fifth Edition (WISC-V), is the most widely used and accepted IQ test for children.[15] A full-scale IQ score of 145 on the WISC-V corresponds to the 99.9th percentile and is considered indicative of profound giftedness. A full-scale WISC score of 160 is the highest possible score without extended norms and equates to the 99.99 percentile. On the WISC-V, a full-scale IQ score of 145–160 is considered profoundly gifted.[2]

IQ Tests Do Not Always Capture Profound Cognitive Abilities

To inclusively capture the multifaceted nature of profound giftedness, we must consider a child's social, emotional, physical, cognitive, and altruistic-moral development—as well as their developmental potential. A single quantitative measurement of cognitive ability does not inclusively identify profound giftedness. While an IQ test may identify profound cognitive ability, it does not capture the other dimensions of profound giftedness outlined above.[3]

Equally important to inclusively measuring profound giftedness is recognizing that IQ scores can underestimate profound cognitive ability.[3] Traditional IQ tests were not originally designed to identify individuals at this level of exceptionality. IQ tests were originally designed to identify profound disability. Due to the very nature of profound giftedness, an IQ test can be an underestimate of a profoundly gifted child's profound cognitive ability. IQ tests are not designed to account for the unique characteristics, tendencies, or overexcitabilities commonly exhibited by profoundly gifted children.[3]

Greater-than-Typical Sensitivities, Intensities, Awareness, and IQ Tests

Profoundly gifted children often exhibit heightened sensitivities, intensities, and awareness.[3] These amplified responses of the nervous system to both internal and external stimuli are known as overexcitabilities.[11,12] Overexcitabilities can manifest in various combinations of emotional, intellectual, imaginational, psychomotor, and sensory experiences. Overexcitabilities often excite, motivate, and propell responses, however, overexcitabilities can also create overwhelming feelings, inability to perform, perfectionism, or fear of failure. These extraordinary forces—sensitivities, intensities, and heightened awareness—can influence how a child participates in and responds to the testing process.[3]

In addition to their unique tendencies, the multiple overexcitabilities commonly seen in highly–profoundly gifted children can influence a range of environmental, interpersonal, and intrapersonal factors during the testing experience—factors that may, in turn, impact the resulting quantitative scores.[3] Some examples of these influences include the child's heightened sensitivity, intensity, and awareness of:

- the relationship, or lack thereof, with the test administrator
- the physical testing environment
- their own internal responses and reactions to the environment
- their physical and emotions and feelings on testing day
- other known or unknown exceptionalities

These factors and influences can affect the outcome of any test and should be considered qualitatively alongside quantitative scores.[3] The physical testing environment—along with the child's internal and external reactions and experiences on that particular day—are all critical variables that must be taken into account.

---

*The term **highly–profoundly gifted** acknowledges the potential for an underestimated IQ score due to overexcitabilities, a hallmark trait of profound giftedness.*

In some gifted children—particularly those who are highly–profoundly gifted—internal and environmental influences may significantly impact performance, leading to an underestimated IQ score. When subtest results do not align with what is known about the child, it becomes especially important to conduct a qualitative assessment of their overall development and developmental potential. This holistic and comprehensive approach is essential for the inclusive and accurate identification of giftedness, especially among highly–profoundly gifted children and adolescents.[3]

Highly–Profoundly Gifted | WISC-V IQ 140–160 | 99.6–99.99 Percentile

To support the most accurate identification of giftedness, the term *highly–profoundly gifted* has been adopted. This terminology offers a more inclusive representation of cognitive abilities, as well as the social, emotional, physical, intellectual, and altruistic-moral development and potential of these exceptional children.

Quantitatively, in terms of IQ scores, the term *highly–profoundly* gifted represents, the cognitive abilities of less than 1% of the population. Qualitatively, the term *highly–profoundly gifted* describes children who share similar traits, developmental patterns, and potential. Most importantly, for the well-being of highly–profoundly gifted children, it is important for us to realize that highly–profoundly gifted children have the most similar educational and developmental needs. The term *highly–profoundly gifted* serves the purpose of more inclusively identifying and addressing the educational and developmental needs of these children.

WISC-V IQ Scores 140–160 have Similar Educational and Developmental Needs

If the goal of gifted identification is to determine and to appropriately support the child's educational and developmental needs, then qualitative assessment is essential. An IQ score provides a starting point of reference for the further assessment of giftedness. Cognitive abilities at or near the 99.6 percentile indicate a very high level of giftedness. The term *highly–profoundly gifted* acknowledges that individuals scoring at or above the 99.6th percentile fall within this range—that is, between the 99.6th and 99.99th percentile—less than 1% of the population.

---

*The term **highly–profoundly gifted** shifts the focus away from a sole reliance on IQ scores—which may underestimate ability due to the very nature of profound giftedness—and instead emphasizes identifying the child's appropriate educational and developmental needs. Children within this range often share similar needs that must be accurately recognized and effectively supported.*

Level of Giftedness—Prior to 1997

At the 2017, World Council for Gifted and Talented Children Conference, Gross and Wood discussed the levels of giftedness—prior to 1997 and the levels of giftedness today. Prior to 1997—IQ scores of 180 or greater were possible. The level of giftedness was determined by IQ score using the ranges: mildly gifted (115-129), moderately gifted (130-144), highly gifted (145-159), Exceptionally gifted (160-179), profoundly gifted (180+). Miraca Gross reported, "unfortunately the test ceiling (the highest measurable score) on most individual IQ tests used nowadays is in the low 160s. We no longer have the capacity to measure intelligence quotients in the high 160s or beyond as was possible some 20 years ago."[1]

Levels of Giftedness—Today

The levels of giftedness—today include gifted and highly–profoundly gifted. *Highly gifted* and *profoundly gifted* may still be used today to differentiate IQ scores. However, if the purpose of identifying the level of giftedness is to best support the educational and developmental needs of the child, the term *highly–profoundly* best supports that aim. Children scoring in these ranges have the most similar educational and developmental needs. What about the term, *exceptionally gifted*? Once again, the term (like *highly gifted* and *profoundly gifted*) was used—prior to 1997 to further differentiate an IQ score at a time when IQ scores of 180 and above were obtainable.

On today's cognitive ability measures, IQ scores beyond 160 are not obtainable unless the assessor is using extrended norms which is not typical. The term, *highly–profoundly* gifted represents the narrow IQ range of this population, but more importantly, the term *highly–profoundly* gifted identifies the distinctly different educational and developmental needs of the children, adolescents, and young adults within this gifted population.

Term	Standard Deviations	IQ Score	Percentile
Norm	less than 1 standard deviation above norm	100-114	50 – 83.9
Above Norm	1 to under 2 standard deviations above the norm	115 - 129	84 – 97.9
Gifted	2 standard deviations above the norm	130 - 139	98 – 99.5
Highly–Profoundly Gifted	almost 3 to 4 standard deviations above the norm	140 - 160	99.6 - 99.99
Profoundly Gifted (Davidson Institute)	3 to 4 deviations above the norm	145 - 160*	99.9 - 99.99

*Greater than 160 with use of extended norms (not typically assessed)

Purpose of Identification is to Fulfill Educational and Developmental Needs

The purpose of identification is to fulfill the educational and developmental needs of the child. Gifted identification is not to simply assign the child a quotient that bears no benefit or intervention for the child. The term *highly–profoundly gifted* more inclusively identifies and supports the child's educational and developmental needs whereas an IQ is simply a label. When assessing the level of giftedness, full scale IQ scores and subtest scores need to be assessed carefully. This is especially true for scores near the 99th percentile and above. Children scoring in the mid to upper end of the 99th percentile have the most similar developmental and educational needs. One of which is like-minded peers. For this reason, the term *highly–profoundly* gifted is used.

Highly–Profoundly gifted is the updated term that acknowledges:

- Human development is naturally asynchronous and fluid. To inclusively identify profound giftedness, it is essential to consider an individual's overall development and developmental potential in conjunction with cognitive ability.

- The current gold standard for the identification of cognitive abilities in children is the WISC-V with a 160 maximum IQ score.
- IQ tests do not always capture the profound cognitive abilities of a profoundly gifted child; they can be an underestimate.
- Greater-than-typical sensitivities, intensities, and awareness—often exhibited by this population—can significantly affect their participation and responses.
- A WISC-V IQ of 140–160 equals the 99.6–99.99 percentile (less than 1% of the population).
- Children with WISC-V IQ scores of 140–160 have the most similar educational and developmental needs.
- Levels of Giftedness—Prior to 1997—are no longer obtainable.
- The purpose of identification is to fulfill the unique educational and developmental needs of the child

References

[1] Gross, M.U.M, & Wood, V.R. 2017. The Unique Barometers of Giftedness Through the Eyes. *World Gifted and Talented Conference*. Sydney, AU.

[2] Davidson Institute. n.d. Davidson Gifted. Accessed [September 2022]. https://davidsongifted.org.

Annals of Cognitive Science 4 [4] Terman, L. M. 1925. *Mental and physical traits of a thousand gifted children: Genetic studies of genius: Vol. 1.* Stanford, California: Stanford University Press.

[5] Hollingworth, L. S. 1942. *Children above 180 IQ (Stanford-Binet): Origin and Development.* Yonkers-on-Hudson, NY: World Book Company.

[6] Dąbrowski, K., & Piechowski, M. M. 1977a. *Theory of Levels of Emotional Development: Vol.1. Multilevelness and Positive Disintegration.* New York: Dabor Science Publications.

Dąbrowski, K., & Piechowski, M. M. 1977b. *Theory of Levels of Emotional Development: Vol. 2. From Primary Integration to Self-Actualization.* New York: Dabor Science Publications.

[7] Columbus Group. 1991. *Unpublished Transcript of the Meeting of the Columbus Group.* Columbus, Ohio.

[8] Clark, Barbara. 1997. *Growing Up Gifted.* Columbus, OH: Merrill..

[9] Gross, M. U. M. 2004. *Exceptionally Gifted Dhildren* 2nd ed. New York, NY: Routledge Falmer.

[10] Webb, J.T., Amend, E.R., Beljan, P., Webb, N.E., Kuzujanakis, M., Olenechak, R.F., Goerss, J., 2016. *Misdiagnosis and Dual Diagnoses of Gifted Children and Adults: ADHD, bipolar, OCD, Asperger's, depression, and other disorders.* Great Potential Press, Inc., 2nd edition.

[11] Dabrowski, K. 1972. *Psychoneurosis is Not an Illness.* London: Gryf Publications Ltd.

[12] Dabrowski, K. 1996. *Multilevelness of Emotional and Instinctive Functions.* Lublin: Towarzystwo Naukowe Katolickiego Uniwersytetu Lubelskiego.

Tessellations School World Council for Gifted and Talented Children Psychology in the Schools

Chapter 2

Highly–Profoundly Gifted and Overexcitabilities

Vanessa R. Wood, Psy.D.

Contrary to popular belief, giftedness is not academic intelligence (alone). By defining giftedness only through the limited lens of academic achievement, we risk missing its core nature and complexity.

Instead, intelligence is a manifestation of giftedness. The heightened ability to take in and interpret vast amounts of information. Giftedness embodies a different Operating System (OS)—an acutely aware, sensory oriented network. A different way of taking in, connecting, and interpreting information. Giftedness is a multi-dimensional, dynamic, free-spirited way of "being." An innate quality projected (or energized) by a heightened sense of awareness. An acute sense of the world. The ability to see the multitude of never-ending paths, connections, and interpretations.

Giftedness is a deep immersion in feelings and perceptions, paired with the ability to efficiently receive and interpret vast amounts of information. It reflects a heightened capacity to synthesize, reflect, and grow from within—a continual drive toward self-actualization. Giftedness is inherent, multi-dimensional, dynamic awareness.

Vanessa R. Wood, 2016

In a two-pronged literature review, Wood and Laycraft[1] found striking similarities between the characteristics, behaviors, and developmental patterns of the highly–profoundly gifted and those associated with overexcitabilities. This chapter explores the unique social, emotional, physical, cognitive, and altruistic traits of highly–profoundly gifted children, recognizing them through the lens of multiple, co-occurring overexcitabilities. Drawing on Dabrowski's human development theory, the theory of positive disintegration (TPD),[2,3] these heightened traits are examined in relation to the advanced—and often asynchronous—developmental trajectory of this population. Giftedness, human development, and potential are presented through the multidisciplinary experience of a psychologist, researcher, educator, program administrator, nonprofit advocate, and parent. *Wood's Assessment Model of Giftedness and Highly–Profoundly Gifted Individuals* is introduced.

Giftedness is Human Development and Potential

Whether giftedness is identified through innate ability, outward achievement, or a combination of both, it is essential to recognize it as a distinct pattern of human development.[1] Giftedness encompasses the whole individual—integrating social, emotional, physical, cognitive, and altruistic-moral development, along with their developmental potential. This potential serves as a unique blueprint for what an individual could realize under optimal social and environmental conditions.

Beyond advanced cognitive ability, giftedness encompasses advanced—and often asynchronous—social, emotional, physical, cognitive, and altruistic-moral development and potential. When supported by optimal social and environmental conditions, an individual's developmental potential can be activated. In such an ideal scenario, giftedness manifests as advanced growth and achievement across these domains.

This supportive environment can lead to high achievement by providing the conditions necessary for optimal growth. In turn, these conditions foster and sustain ongoing positive development.

Conversely, if the educational environment does not align with a child's educational and developmental needs, their developmental potential may be compromised.[1] For example, a child who lacks access to like-minded peers, mentors, or informed practitioners misses crucial opportunities for self-validation and mentorship.

The identification of giftedness lies in the perception of giftedness. If giftedness is only thought to be cognitive ability, then giftedness is a high IQ (intelligence quotient). If giftedness is only thought to be academic achievement, then giftedness is a high GPA (grade point average). However, when giftedness is viewed through a humanistic lens—as a unique, and at times radically unique, lived experience —it becomes clear that giftedness extends far beyond advanced cognitive abilities. It also encompasses advanced, and often asynchronous, social, emotional, physical, cognitive, and altruistic-moral development and potential.[1]

To properly assess the holistic, human nature of giftedness, we must uncover the individual's authentic characteristics and behaviors, along with their advanced and asynchronous social, emotional, physical, cognitive, and altruistic-moral development.[1] Additionally, evaluating the individual's developmental potential is essential for identifying discrepancies and recognizing opportunities for growth.

Giftedness is More Than Advanced Cognitive Ability and Achievement

An IQ score alone only assesses one component of giftedness, cognitive ability. An IQ score, when combined with an assessment of potentially advanced social, emotional, physical, cognitive, and/or altruistic-moral development and developmental potential, reflects the interconnected nature of giftedness.[1] This comprehensive approach supports a more equitable, holistic, and authentic identification of gifted individuals.

The pioneers in the study of giftedness and the highly–profoundly gifted population—Terman[4], Hollingworth[5], and Gross[6]—recognized that advanced cognitive development is not solely the result of intellectual ability, but rather the outcome of an interconnected relationship across all areas of development.[1] Despite this understanding, giftedness in U.S. school systems has largely been identified through a narrow, quantitative lens, relying primarily on academic achievement and group cognitive ability tests. There are no federal mandates supporting the identification of giftedness; instead, identification practices are determined at the state and local district levels.

Highly–Profoundly Gifted—Multifaceted Development

As discussed in the previous chapter, levels of giftedness have historically been defined strictly by IQ scores, with various terms—including moderately gifted, highly gifted, exceptionally gifted, and profoundly gifted. More recently, the term *highly–profoundly gifted* has been adopted by The International Gifted Consortium (IGC), Research Center for Highly–Profoundly Gifted, to shift the focus away from a unilateral reliance on IQ scores and to acknowledge the multifaceted, interconnected nature of profound giftedness.[1] In this broader context, cognitive ability and its connection to all areas of development—including social, emotional, physical, cognitive, and altruistic-moral—are considered, along with the individual's developmental potential.

We cannot overlook the authentic nature of profound giftedness or the lived experience of a highly–profoundly gifted child. Whether an individual is identified as highly gifted or profoundly gifted, both designations reflect significantly advanced cognitive ability in combination with advanced development and/or potential across multiple domains.[1]

Profound giftedness is statistically rare and occurs in .01% of the population according to the Bell curve. Quantitatively, the Davidson Institute defines profoundly gifted individuals as those who score in the 99.9th percentile on achievement and cognitive ability tests, corresponding to an IQ of 145 or higher on the WISC-V, the most widely accepted instrument for the measurement of cognitive ability in individuals 6 years and older.[7]

Perhaps more importantly, in recognizing the authentic nature and diversity of highly–profoundly gifted students, The International Gifted Consortium, Research Center for the Highly–Profoundly Gifted, defined the distinct qualitative differences commonly observed within this population. Profound giftedness is:

- significant advanced cognitive abilities and development, as compared to those of peers in the chronological age group
- experienced through heightened sensitivity, intensity, and awareness
- identifiable through social, emotional, physical, cognitive and/or altruistic-moral behaviors, developmental milestones, and life experiences across the lifespan
- intuitive and often asynchronous, human development
- at high risk of misunderstanding, misidentification, and misdiagnosis (the 3Ms)

Profound giftedness requires support and scaffolding from like-minded peers, mentors, and practitioners to meet the profoundly gifted individual's exceptionally unique educational and developmental needs, and to provide fitting opportunities for positive growth and well-being.[1]

Asynchronous Development

The development of highly–profoundly gifted children and adolescents is often accelerated and markedly asynchronous—advanced or significantly advanced in some areas, while less advanced or typical in others.[1] In some cases, this disparity can be extreme, in other cases, not as much. Some individuals may be considered *globally gifted*, meaning development is accelerated across many or most areas of development. In this context, it is important for us not to undermine any areas of development that may not appear as strong as the most advanced areas of development. In the developing highly–profoundly gifted child, areas of strength or passion typically are the focus, however, that doesn't always mean the other areas of development are under-developed. Human development is naturally scattered—when significant advanced development is present, other areas will be asynchronous—relative to the advanced development. This asychrony is self-contained and only asychronous relative to the individual's own development. We must be careful not to make assumptions regarding development. It is important that we do not overlook, misinterpret, or downplay the development of the globally gifted individual.

Parents, teachers, counselors, psychologists, and pediatricians need to be very careful in their understanding of asychronous development especially in the developing highly–profoundly gifted child, adolescent, or young adult. Asychronous development can be different in the globally gifted child and needs to be understood as such. Asynchronous development may reflect external presentation rather than the child's true underlying ability. For example, a six-year-old, who is light-years ahead in math, just started learning to ride a bike with his brother. It wasn't due to a lack of physical development that he didn't begin riding a bike earlier—it was simply that he wasn't interested until his four-year-old brother was riding a bike too. This example also demonstrates the influence of like-minded peers and the opportunities they present for camaraderie, mirroring, and growth. The exponential influence of like-minded peers is applicable across all areas of development.

The development of the highly–profoundly gifted child can be so extreme that other children or adults can simply not relate. The extraordinarily advanced development of highly–profoundly gifted children is often dismissed as 'not possible,' 'unconventional,' or 'atypical,' and therefore perceived as 'wrong'—simply because they are doing things that their older, and sometimes much older, peers are doing. Rather than being recognized as advanced or beyond their years, these children are sometimes mistakenly viewed as 'defiant' or 'non-compliant.' For example, one teacher remarked, "why can't he just do what everyone else is doing?" To the inexperienced or untrained eye, such extreme development and asynchrony is frequently misunderstood.[1] As a result, the disparity in development—rather than the ability itself—can become the focus, overshadowing the recognition of the child's extraordinary growth or potential.

It is essential, for anyone working with children, to understand the full spectrum of human development and potential. Teachers, school administrators, psychologists, pediatricians, and other practitioners must be equipped to recognize not only typical development, but also the advanced and asynchronous development characteristic of giftedness—and the significantly advanced development and potential seen in profound giftedness. The presence of both advanced and asynchronous development is an indicator of high developmental potential.

Advanced and Asynchronous Development and Developmental Potential

As parents and advocates for the well-being and development of our children, it is essential that we first recognize giftedness as a facet of human development and potential. This authentic perspective allows us to identify giftedness holistically, taking into account the full range of a child's development and/or developmental potential—not just academic achievement or performance on standardized tests.[1]

In addition to advanced cognitive ability, giftedness involves a combination of advanced and/or asynchronous social, emotional, physical, cognitive, and altruistic-moral development.[1] When we understand giftedness qualitatively, within the broader context of human development, the presence of overexcitabilities begins to make sense. As the five forms of overexcitability are described, it becomes clear that combinations of multiple overexcitabilities—and higher levels of development—help explain the intrinsic motivation and inner intensity behind the unique development of the highly–profoundly gifted child.

Assessing overexcitabilities provides a comprehensive, humanistic view of the individual—capturing characteristics, behaviors, and developmental patterns that are often missed by traditional, quantitatively focused assessments. [1] This type of assessment, across all domains of development, is essential to the holistic identification of highly–profoundly gifted children.[1]

This is especially critical for the unidentified highly–profoundly gifted child who may be underachieving. Underachievement can result from a range of factors, including the absence of like-minded peers, mentors, or practitioners who understand and validate the child's experience; misidentification or inappropriate placement in remedial programs; or other social-environmental conditions that fail to meet the child's educational and developmental needs—such as a lack of cognitive challenge, physical engagement, or meaningful stimuli within the learning environment.

Overexcitabilities Explain Greater-than-Typical Behaviors and Development

Overexcitabilities are heightened neurological responses to internal and/or external stimuli.[2,3] They represent the unique forces behind the differentiating sensitivity, intensity, and awareness often observed in highly–profoundly gifted individuals.[1] The five forms of overexcitability include emotional, intellectual, imaginational, psychomotor, and sensual.[2,3]

1. Emotional overexcitability is considered the core of the five forms of overexcitability and is typically expressed in combination with at least one other type. It involves heightened emotional sensitivity, deep feelings, and an intense compassion for others. Emotions are processed and displayed deeply. It is often seen as a strong passion, attachment, or desire to help others.

2. Intellectual overexcitability is the heightened exploration of truth and understanding. A remarkable passion for learning and problem solving. The natural ability to see nuances, connections, and relationships. The pursuit of development of theories and understanding.

3. Imaginational overexcitability is the heightened play of the imagination, visualization, and association. The innate need to create or expand. Those high in imaginational overexcitability can see many opportunities and limitless possibilities.

4. Psychomotor overexcitability reflects heightened excitability of the neuromuscular system and is characterized by high energy levels, intense physical activity, and a constant need for movement or action. It may manifest through both fine and gross motor activity and often works in tandem with emotional, intellectual, and imaginational overexcitabilities—serving as a physical outlet that supports or amplifies their expression.

5. Sensual overexcitability involves an intensified experience of sensory input, amplifying both pleasure and discomfort across the senses—sight, sound, smell, taste, and touch. Individuals with this form of overexcitability may experience deep enjoyment from aesthetic or sensory experiences, as well as heightened sensitivity or aversion to stimuli that others might find neutral. [2,3,8-12]

Overexcitability, a neurologically based trait, was first recognized in the medical literature in 1899 by Scottish physician Thomas Clouston, who described it as "an undue reactiveness to mental and emotional stimuli which in ordinary children would evoke only a slight response."[13] In 1972, Polish psychiatrist and psychologist Kazimierz Dabrowski expanded on this concept by introducing five distinct forms of overexcitability to the field of psychology as part of his broader theory of human development.[2] Dabrowski developed the theory of positive disintegration (TPD) to explain the multiple levels of human development and the qualitatively different developmental experiences associated with higher levels of personal growth. He recognized this naturally asynchronous and/or turbulent process as *positive disintegration*. As an individual reaches for higher levels of development, lower levels are disintegrated. This is the natural and sometimes chaotic process of human development; development in motion.[2,3,14]

The theory of positive disintegration (TPD) is particularly well-suited to gifted individuals, as it remains the only developmental theory that specifically addresses the unique nature, physiology, and developmental trajectory of giftedness.[15] Its recognition of both scattered and advanced levels of development—across social, emotional, physical, cognitive, and/or altruistic-moral domains—alongside the heightened sensitivity, intensity, and awareness associated with overexcitabilities, aligns closely with the lived experiences of highly–profoundly gifted individuals. Gifted adults, parents, children, adolescents, and practitioners who have worked with this population often find deep resonance with the principles and insights of Dabrowski's theory.[1]

Highly–Profoundly Gifted and Overexcitabilities

Three key insights emerged from the International Gifted Consortium's (IGC) literature review on the highly–profoundly gifted and overexcitabilities. These findings are essential to developing a foundational understanding of the unique development of highly–profoundly gifted individuals.

First, overexcitabilities are neurologically based physiological responses, exhibited through heightened sensitivity, intensity, and awareness, and may be expressed either inwardly or outwardly.[1] In both forms, overexcitabilities can be misunderstood or entirely overlooked by untrained professionals.[16] Inward expressions may be misinterpreted as disengagement or disinterest, while outward expressions can be mistakenly labeled as oversensitivity or hyperactivity.

Second, the combination of multiple overexcitabilities expressed by the highly–profoundly gifted is qualitatively different from the expression of one or two overexcitabilities in isolation. Dabrowski's theory of human development suggests that the integration of multiple overexcitabilities including emotional, intellectual, and imaginational begins to emerge at higher levels of development (Level III and above).[17]

For example, self-education illustrates the interaction of emotional and intellectual overexcitability: a passion or strong emotional drive (emotional OE) combines with a deep pursuit of understanding (intellectual OE). At higher developmental levels, imaginational overexcitability is also present, tapping into creativity and intuition. Psychomotor and sensual overexcitabilities—sometimes referred to as secondary OEs—can further enhance the self-educational experience.[2,3] All five forms of overexcitability may be present in such higher-order developmental expressions.[1]

Third, in the research literature, IGC researchers found multiple overexcitabilities—particularly emotional, intellectual, and imaginational—are often expressed introspectively.[1] For example, a child who engages in voracious reading or deep, sustained study may be demonstrating intellectual overexcitability (in pursuit of truth), emotional overexcitability (through attachment, empathy, or joy), and imaginational overexcitability (via abstract thinking, visualization, or association). Due to this introspective nature, these forms of heightened sensitivity, intensity, and awareness—the hallmarks of giftedness—can be easily overlooked.[1]

In the IGC–University of Antwerp mixed-methods study of highly–profoundly gifted children, Wood et al.[18] found that the most prevalent overexcitability profile included all five forms. Quantitatively, 76% of the children and adolescents assessed with the OEQ-II (Adapted IGC) exhibited three or more overexcitabilities, most commonly emotional, intellectual, and imaginational. This trend was consistent across gender and location, with no significant differences between children in the United States and Belgium. Qualitatively, 99% of interview transcripts included clear evidence of three or more overexcitabilities, again including, emotional, intellectual, and imaginational.[1]

This developmental pattern—where multiple overexcitabilities evolve into developmental dynamisms—is best understood through the lens of Dabrowski's human development, the theory of positive disintegration (TPD). In the next section, we will explore Dabrowski's theory alongside the unique characteristics, behaviors, and developmental trajectories of highly and profoundly gifted individuals.

Theory of Positive Disintegration and Highly–Profoundly Gifted

Five Levels of Development

The theory of positive disintegration (TPD), a human development theory proposed by Kazimierz Dabrowski, is structured around five ascending levels of development. As an individual progresses through these levels, the dominance of the egocentric self gradually diminishes.[2,3] At Level I, development is characterized by a self that is all-powerful and egocentric in nature—the individual views themselves as the center of their own universe, with little awareness of or concern for broader moral, social, or emotional complexities. As one ascends, the self becomes less and less the focus. It is typical to ascend and descend through higher developmental stages. In level V, one is said to be self-actualized, life giving, and selfless. It is not typical to reach the peak of level V; in fact, few do.[2,3] Much like climbing Mt. Everest, only those who persevere through self-reliance reach a state of transcendence—the culmination, or peak, of the extraordinary human experience.

Multi-Level, Greater-than-Typical Sensitivity, Intensity, and Awareness

Greater-than-typical sensitivity, intensity, and awareness—combined with asynchronous development—help explain the intensified human developmental process experienced by highly–profoundly gifted individuals.[1] Unlike traditional developmental theories that follow a typical, linear, age-based sequence, Dabrowski's theory of positive disintegration (TPD) presents development as an organic, dynamic, and multi-level manifestation of the individual.[2,3]

TPD embraces the often chaotic, disruptive, yet necessary nature of advanced development and self-actualization. *Positive disintegration* refers to the natural breaking down of internal psychological structures or barriers that limit growth and potential. While this process is often unsettling, it is essential for transformation, making way for higher levels of functioning, authenticity, and inner harmony.[2,3]

Overexcitabilities serve as both catalysts and companions in this process. They provide the energy and heightened responsiveness that fuel internal conflict, reflection, and ultimately, developmental growth. These intensities help propel the individual forward—motivating their movement through Dabrowski's levels of development.

To fully understand overexcitabilities in the context of the highly–profoundly gifted, an integrated framework is essential. This includes recognizing:

- Developmental potential
- The five forms of overexcitability
- The combination of multiple overexcitabilities at higher developmental levels
- The formation of developmental dynamisms

Together, these elements provide a comprehensive understanding of the complex and nonlinear developmental progression that is characteristic of highly–profoundly gifted individuals.[1]

Developmental Potential

Developmental potential refers to the level of growth an individual may achieve when provided with optimal physical, emotional, and environmental conditions.[2,3] Dabrowski identified five core factors and influences that contribute to an individual's developmental potential. These elements interact to shape the course of one's growth and the capacity to reach higher levels of personal and moral development:

- The First Factor—the innate and biological potentialities of the organism
- The Second Factor—the social and environmental influences
- The Third Factor—autonomous forces, self-processes, and guidance such as internal conflicts, self-awareness, self-reflection, and choices and decisions related to personal growth. The Third Factor is often referred to as the "internal compass" of the individual

- Overexcitabilities and the combination of multiple, higher-level overexcitabilities leading to developmental dynamisms
- Special abilities and talents[2,3]

An individual's developmental potential is entirely unique and shaped by a combination of factors, including special abilities and talents, the presence of overexcitabilities, autonomous or self-directed inner forces, social and environmental influences, and the individual's genetic makeup and familial history.[2,3]

Developmental Potential and Highly–Profoundly Gifted

The First Factor

The early developmental milestones and biological research on highly–profoundly gifted individuals reflect Dabrowski's First Factor of developmental potential—*the biological potentialities of the individual.* These individuals often exhibit significant differences in early development when compared to their age-mates. Common early indicators include:

- acute awareness from infancy
- early onset of movement
- early onset of verbal communication
- fast acquisition of language[4-6,19]

Examples of greater-than-typical biological development commonly observed in highly–profoundly gifted individuals include:

- functional bilateralism and inter-hemispheric communication[20,21]
- advanced processing capabilities[20,21]
- physiological sensitivity as reported in the greater occurrence of autoimmune, allergy and asthmatic reaction[19,22]
- family history of giftedness. The IGC-University of Antwerp study[18] found that 89% of the highly–profoundly gifted children studied had a family history of giftedness. It has been

reported that siblings tend to be within ten IQ points of each other. Similar relationships were also reported for parents and grandparents.[23]

The Second Factor

The social and environmental influences experienced by highly–profoundly gifted individuals align with Dabrowski's Second Factor of developmental potential.[1] In terms of social development, the International Gifted Consortium (IGC) literature review found that highly–profoundly gifted individuals often exhibit:

- a lack of like-minded peers
- a lack of like-minded mentors among highly–profoundly gifted students
- a need for intellectual peers and nurturing environments designed to fit their unique development.[1]

Dabrowski found that the higher the developmental potential of an individual, the greater the effect of social and environmental influences.[14] Some symptoms exhibited by highly–profoundly gifted students in an unfit social environment include:

- opposition and defiance or lack of care or indifference which Dabrowski said attributed to unharnessed psychic excitability
- social alienation which Dabrowski said leads to nervousness or anxiety
- underachievement or what Dabrowski identified as inhibited development[1]

The Second Factor is a crucial component of developmental potential, as it is where we can positively influence the development, developmental potential, and well-being of our children and students. The First Factor is already determined by the child's innate genetic make-up. The Second Factor, however, is not pre-determined and is directly shaped by social and environmental influences. The adults responsible for the well-being of children—parents, teachers, school administrators, psychologists, and pediatricians—play a critical role in influencing their development and developmental potential. Therefore, it is essential that we consider:

- the environment a child grows up in at home, at school, and in their community
- the social context of their upbringing at home, at school, and in their community
- the peers, teachers, role-models, and practitioners with whom they interact and rely on at home, at school, and in their community

Please reference the 2024 IGC–University of Antwerp study[18] for examples of social and environmental influences experienced by highly–profoundly gifted children.

All of these influences play a role in the developmental potential of an individual. To positively support the development and developmental potential, highly–profoundly gifted children need a supportive environment including:

- like-minded peers
- like-minded mentors
- like-minded practitioners[1]

Parents and teachers, as well as other vital stakeholders (school administrators, counselors, psychologists, pediatricians) must provide fitting experiences with like-minded peers, mentors, and practitioners. Like-minded peers, like-minded mentors and like-minded practitioners are essential to the well-being and development of highly–profoundly gifted individuals.

Maslow's Hierarchy of Needs[24] reminds us that one of our most basic needs as human beings is to feel an authentic sense of belonging. To experience a sense of belonging, validation, and purpose, we need a reciprocal exchange of perceptions, thoughts, experiences, and feelings.

Els De Wit captured this essential concept in her analogy of the sleeping lion.[25] Highly–profoundly gifted children and adolescents need opportunities to see themselves in others. This mirror effect provides opportunities for positive self-reflection and development. Without peers and mentors, with whom we can connect, we have no mirror.

The Third Factor

The significantly greater-than-typical sensitivity, intensity, and awareness exhibited by the highly–profoundly gifted, combined with their advanced cognition, allow for heightened metacognitive and introspective capabilities.[1] This deep self-awareness and self-guidance reflect the Third Factor of developmental potential. The Third Factor is an essential dynamism—a combination of multiple, higher-level overexcitabilities—that influences the formation of other dynamisms.[10] [11] It functions as the individual's internal compass, rooted in intrinsic motivation, personal values, and a sense of purpose.

The Third Factor is not only present but fully active at the highest levels of developmental potential.[2,3] It is influenced by both the First Factor (genetic potentiality) and the Second Factor (social–environmental influences). When fully developed, the Third Factor becomes the guiding dynamism that leads to higher stages of development and self-actualization. This instinctive activation of self-directed growth emerges naturally at the onset of multi-level development (Level III). Initial signs of development include self-initiated activity, independence, and strong will. The development of the self through autonomous forces is the Third Factor. It is an organic developmental process.[2,3] Evidence of the Third Factor was prevalent in the IGC-University of Antwerp study of highly–profoundly gifted children and adolescents.[18]

Parents, educators, mentors, pediatricians, and practitioners can nurture the development of the Third Factor by:

- encouraging autonomy, responsibility, accountability, and self-reflection
- purposefully scheduling autonomous downtime
- providing rest for the mind, body, and spirit of the child

The Five Forms of Overexcitabilities

The five forms of overexcitability express and develop greater-than-typical sensitivity, intensity, and awareness.[2,3] Sensual overexcitability is exhibited through heightened sensory experiences, including both extreme pleasure and discomfort. This may involve an intensified tactile response, such as irritation from a shirt tag, or an overwhelming appreciation of beauty, such as the sight of a sunset. Psychomotor overexcitability is expressed through neuromuscular activity, high energy levels, or a persistent need for movement and action. Energy can be expressed through rapid speech, tapping feet, biting nails or from an internal psychomotor drive. Imaginational overexcitability allows an individual to envision the abstract, make associations, and imagine a wide range of possibilities. Intellectual overexcitability is often expressed as a passion for learning or an unstoppable desire to understand and make sense of the world. Emotional overexcitability exists as the core motivator of all the overexcitabilities. Greater-than-typical sensitivity, intensity, and awareness are expressed in all the overexcitabilities including emotional overexcitability. Emotions are deeply processed and displayed strongly. Deep care and compassion are evident. Additional examples are listed below from the IGC article "How Can We Better Understand, Identify, and Support Highly Gifted and Profoundly Gifted Students? A literature review of the psychological development of highly–profoundly gifted individuals and overexcitabilities."[1,11-13]

Multiple, Higher-Level Overexcitabilities and Highly–Profoundly Gifted

Individual or independent overexcitabilities behave distinctly differently from the combination of multiple overexcitabilities.[2,3] At higher levels of development, the combination of multiple overexcitabilities is often reflected in the heightened sensitivity, intensity, and awareness observed in highly–profoundly gifted individuals across multiple areas of development.[18]

Overexcitabilities serve different roles at different levels of development.[2,3] Levels I and II of Dabrowski's developmental framework are considered "unilevel," referring to the independent and undifferentiated nature of development at these stages. At levels I and II, there is little or no development, introspection, and inner conflict. Multilevel development begins at level III and progresses through levels IV and V. These stages are complex, containing layers upon layers of developmental patterns and the coexistence of multiple overexcitabilities. These overexcitabilities serve as both the driving force and the dynamic flow behind developmental progression—as well as periods of regression—shaping and forming the psychic milieu within an individual's multilevel development.

During growth periods, overexcitabilities are fully active and engaged. Combinations of overexcitabilities work together to encourage and support the continued development of the individual. For examples of multiple-level overexcitabilities in combination, see the IGC–University of Antwerp study.[18] When all five forms of overexcitabilities are working together, they lift the individual to higher levels. Similarly—though in a different form—multiple higher-level overexcitabilities can converge to inspire quiet introspection, reflection, or unconscious processing.[2,3] This represents the inner development of self-actualization.

Higher-Level Overexcitabilities and Advanced Development

Higher-Level Emotional Overexcitability and Advanced Emotional Development

The heightened sensitivity, intensity, and awareness characteristic of emotional overexcitability at higher-levels is reflected in the advanced emotional development of the highly–profoundly gifted.[1] For example:

- Heightened or greater-than-typical discernment is characteristic of highly–profoundly gifted children and corresponds to level III emotional overexcitability combined with intellectual overexcitability. The ability to pick out nuances, to see differences or to pick up on relationships, feelings, or objections, especially in abstract form. To see through things.

- Heightened or greater-than-typical response to aesthetics—also characteristic of highly–profoundly gifted children—reflects level IV emotional overexcitability combined with sensual overexcitability. This is the extreme joy expressed by the epitome of visually appealing stimuli and emotional gratification. Responses are unique to the individual and the experience represents some form of connection.
- Heightened or greater-than-typical sensitivity to others—common among the highly–profoundly gifted—corresponds to Level III and level IV of the empathy dynamism. Dynamisms can be thought of as the combination of advanced overexcitabilities and begin to form at level III. The empathy dynamism is the development of innate, authentic care for and expression of compassion for others. An individual who has developed the empathy dynamism experiences such deep care for another person or living creature that they become emotionally connected and can actually share in the experience. Those with a highly developed empathy dynamism can actually feel what the other person is experiencing.[1]

Other characteristics, behaviors, and aspects of emotional development that correspond to the heightened sensitivity, intensity, and awareness exhibited by the highly–profoundly gifted include:

- introspection and introversion
- a strong sense of right and wrong
- an internal guide from within (The Third Factor)
- multi-dimensional, accelerated, and asynchronous emotional development
- feeling out-of-sync[1]

As acknowledged by Dabrowski this sense of chaos is common at higher levels of advanced development and is a natural part of the growth process experienced by individuals with high developmental potential.[14]

Higher-Level Intellectual Overexcitability and Advanced Cognitive Development

This heightened sensitivity, intensity, and awareness is also evident in the advanced cognitive development of highly–profoundly gifted individuals.[1] For example:

- An early ability to read, coupled with a desire for frequent and sustained reading, is correlated with the combination of intellectual overexcitability and emotional overexcitability.
- Self-acceleration, a compulsion to learn everything, a desire for complexity, perceptive insights, and the ability to skip steps are all correlated with level III and level IV intellectual overexcitability and emotional overexcitability.
- Divergent thinking capabilities, the ability to see patterns, and the capacity to comprehend abstract concepts by simplifying are correlated to level IV intellectual overexcitability, combined with emotional and imaginational overexcitability.[1]

Other characteristics, behaviors, and cognitive development that correspond to heightened sensitivity, intensity, and awareness include deep reflective thinking, a need to ponder, and a need to make sense of the world, the universe, and the self.[1]

Higher-Level Overexcitabilities and Advanced Altruistic-Moral Development

Heightened sensitivity, intensity, and awareness can also be seen in advanced altruistic-moral development.[1] For example:

- The need to contemplate and sit in silence—commonly found in the highly–profoundly gifted—is associated with the combination of all five forms of overexcitability at levels III and IV.
- The highly–profoundly gifted individual's inquisitive questioning of the mind, along with a deep appreciation for and connection to the human spirit, reflects a combination of all five overexcitabilities at level IV.

- Unique and distinctive altruistic development, often found in the highly–profoundly gifted, begins at level III and IV and includes feelings grounded in increasing awareness and the formation of altruistic attitudes based on one's own hierarchy of values.
- Greater-than-typical sensitivity, intensity, and awareness are all activated elements observed in advanced altruistic development and higher-levels of developmental potential.[1]

Dynamisms—Distinct Differences of Highly–Profoundly Gifted

Dabrowski identified the Third Factor as the most influential dynamism in an individual's developmental potential.[2,3] It represents all the autonomous forces within a person and serves as the guiding component of self-actualization. The Third Factor is especially recognizable in individuals who possess an innate sense of knowing and who subconsciously follow their internal guidance.

The IGC literature review of the highly–profoundly gifted and overexcitabilities found that the most distinct developmental differences in the development in this population were synonymous with the combination of higher-level overexcitabilities and the formation of dynamisms.[1]

"Dynamisms are instincts, drives, and intellectual processes, combined with emotions, p.294"[10] They are the developmental outcome of the combination of all forms of higher-level overexcitabilities. Other dynamisms include:

- empathy
- responsibility to others
- autonomy
- authentism
- intuition
- self-control
- self-awareness
- self-preservation

- auto-psychotherapy
- education-of-oneself
- subject-object in oneself—the ability to look critically at oneself, as if from the outside
- inner psychic transformation
- personality ideal[17]

It is important to recognize that overexcitabilities play different roles at different levels.[2,3] While overexcitabilities can exist independently at levels I and II, they function quite differently at these lower levels compared to higher levels. At level III, overexcitabilities begin to combine, generating new, enriched energy and opportunities for development. As they continue to interact and evolve, overexcitabilities can lead to the formation of dynamisms and support advanced developmental growth.[14]

The assessment of development and developmental potential—including overexcitabilities and emerging dynamisms, as outlined in Dabrowski's human development theory—offers the most accurate reflection to date of the unique characteristics, behaviors, development, potential of highly–profoundly gifted individuals.[1] It is a comprehensive approach to the equitable identification and support of highly–profoundly gifted students.

Assessing Giftedness Based on Advanced Development and Developmental Potential

Wood Assessment Model of Giftedness and Highly–Profoundly Gifted Individuals

How do parents, holistically assess the development and developmental potential of their children? How do teachers, school administrators, and gifted coordinators assess the development and developmental potential of their students? And how do pediatricians and other practitioners support the development, developmental potential, and well-being of their patients?

Considering the social, emotional, physical, cognitive, and altruistic-moral development of an individual—as well as their developmental potential, based on Kazimierz Dabrowski's five factors and influences—the *Wood Assessment Model* offers a comprehensive and equitable framework for identifying giftedness and highly–profoundly gifted individuals. This theoretical assessment model is recommended in conjunction with an evaluation of achievement and cognitive ability subtest scores from the most appropriate IQ test.

Currently, the gold standard for the measurement of cognitive abilities in children and adolescents is the Wechsler Intelligence Scales for Children, Fifth Edition (WISC-V).[23] It is essential that the WISC-V be administered by a professional trained in profound giftedness.[1]

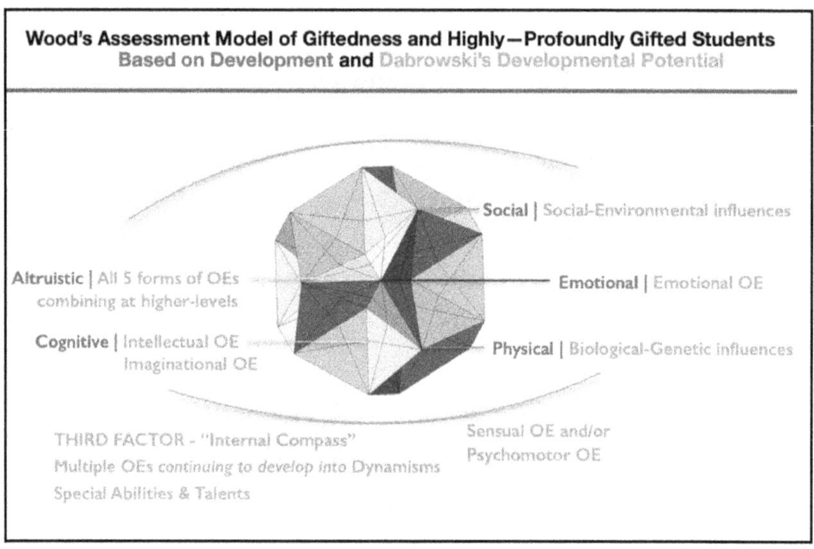

Use of this model trains teachers, school administrators, and psychologists to recognize and consider the authentic characteristics, behaviors, development, and developmental potential of gifted and highly–profoundly gifted students. It supports a holistic assessment of the child's development while also taking into account their developmental potential—including familial history, social and environmental influences, combinations of the five forms of overexcitabilities, and the child's special abilities and talents.

This is the most inclusive and equitable assessment and identification process because it is based in the holistic development and developmental potential of the child. It can be combined with academic achievement and cognitive ability scores to provide the most comprehensive assessment available. This model conceptually identifies the diversity within the highly–profoundly gifted population, including those who have historically been overlooked or left unidentified due to negative social and environmental influences and/or underachievement. Additionally, this model can help identify students who were previously misidentified. The Wood Assessment Model of Giftedness and Highly–Profoundly Gifted Individuals may be used as a screening tool for both the identification of giftedness and the support of developmental potential in highly–profoundly gifted individuals.

Proper assessment and identification are essential for the appropriate education and development of highly–profoundly gifted individuals.[1] *All human beings require a sense of belonging and support to achieve well-being and self-actualization, as outlined in Maslow's Hierarchy of Needs.*[24]

Below is a summary designed to aid in the identification and support of the five forms of overexcitability, intended for parents, teachers, school administrators, psychologists, pediatricians.

For additional information, refer to the latest research study,[18] *Prevalence of Emotional, Intellectual, Imaginational, Psychomotor, and Sensual Overexcitabilities: A mixed-methods study of development and developmental potential.*

Additionally, see the IGC literature review by Wood and Laycraft[1], *How Can We Better Understand, Identify, and Support Highly Gifted and Profoundly Gifted Students? A Literature Review of the Psychological Development of Highly–Profoundly Gifted Individuals and Overexcitabilities*[1]. PDFs of the research are available at GiftedConsortium.org

Understanding and Supporting Overexcitabilities

Psychomotor Overexcitability

When we understand psychomotor overexcitability, we recognize it as a physiological experience.[26] It is not merely a desire for movement, but a genuine need for it. Psychomotor overexcitability powers other overexcitabilities and the neuromuscular system at large. Parents and teachers can support psychomotor overexcitability by:

- nurturing awareness, tolerating movement, and encouraging mind-body connection
- building activity and movement into the day's experiences, breaks, and curriculum
- bringing learning outdoors and integrating nature
- encouraging self-advocacy while respecting the collaborative community[26]

Sensual Overexcitability

When we understand sensual overexcitability, we recognize that heightened senses are actually enhancements.[26] It reflects an extraordinary ability to receive and perceive stimuli in its greatest depth. Parents and teachers can support sensual overexcitability by:

- Recognizing that the environment—and the stimuli within it—can have a dramatic effect on individuals helps us understand that, at times, less can be more.
- Empathizing with feelings associated with acute awareness. Direct attention or being put on-the-spot can be humiliating or crippling.
- Providing opportunities to talk about feelings and aesthetics.[26]

Intellectual Overexcitability

When we understand intellectual overexcitability, we recognize it is an innate need to know—an intrinsic drive for depth and complexity.[26] We come to realize that traditional academic expectations may not align with this need, prompting us seek out or create experiences that appropriately nurture and support the individual's existing development.

Parents and teachers can support intellectual overexcitability by:

- incorporating Socratic learning
- offering opportunities to debate
- grouping like-minded peers
- finding like-minded mentors
- offering acceleration, with appropriate scaffolding, to provide appropriate challenge[26]

Imaginational Overexcitabilities

When we understand imaginational overexcitability, we recognize that individuals with this trait create, develop, and refine ideas within their mind.[26] We come to understand that their creations or insights are not always visible to others. Parents and teachers can nurture imaginational overexcitabilities by:

- developing executive functioning skills to help execute ideas
- engaging in role playing and creative writing
- providing opportunities for divergent thinking
- setting goals, taking time to reflect and celebrating progress[26]

Emotional Overexcitabilities

When we understand emotional overexcitability, we recognize that emotional impressions are often deeply felt and become embedded as life experiences.[26] We understand that individuals high in emotional overexcitability are highly perceptive and absorb a significant amount of emotional stimuli. Organizing and processing an influx of data can require an exorbitant amount of energy. Parents and teachers can nurture emotional overexcitability by:

- appreciating the intensity of heightened self-awareness and empathy for others
- empathizing with the difficulty or excitement that can arise with transitions, in new environments, or when meeting new people

- validating and respecting strong feelings and perceptions
- providing opportunities for moral, ethical, and judicial expressions
- discussing, visualizing, or role-playing new or unexpected experiences
- allowing extra time to acclimate[26]

References

[1] Wood, V., and K. Laycraft. 2020. "How Can We Better Understand, Identify, and Support Highly Gifted and Profoundly Gifted Students? A Literature Review of the Psychological Development of Highly–Profoundly Gifted Individuals and Overexcitabilities." *Annals of Cognitive Science.* 4(1).

[2] Dąbrowski, K. 1972. *Psychoneurosis Is Not an Illness.* London: Gryf Publications Ltd.

[3] Dabrowski, K. 1996. *Multilevelness of Emotional and Instinctive Functions.* Lublin: Towarzystwo Naukowe Katolickiego Uniwersytetu Lubelskiego.

[4] Terman, L. M. 1925. *Mental and Physical Traits of a Thousand Gifted Children: Genetic Studies of Genius*, Vol. 1. Stanford, CA: Stanford University Press.

[5] Hollingworth, L. S. 1942. *Children Above 180 IQ (Stanford-Binet): Origin and Development.* Yonkers-on-Hudson, NY: World Book Company.

[6] Gross, M. U. M. 2004. *Exceptionally Gifted Children.* 2nd ed. New York, NY: Routledge Falmer.

[7] Davidson Institute. n.d. https://davidsongifted.org

[8] Dąbrowski, K., and M. M. Piechowski. 1977a. *Theory of Levels of Emotional Development: Vol. 1. Multilevelness and Positive Disintegration.* New York: Dabor Science Publications.

[9] Dabrowski, K., and M. M. 1977b. *Theory of Levels of Emotional Development: Vol. 2. From Primary Integration to Self-Actualization.* New York: Dabor Science Publications.

[10] Piechowski, M. M. 1999. Overexcitabilities. In *Encyclopedia of Creativity*, Vol. 2, edited by M. Runco and S. Pritzker, 325–334. San Diego, CA: Academic Press.

[11] Daniels, S., and M. M. Piechowski. 2009. *Living with Intensity.* Scottsdale, AZ: Great Potential Press.

[12] Lind, S. 2011. "Overexcitabilities and the Gifted." Retrieved from https://www.sengifted.org/post/overexcitabilities-and-the-gifted.

[13] The Lancet. 1899. "States of Over-Excitability, Hyper-Sensitiveness, and Mental Explosiveness in Children." *The Lancet*154 (61): 292.

[14] Dabrowski, K., A. Kawczak, and M. M. Piechowski. 1970. *Mental Growth through Positive Disintegration.* London: Gryf Publications.

[15] Colangelo, N., and G. A. Davis. 1991. *Handbook of Gifted Education*. Boston: Allyn & Bacon.

[16] Webb, J. T., E. R. Ammern, P. Beljan, N. E. Webb, M. Kuzujanakis, F. R. Olenchak, and J. Goerss. 2016. "*Misdiagnosis and Dual Diagnosis of Gifted Children and Adults: ADHD, Bipolar, OCD, Asperger's, Depression, and Other Disorders*." 2nd ed. Scottsdale, AZ: Gifted Unlimited.

[17] Piechowski, M. M. 1978. "Self-Actualization as a Developmental Structure: A Profile of Antoine de Saint-Exupéry." *Genetic Psychology Monographs* 97 (2): 181–242.

[18] Wood, V. R., et al. 2024. "Prevalence of Emotional, Intellectual, Imaginational, Psychomotor, and Sensual Overexcitabilities in Highly and Profoundly Gifted Children and Adolescents: A Mixed-Methods Study of Development and Developmental Potential." *Education Sciences* 14 (8): 817. https://doi.org/10.3390/educsci14080817.

[19] Rogers, K., and L. Silverman. 1997, November. "The Construct of Asynchrony." Paper presented at the 44th Annual Conference of the National Association for Gifted Children, Little Rock, Arkansas.

[20] Alexander, J. E., M. W. O'Boyle, and C. P. Benbow. 1996. "Developmentally Advanced EEG Alpha Power in Gifted Male and Female Adolescents." *International Journal of Psychophysiology* 23 (1–2): 25–31.

[21] O'Boyle, M. 2008. "Mathematically Gifted Children: Developmental Brain Characteristics and Their Prognosis for Well-Being." *Roeper Review* 30 (3): 181–186.

[22] Benbow, C. P. 1986. "Physiological Correlates of Extreme Intellectual Precocity." *Neuropsychologia* 24 (5): 719–725.

[23] Silverman, Linda K., and Barbara J. Gilman. 2020. "Best Practices in Gifted Identification and Assessment: Lessons from the WISC-V." *Psychology in the Schools* 57 (10): 1569–1581.

[24] Maslow, Abraham, and K. J. Lewis. 1987. "Maslow's Hierarchy of Needs." *Salenger Incorporated* 14 (17): 987–990.

[25] Wit, Els De. 2020. *Slapende Leeuwen: Uitzonderlijk Hoogbegaafd. Is Dat Nu Écht Zo Anders?*

[26] Wood, V. R. 2018, February. "Shaping Our Future: Giftedness through the Eyes of the Highly–Profoundly Gifted." Lecture presented at the *Arizona Association for Gifted and Talented (AAGT) Conference*, Phoenix, Arizona, USA.

Chapter 3

Theoretical Minimum of Highly–Profoundly Gifted

Els De Wit, M.A.

Exceptionally Normal

He is five when he reads like an eight-year-old. He does math with his food during dinner time.

At the age of nine she learns to program by herself and wants to learn the mathematics of high school. However, understanding exam questions, she finds very complicated.

By the age of five, he had visited almost every museum in the country. Adults don't take him seriously. They see his height, not his capabilities. Now that he is a teenager, cynicism has become his style of speech. His unappreciated passion has harsh undertones that few people appreciate.

These children are a forgotten and underestimated group. They too are among the gifted. Yes, they are exceptional in speed of thought, in making connections, in remembering, in level of thought, in intensity. But they are also exceptionally normal. This group dances along to the steps they see in role playing games; they laugh themselves silly with YouTube videos; they may "just not be in the mood" today—and may also feel like they'll never, ever be able

> *to master something. And this group wonders every day: is it just me?*
>
> *These children do not gain satisfaction from workbooks. They see through the "fun" of lessons and yearn to understand the system behind the language, the structure of a formula, and the connections within scientific laws. In school, these children may be asked to write three characteristics of an animal, while at home they study the physics and laws of the universe.*
>
> *Writing about three characteristics can become a very difficult question. There are so many characteristics. And again, they wonder: is it just me?*

The Theoretical Minimum

What makes highly–profoundly so different from gifted? Are these children smarter? Faster? What is it about them that makes them highly–profoundly gifted? And how do you explain this type of giftedness to others? When you consult the literature on highly–profoundly gifted children, the first thing you will find are the so-called "prodigies." These children seem to fly through life. They pick up a book and immediately understand it; they display their talents without hesitation and seem unconcerned about what others think of them. Their emotions and their motor skills do not seem to get in their way.

But that is not necessarily your child. Your child may live on cloud nine. Your child may be too shy to show their talents but at home they run through the house always busy with something, but never with what you asked.

When your child looks up how to draw a house using perspective on YouTube, they suddenly know the right keywords, have all the patience in the world—and you could play a tambourine beside them without them even noticing. This can't possibly be the gifted child you read about in the literature. Gifted people perceive the world in a unique way. Brain research shows that there is indeed such a thing as a gifted brain.[1]

Based on both research and my own experiences with highly–profoundly gifted children, I have compiled an overview of what profound giftedness truly entails. My goal was to provide a way to explain profound giftedness to your family, your friends, and to others. This chapter addresses the question: What is the absolute minimum you need to know about giftedness and highly–profoundly gifted individuals?

In this chapter, you will discover how I explain high-profound giftedness to others. I focus the discussion on children, but it is also relevant for adults who need to explain their giftedness and its impact on their environment. Extreme giftedness is not always visible on paper. Intelligence quotient (IQ) tests do not always show one's true intelligence. Furthermore, IQ scores do not account for holistic development; they attempt to measure only the cognitive ability of an individual. If you only cater to the cognitive side of the highly–profoundly gifted individual, the rest of giftedness is neglected. The very nature of the profoundly gifted child may be hindering their cognitive abilities from being captured.

The most visible characteristics will be discussed in five domains:

- Intensity
- Immersion
- Idealism
- Asynchronous development
- Lack of experience

These are the characteristics that distinguish a highly–profoundly gifted child from a high-achieving child. Highly–profoundly gifted children are intense, hold high expectations for themselves and from the world around them, and are not always as mature as one might expect. As bright as they are, they are still children after all.

Little has been written about the fifth domain, lack of experience. Lack of experience leans towards asynchronous development. However, if we want to better understand the highly–profoundly gifted child, a lack of experience deserves its own place on our theoretical minimum. It is important for people to realize that talent does not always develop by itself. To develop, we need chances to learn, to experiment, to flourish, and to fail.

Intensity

Sleeping Lions

Your child is gifted. But what does that mean? You read books about giftedness, but it may not always feel like they are talking about your child. A bit, but not completely. Somehow, what is said, isn't complete. Somehow it feels different. You go to your child's school, and you talk to their teachers. They tell you not to worry. Your child's school may want to accommodate your child, they may try to, but your child still doesn't fit. Your child may be more like a "sleeping lion."

Inside your child, there is a lion. A lion hunting for knowledge, who wants to enjoy the richness of its environment. A lion who wants to see and hear everything and receive acknowledgment for its curiosity and capacities. On the inside, there is more greatness than what one may see in the classroom. Your child does not feel challenged spending an hour a week in a gifted class or solving puzzles in the workbooks made for gifted children.

There is a constant hunger: a hunger to learn. No matter how much you offer, it never seems enough. The amount of knowledge they engulf is enormous. Every answer is countered with another question.

Complex = simple. What is typically complex for most may be overly obvious for the lion. For example, Lions, by nature, understand how to hunt best. Their speed, their mass, their jumping agility, their efficiencies; they know how hard and where to bite. It is hard to explain. How do you explain something that is innate?

Having to do too little for too long makes a lion lazy. Even if the gazelles are dancing in front of its eyes, when a lion is not in its natural environment, it will not move. The lion is not in the mood anymore; it has given up. Its intrinsic hunger to learn is gone. The lion has been on a diet for too long.

The simple is complex. A lion is not born to accept things the way they are just because that's the way they are. A lion doesn't only want to know, it needs to know. After being starved from its natural desire to learn, it is very difficult for the lion to re-engage. They may not even know anymore what they once desired. When they look into the mirror, they are startled by what they see. **Who am I? Once a big lion, now, I see a small cat.**

Intensity can be seen in all areas and life experiences.[2] Emotional intensity is often overlooked as childish behavior. This misunderstanding can rule out the option for acceleration at school. Some examples, of emotional intensity include the drama when you comb your child's hair or when your child scores "only" 9.5 out of 10. It is the inexplicable stomachaches and headaches, for which you can no longer count the hospital visits. It is extremely shy behavior. The vicarious guilt. Emotional intensity is your child playing deaf and mute for weeks until they have figured everything out in their head.

Often, parents first notice the emotional intensity of their child. It is often reported as inexplicable headaches, stomachaches, fatigue, or persistent illnesses that present in extreme ways or fail to resolve over time.

Giftedness is often diagnosed much later. Moreover, giftedness is often first noticed by others. Emotional intensity can send children into a spiral of investigations and counseling that were "just not that."

Emotional intensity also has its beautiful side. It is a child who is moved by a beautiful piece of music, a child who is mesmerized by a painting, a child who, without direction, cares for their brothers and sisters. A child who gives you a hug as if their life depends on it. A teacher who understands these children, and doesn't underestimate them, can be the lifeline they cherish for years.

Intellectual intensity is recognized most easily in *maladaptive* children. I use *maladaptive*, just like Dabrowski,[3,4] in a positive way. These children aren't hiding their capacities from the rest of the world. They connect with the world and their mind is always "on." Nothing is ever too much; it is never enough. These children always want to go deeper. The questions do not stop, and this high intellectual curiosity can be the cause of sleeping problems. Emotional intensity can also be involved here. These children are often told, "you think too much". But this is not by choice, this is how they are wired. Every answer paves the way for at least one new question. They want to grasp the world. Not tomorrow, but now. Sleep problems can be common among gifted teenagers as well; the endless worry about the pitfalls of the world bother them just as much as you.

This emotional intensity is often evident in conversations and is frequently the source of broken friendships, misunderstandings, or social exclusion. Your child is enjoying the tension, the disagreement and is looking for arguments to prove it is right. The other party, on the other hand, just wanted to have a pleasant talk. Usually, the children themselves are the last to realize why friendships don't always work out.

In our groups for the highly–profoundly gifted, discussions go on for hours with no problems, and it often gets competitive. During these discussions, it is the content that prevails. Participants don't always interact warmly in the moment—there's no time for that; they want to uncover the truth, identify errors, and investigate. Bystanders are surprised at the speed at which topics pass by in an hour. It is not uncommon to start with today's news, take a few detours through the universe, history, an inventor, a funny quote —and end right back where you began, with today's news. And somehow, it all makes sense to them.

This is very normal for them. These in-depth discussions create a closer bond. It is a way to really get to know each other beyond "my favorite color, hobbies, and "when I grow up, I want to be." They gain each other's respect through sound arguments and discourse. As peers, they hold each other accountable. They must be ready to back up what they say. That are not always used to these types of reciprocal conversations. The opportunity for them to debate on their level is a much-needed outlet and a significant form of intellectual stimulation. In these discussions they can rise rapidly to an abstract level, to explore underlying principles.

There are usually three types of participants: the moderator, the hard-core, and the silent thinker. The moderator does not really take part. The moderator is above the discussion on a meta level. The hard-core participant has an opinion that must be known. They are the driving force behind the conversation, keeping it going—because to them, it's hard to imagine how you *don't* see their perspective. The silent thinker analyzes and considers the arguments in his head until he knows what to say to the participants. The silent thinker dismisses half of the discussion in just a few words.

For deeper insight on intensity, I highly recommend reading the chapter on Dabrowski by Vanessa R. Wood.

Immersion

Adam grasped concepts holistically and intuitively.
Once he acquired the basic framework, he filled in the particulars.

From all that I have observed, immersion is the bridge
between potential and the realization of one's gifts and talent.[5]

Taking the Plunge

Immersion is plunging into a certain domain. Losing yourself in a topic until you know everything you want to know, and then letting it go just as quickly or easily as you started. For example, when searching on Google, most people find satisfaction quickly, on the first page with the first five hits.

Immersion, on the other hand, is clicking through on Google for many, many hours, seeking precision in knowledge. Immersion means considering the totality of an idea, multiple views, and alternative perspectives. For example, you might ponder, when using the word x, do you imply the same meaning as me? You likely open 53 tabs until your computer almost crashes, and only then do you decide you know enough, for now. Highly–profoundly gifted people are able to acquire knowledge from an early age autodidactically.

A gifted person has this tendency too, but they usually hit a wall of "knowing enough." For the highly–profoundly gifted, however, this wall does not seem to exist.

Learning comes naturally and they can lose themselves deeper and deeper into a domain. It is their way of learning; the conflict with step-by-step learning in school immediately becomes clear.

Most people are rote learners. They learn through a step-by-step, repetitive process. Giftedness leans more towards intuitive and meta-cognitive processes. Gifted individuals enjoy thinking about their thought processes. This is the way they learn and process the world around them. They often consider the end-result first and work backwards in a non-linear way to the understand the big picture. They are big picture thinkers. This thought process naturally enables them to find connections between different concepts[6,7].

This process enables highly–profoundly gifted individuals to adopt more efficient learning strategies very quickly. Understanding their unique learning process helps explain why they are able to grasp concepts more rapidly than their mildly gifted peers. For more information, refer to Vanessa Wood's Assessment Model of Giftedness and Highly–Profoundly Gifted Students.

Brackmann[8] mentions the connection between abstract concepts and emotional reactions. For instance, feelings can represent numbers. Emotions and learning tend to be inextricably linked in highly–profoundly gifted children. Emotional energy drives their interests, their passions. You can safely say that they are emotionally attached to their passionate interests.

Grobman,[5] who has provided psychotherapy to exceptionally gifted teenagers for decades, described this inner urge as an obligatory force of nature. When they are all in on a topic, they can be so hyper-focused that it's like the rest of the world doesn't exist. Whereas gifted children tend to more easily separate themselves from the project that they are working on. This is a distinctly more intense commitment to thought, creative process, and/or autonomous force. They are less likely to veer from this "need to know."

Autodidact

The highly–profoundly gifted are autodidact by nature. Their senses are naturally very sharp. From a young age, they tend to teach themselves to read, calculate, use the times tables, to work on the computer. For them, this is self-evident, and it is very often done intuitively.

They pick up and incorporate everything into their knowledge. They may overhear a conversation, something on television or pick up something new in a bedtime story. They seek strategies of their own to understand the world around them. These strategies, incorporated into their development at a very early age, cause everything to speed up. The puzzle pieces seemingly fall into place automatically.

For example, at an earlier age than typical they may be sitting, crawling (or skipping crawling all together), standing and walking. They may be coloring, reading, calculating numbers, and they may lose their temper when they are interrupted or get help offered. One of the most popular phrases I hear in my work with these children is, "okay, okay, okay, I know," followed by a gesture of, I've got this.

It's only when they test themselves against their environment and observe how other children work they may realize their way isn't always the way for everyone else. Most children do not know all the colors or learn to count on their own. Typically, children need a lot of practice.

In the highly–profoundly gifted, everything appears to seep quickly to long-term memory. They tend to be autodidact, meaning they are synthetic thinkers. Examples of autodidact learning include leaps in thought, total immersion, and the integration of new information into working memory.

Autodidact learning, however, differs completely from typical learning modalities. Typically, learning is presented and processed in a linear, sequential, and structured manner that supports traditional executive functioning. Being autodidact means having the ability to immerse yourself fully in the learning process, following an organic and self-directed train of thought.

However, this autodidact approach may gradually be lost if it is not used or supported. In traditional learning environments, children often learn that the way they approach new material—such as reading and math techniques—is considered incorrect. They may be told that they are missing steps in the way they solve a math problem. These children rarely appreciate having to show their work. This can be very frustrating to them as they do not always "see" the steps as necessary or efficient. Or they may not follow formal writing techniques. It is more important to them that the story be just so than to worry about the capitals and spelling. They often find their independent, self-guided nature does not always pay off; they are repetitively told that they are doing it "wrong." Some care, and wait for the teacher to explain, some don't, but over time there is an impact either way.

> *In the first grade, Sophie was four. The teacher told her she would learn multiplication next year. At home she asked, "Mommy, if this is multiplication, then how do you divide?" One example was all she needed. "Okay," she said, and off she went. Sophie needed no further explanation.*
>
> *During the first grade, she was given a test with multiplication. Sophie skipped those questions because she was told by her teacher that you don't learn multiplication until*

> *the second grade. She skipped the multiplication questions because, "if I can do this, they will find it strange," she said.*

This authentic process of gaining and understanding knowledge is the most engaging way to learn. It is filled with passionate enjoyment, self-motivation and self-direction. It is a trait to cherish and to keep alive. The traditional learning environment may be too slow to engage their motivation. The ability to acquire knowledge independently, knowing where to find it and how to approach it, are all valuable skills; for the autodidact learner, this is an innate process.

This intense desire for knowledge and understanding can be supported through differentiation. Autodidact learners can maintain their own learning pace while the teacher directs the classroom pace. This enables teachers to look beyond the standard curriculum, providing the breadth and depth autodidact learners need. The highly–profoundly gifted have a natural tendency towards breadth and/or depth in their areas of interests. By nurturing their natural inclination, you also nurture their passionate curiosity and allow them to engage in their own authentic learning process.

Problem Seekers

Gifted individuals tend to be natural problem solvers. This is especially true for highly–profoundly gifted individuals, who often see an endless array of solutions and possibilities. A topic is rarely complete for them. For every answer, there is at least one new question, or problem that must be solved. They have an efficiency about them as they follow their own sense of direction, creating their own strategy, approach, and method. Complexity is what drives them. Generally accepted theories are not always followed.

Integrated Thinkers

Highly–profoundly gifted children combine synthesis and analysis. Analytical thinking breaks down a problem step by step in order to reach a result, while synthesis allows for leaps in thought by merging concepts across domains. Highly–profoundly gifted people typically combine both. They can zoom-in on the details and see them as part of the larger and sometimes abstract whole.[10]

Self-Induced Structure

Overall, highly–profoundly gifted individuals thrive on creating structure for themselves. Step-by-step education can be contrary to their very nature. They make leaps between thoughts that seemingly have little to do with each other, and then intricately fit them all together. It may appear as pure chaos to a bystander, however, it is often an intuitive process. Tests that only allow for one answer, may be very difficult for them. Often, they are creating their own logic systems, which can make it difficult to follow someone else's structure or prescribed methods. It's important for the developing child to recognize that there is a world where they can explore and play with their own theories and strategies—and a world where they must learn to follow established rules. Both can exist next to each other, and each world might even benefit from the other.

Idealism

> *"The root of excellence is perfectionism. It is the driving force in the personality that propels the individual towards achieving higher goals. There is a strong correlation between perfectionism and giftedness. I have yet to meet a gifted person who wasn't perfectionistic in some way."*[7]

Perfectionism is one hallmark of giftedness. However, highly–profoundly gifted people tend to want more than perfection. They want *more than* to comply with the rules exactly as they were told or to get excellent grades because that's what you're supposed to do. There is perfectionism and then there is idealism. Idealism is difficult to encompass. It's a big idea with a self-imposed hierarchy or value-system.

In my practice, I often see a different drive in these children than you would expect for their age. They have a very strong inner drive to pursue their own ideals. They might know that this ideal—which they can perfectly imagine—is not actually achievable, but they might not. They might believe that anything you can imagine is possible. We want our children to believe this! They often know all too well what reality looks like. They can see the gap between reality and their ideal, but they have a difficult time accepting it. Often, according to their value-system, it shouldn't be that way; and they can feel obligated to effect change. Effecting big change is difficult and can take time. Children who feel deflated can benefit from grit and the developmental of resilience. We all need coping mechanisms for how we respond to the realities of our imperfect world. Highly–profoundly gifted children, like all children, need grit to pursue their dreams and resilience to persevere—even when the task or situation feels impossible.

The ability to imagine what is possible and to idealize is a rare human trait. Frustration often arises when a highly–profoundly gifted child realizes—or feels—that what they envisioned may not be achievable. At the same time, they can often see an endless number of alternatives or improvements. They can keep the parent problem, the abstract aspiration in mind. At school, this can manifest as the child being the ideal student or teacher pleaser, always knowing the answers, masking their true abilities, or intentionally avoiding higher grades than a friend. As these children get older, their experiences and their world evolve along with their ideals.

> *Idealism exists among gifted people, where there's a sense of disparity between what we are and what we could be, and that disparity becomes the fuel for an inner self-becoming toward perfection.*[12]

Viewing the world as how things should be can lead to disappointment when realization sets in. They may try to understand life by rules and norms and find out that there are a lot of exceptions, for everything, that can't always be justified. Cynicism can be a well-known weapon for these young people. It is estimated that nearly all highly–profoundly gifted individuals experience at least one episode of existential depression in their lifetime.[13]

> *This sense of disappointment can lead to existential depression, which is more common among gifted individuals. Once experienced, existential depression must be continually addressed. Depression doesn't always arise from disillusionment with life; however, existential concerns are often present in depressive episodes. Depression in children and teens is more likely to be expressed as an irritable mood and angry outbursts. Signs of depression might include fighting, rudeness, restlessness, sulking, substance use, or being withdrawn and quiet. Identifying depression in teens can be challenging, as early symptoms— such as underachievement, rebelliousness, or irritability— are often attributed to other causes. Struggling with existential issues can leave the individual feeling estranged from their peers, especially when their concerns are met with confusion, hostility, or dismissal, often leading to inner conflict or tension with others. This struggle and feelings of loneliness can lead to social and emotional distress.*[14]

Existential Questions

> *Incidentally, it is proof of a good mind when a person knows how to ask good questions. —Immanuel Kant*

Existentialism entails your vision of how things are, how you are, and what the world is like. Idealism can get in the way. Those experiencing existential conflict see how things should be versus how things are. They seek universal rules and answers, but they also see the injustices, the contradictions, and the hypocrisy in the world. Gifted individuals are more likely to suffer internal conflict when they see the difference between "what is" and "what ought to be." Dabrowski saw existential conflict as a positive indicator of potential development.

> *Asking questions means waiting, even for a lifetime.*
> *—Heidegger*

Here are some examples of existential questions:

- *Who or what provides meaning in life?*
- *Is everything coincidence or fate?*
- *Are our lives predetermined?*
- *What is the purpose of my life?*

We sometimes hear these questions from people during a midlife crisis. However, they also occur in children who have yet to go through puberty. Children as young as six years old can be overwhelmed by the question of whether their life is fixed.

These children may also feel disappointment in themselves when they realize they cannot consistently live up to their own value system and beliefs. Sometimes their behaviors and their value systems may collide. This can lead to a cycle of recognition, denial, frustration, low self-esteem, a sense of meaninglessness, and many conflicting thoughts—often resulting in of concern, reflection, and contemplation.

Children experiencing existential conflict want to make changes in the world but also see their limited impact. The result is often frustration and feelings of powerlessness. Their awareness can fixate on their lone expression of one compared to the monstrosity of the universe at large. Who are we to bring about change?

> *Why does someone ask you how you are when they don't even have time to really listen to your answer?*
>
> *I don't understand how people can get satisfaction from an average result.*
>
> *How can we change the world? They don't even listen to us. People just do the same thing they did a hundred years ago, only now they are better equipped at doing it. Like when people nod along with the dumbest boss just because they can't think for themselves or because they're scared.*

The feeling that there is never enough time, money, or resources available to pursue your goals—or to excel in what matters most to you— can be deeply frustrating. When that frustration turns into a belief that nothing can be done, it may lead to feelings of learned helplessness. They often reduce their ownership and decide to let others solve it.

> *Treating the depression instead of trying to improve the environment is like trying to stop a leaking roof by mopping the floor. Gifted children may also experience existential depression when they become preoccupied with questions of existence or distressed by the gap between the ideal world in their minds and the reality around them.*[16]

Depression can be inflicted by an awareness of personal energy and talents combined with the lack of place to go or meaningful place to use it. Their perceptions of meaning or meaningless are often very acute. They seem to possess a need for alignment between meaning, themselves, and their environment.

Existential depression is more common in highly–profoundly gifted people. The form of questioning that precedes existential depression is closely related to the type of questions highly–profoundly gifted individuals tend to ask themselves more frequently and more deeply.

It is important to realize that these hours of self-reflection are not necessarily bad. Dabrowski[17] believed that this is a part of life, and that we all need conflict to reflect, evaluate, and potentially change. The potential lies in accepting these experiences as natural parts of life and allowing the motivation behind your dissatisfaction to propel you forward.

As much as they may suffer from dealing with these existential questions, looking for meaning in life can become a high-powered engine. These existential questions can make them re-evaluate life and what they want to do with it. Understanding why you do what you do—and having a sense of purpose that is intertwined with emotion, as is often the case with highly–profoundly gifted children—is a powerful engine for living an authentic life.

It can be a potent source of motivation, a powerful energy source that you can tap to close the gap between what is and what should be. A steppingstone to a higher level of consciousness, a sharper, more clear view of life for which you must first let your old foundation crumble. Or, as I say during my counseling, it is better not to build a new house on the demolition waste of the previous house.

Given the philosophical nature of their questions, it is both useful and instructive to seek for answers through the practice of philosophy. Philosophical conversations can be very beneficial given their abstract nature and open-minded thinking. It is not about the individual or about right or wrong, but about the thought process and what we think in the here and now. A difficult pursuit for a teenager who has already tormented many egos.

Sadistic Friend

A sadistic friend is an imaginary "friend," someone who will walk by their side for years. A friend who constantly undermines them from within. With degrading, perpetual thoughts such as "you are not gifted, you can't do that." Everything that could go wrong is assumed. If that friend is listened to long enough, he will eventually prove himself right; nothing or no one is infallible. At the same time, there is something satisfying about listening to this sadistic friend, it proves your worst thoughts to be right.

Imposter syndrome is also a common occurrence, in which the qualities of their giftedness are minimized or denied. The cause of positive outcomes shifts from success to luck—from "a job well done" to "it was an easy task," or "If they only knew what I'm really capable of, they wouldn't give such compliments!"

This sadistic friend can cause powerful feelings of guilt. Because of their multipotentiality, highly–profoundly gifted young people may experience these feelings more frequently and with greater intensity.[18]

> *For me, it just happens, while others have to put in a lot of effort. I didn't work hard.*
>
> *I would not say that I have the best marks in the class, I forgot to prepare for the test.*
>
> *My classmates are full of praise for me, but I don't believe it.*
>
> *Why is he being so kind to me? What is he going to ask me to do?*
>
> *I'm not going to say I know the answer, they'll think I'm a know-it-all.*

One might feel that they are not accepted, but it could also be a reflection of their own thoughts. There are, however, plenty of examples of people eager to show these children, "you're really not as smart as you think you are"—a fleeting moment glory for our sadistic friend.

Personal Idealism vs. Worldly Ideals

It is better to discover and define your own norms and values organically through experience—even if they deviate from "the norm" or others' expectations. For developing children and young people, trying to conform can be emotionally exhausting and becomes a source of disappointment and self-denial. In my counseling sessions, I help children understand the difference between personal idealism and worldly idealism. Worldly ideals are the cliché-type of idealism: ending world poverty, world peace, no child left behind, fair wages for everybody. These are worldly ideals that no one person on their own can accomplish, if ever. These ideals require big, powerful forces, and many good-willing people.

What one can try to accomplish, however, are personal ideals. For example: helping your family, donating to a charity, fundraising with a bake sale, doing your best at school, learning from your mistakes, or having a bedroom you love because you decorated it yourself. These are all goals your child can achieve with a little outside help. These goals are doable for them and when they engage in them, it can make their world and the world of those close to them a bit better.

The What-if Continuum

> *You see things, and you say, "why?", But I dream things that never were, and I say, "why not?"*[19]

From my experience, idealism—when combined with imaginational overexcitability (OE; see the section on overexcitabilities)—allows highly–profoundly gifted individuals to perceive the real world and the imaginary world as a continuum. The gap between "what is" and "what if" does not exist. They see a strong need and often feel a powerful pull towards a solution that would make the world a better place. They can easily imagine a world where their "if" already exists.

As discussed in Brackmann's contribution, highly–profoundly gifted individuals "usually have an ideal in their head that far exceeds the real world." They do not see a gap between "what is" and "what if" and therefore experience no obstacles just because what they envision does not exist yet. The world of possibilities suddenly becomes much larger because they can see this ideal—the "what if." They experience great discomfort as they see the problem. They imagine the ideal situation and must take action. To them, they have no choice. It is the right thing to do so they must do it.

This is a beautiful trait which we must cherish in them. Their ability to envision the world as it should, can help make it a better place—but we must allow them the confidence to trust their innate idealism and support them in bridging the gap between "what if" and "what is."

Asynchrony

> *Giftedness is asynchronous development, in which advanced cognitive abilities and heightened intensity combine to create inner experiences and awareness that are qualitatively different from the norm. This asynchrony increases with higher intellectual capacity. The uniqueness of the*

> *gifted renders them particularly vulnerable and requires modifications in parenting, teaching, and counseling in order for them to develop optimally.*[20]

Asynchrony is the mismatch between cognitive, social, and emotional development. Adults working with highly–profoundly gifted children can wonder how such a brilliant child has no awareness of things you should or should not say in public (the easiest explanation is that they want to know!). Parents might wonder why their highly verbal child might find solving puzzles challenging. Or, why their very responsible child—who rarely seems to do anything wrong—can suddenly throw themselves on the floor screaming because you turned off their favorite TV show to visit their grandparents.

The greater the intellectual capacities, the greater the asynchrony. A child may be very advanced in math but have trouble with reading skills or gross motor skills.[21]

Asynchrony is so common among the highly–profoundly gifted that it is considered a typical trait for them[22]. It is part of their personal fingerprint, meaning each child must be approached individually when planning differentiation. There is no one-size-fits-all solution for these children; every child's needs, must be reviewed and adapted accordingly. We notice that once they are engaged in their development, the jumps can be gigantic. The older they become, the less you may notice the asynchrony.

More than Intelligence

When the focus is solely the intellect of the child, the asynchronous gap can become bigger. It can place too much emphasis on the child's intellectual achievements, allowing those accomplishments to define their identity or self-image, rather than recognizing the child as a person. Gibello[23] calls this cognitive disharmony.

These children often have a "prove-it or lose-it" mentality based on their own perfectionism. They often move through a fixed comfort zone where they can enjoy and be proud of what they have accomplished. They are used to always being the best, however, they find it hard to prove that they are gifted.

Guiding these children often involves finding a balance between satisfying their intellectual hunger and providing space for physical and creative development. There are no one-size-fits-all solutions—only individualized approaches based on each child's unique development and educational needs.

A highly–profoundly gifted child is not always a high performing child. Often, the traditional educational environment does not meet the needs of these children. They may not be engaged in the environment and therefore not performing or achieving as expected. The environment is not providing what they need to develop. The environment may not be conducive to their social, emotional, physical, cognitive, and/or altruistic needs. Most likely, their needs are not being met in a combination of these developmental areas.

Giftedness does not equal achievement when the learning environment fails to meet the child's educational or developmental needs. When we judge giftedness only on what the child is achieving, we miss some of our highly–profoundly gifted children completely. They may remain under the radar or overlooked completely. Cognitive ability is only one factor of giftedness.

We must remember that a child, no matter how intelligent, is more than just its intelligence or its achievements. Highly–profoundly gifted individuals can often feel the pressure of the environment. The pressure of the environment is the ill-fit; the mismatch between their needs and what the environment is offering them. They may respond to this mismatch by independently pursuing their intellectual or creative interests—or by disengaging entirely.

Lack of Experience

> *A boy asks a woman in the toy store how many pieces there are exactly in the kit. The lady replies that he is much too young for that and that the toys in aisle three are better suited for his age.*
>
> *Your child accompanies you into a store and asks you countless questions. Nothing out of the ordinary for you. The cashier smiles, however, the gentleman to your left looks appalled when you give your child a mature, in-depth answer. You know to give your child the full picture all at once.*
>
> *You go to register your child for an activity you know your child will really enjoy. However, you are told, "you will have to wait another two years when you child is the appropriate age."*

Highly–profoundly children may sense that others may or may not admire them for their ideas and achievements. This may induce pressure to perform and over time they may also become dependent on praise and external affirmations from others. Overvaluing achievement can restrict a child's natural learning process, curiosity, or self-initiated exploration.

A focus on chronological age and linear, sequential learning can also limit the learning process of a highly–profoundly gifted child. Waiting until they are the "required age" often leaves them disappointed and does not support their natural readiness. They can be ready much earlier than their age-mates.

Through countless conversations and activities with preschoolers, children, and young people, I have learned that asynchronous development often brings with it a peculiar kind of mismatch. I call it "lack of experience." This is the mismatch between their capabilities and the world around them. I have noted two forms: lack of experience due to age or lack of experience due to opportunities.

I tend to call experience a euphemism. It is a very pretty word for falling on your face enough times to learn how to get back up again. Falling is how you learn you will survive—if you start by crawling back up again.

As a toddler, you go through the process of learning to walk. When you fall, you have two choices: you can either keep lying on the floor or you can crawl back up again. There are two reasons you might not get up again: either you can't because your muscles aren't ready yet (due to age), or you don't know you're supposed to stand up and try again (due to opportunity). This is where a supportive environment is the answer. A supportive environment teaches them how to stand up again, step by step, encouragement by encouragement. You support them, they get up again, and as they gain strength and stability, they learn to crawl—and you let go.

Lack of Experience Due to Age

With limited life experience due to age, a child has an increased awareness of the world around him—for example, a theoretical understanding of what war is might include the data on deaths and injuries and the knowledge of strategies used. However, because of their young age, they lack the experience needed to process it adequately. This often results in a lot of frustration and insecurity. They physically can't swallow the emotional aspect of war. With respect to motor skills, they might see or be able to visualize what they want to build or create, and they know how to do it, but the physical development of their motor skills might not be able to do what their mind visualizes or knows how to do.

Complex pieces of knowledge that they may divulge in great number to their class may be ignored or shut down. The teacher may completely disregard the child's knowledge because the other students either don't understand it, aren't ready for it, or may feel uneasy about the information. Statements such as "you are still too young for that," "you should not take that into account," "that is not correct" may be heard. These thwarted comments or dismissive solutions—without proper explanation—can create feelings of guilt or uneasiness in the child.

Appropriate differentiated material can be an excellent solution. Learning materials can be dense in content and offer the complexity these children need—while also being emotionally appropriate.

Lack of Experience Due to Lack of Opportunities

> *The path between raw talent and achievements is paved with chances of failure —Els De Wit*

Another type of asynchrony, often seen as a problem rather than a skew, is the gap between raw talent and achievement. Their talent may have naturally led them to achievements as a matter of course. However, part of the path must also include sufficient opportunities for potentially less pleasant experience—such as added challenges or new perspectives—that can foster additional growth and learning. Indeed, we must grant them this too. This gives the child the opportunity to develop grit, emotional resilience, and long-term growth potential.

The opportunity to encounter and experience less-than-expected outcomes is essential for holistic growth and development. It is indeed a skewed growth. Growth is not always realized immediately; rather, it is a developmental opportunity that accumulates and reveals itself over time. This is the opportunity for experience. They may be accustomed to immediate success from an early age, due to a lack of opportunities. In crawling for example, this is also what happens when we keep our child in the cradle for too long. They haven't been given the chance or the opportunity. Providing opportunities for growth includes allowing the child to experience failure and develop emotional grit and resilience, thereby supporting their holistic development.

It is important that these children receive feedback on their thinking processes—without underestimating their intellectual capacities. However, we also can't overestimate their emotional maturity. We must not forget, most importantly, that they are developing children.

References

[1] Persson, Roland S. 2015. "Through the Looking-Glass: Understanding the Social Dynamics of Human Nature and Gifted Identity." In *Make Them Shine: Identification and Understanding of Gifted Children and Consideration of Their Social and Emotional Needs*, edited by R. Klingner, 37–76. Zürich, CH: LIT Verlag.

[2] Sword, Lisa. 2001. "Emotional Intensity in Gifted Children." Retrieved from https://www.sengifted.org.

[3] "De theorie van positieve desintegratie." Last modified 2021. http://www.positievedesintegratie.nl.

[4, 15, 17] Daniels, Susan, and Michael M. Piechowski. 2008. *Living with Intensity*. Scottsdale, AZ: Great Potential Press.

[5] Albert, Robert S. 1994. "Talent Development, II: The Contribution of Early Family History to the Achievement of Eminence." In *Talent Development, II*, edited by Nicholas Colangelo and Susan Assouline. Ohio: Psychology Press.

[6] Sallin, J. H. 2020. "High, Exceptional and Profound Giftedness." Last modified 2020. https://giftedconsortium.com.

[7, 10, 21] Lovecky, Deirdre. 1994. "Exceptionally Gifted Children: Different Minds." *Roeper Review* 17 (2): 116–120.

[8] Brackmann, Andrea. 2020. *Extrem Begabt: Die Persönlichkeitsstruktur von Höchstbegabten und Genies*. Stuttgart: Klett-Cotta.

[9, 18] Grobman, Julian. 2021. "A Psychodynamic Psychotherapy Approach to the Emotional Problems of Exceptionally and Profoundly Gifted Adolescents and Adults: A Psychiatrist's Experience."

[11] Silverman, Sharon. 2019. "Perfectionism and the Gifted Child." https://www.hoagiesgifted.org/perfectionism.htm.

[12] Heylighen, Francis. 2013. "Gifted People and Their Problems." https://www.davidsongifted.org.

[13, 14] Webb, James T. 2008. "Dabrowski's Theory and Existential Depression in Gifted Children and Adults."

[16] Probst, Barbara. 2007. "When Your Child's Second Exceptionality Is Emotional: Looking Beyond Psychiatric Diagnosis." https://www.davidsongifted.org.

[19, 22] Neville, Christine, Michael Piechowski, and Stephanie Tolan. 2017. *Off the Charts: Asynchrony and the Gifted Child*. New York: Royal Fireworks Press.

[20] Vaivre-Douret, Laurence. 2011. "Developmental and Cognitive Characteristics of 'High- Level Potentialities' (Highly Gifted) Children." *International Journal of Pediatrics* 2011: Article ID 420297. https://doi.org/10.1155/2011/420297.

Part 2
Giftedness from a Historical and Socio-Cultural Perspective

Chapter 4

What Can We Learn from Highly–Profoundly Gifted Personalities through History

Andrea Brackmann

There are generally two predominant perceptions of brilliant personalities: they are viewed either as child prodigies, outstanding masterminds, and successful high-flyers—or as misunderstood, unstable, lone fighters—often referred to as "genius" and "madness." This contradiction can also be found in the doctrines of psychological research. Gifted individuals—including many who are highly–profoundly gifted but unrecognized—are often perceived in extremes: either excelling academically or professionally, or as social misfits. They are seen as either more physically, socially, and emotionally stable than their peers[1], or as being associated with school problems, social awkwardness, and emotional difficulties.[2] For the highly gifted and geniuses, however, neither one nor the other extreme is fair. Their reality is far more differentiated and complex.

Indeed, well-known geniuses often exhibited outstanding talent and a powerful drive to achieve from an early age. Many had difficulties to contend with at the same time. It often required specific conditions—and sometimes fortunate circumstances—for them to discover their unique abilities, believe in themselves, and fully develop their talent.

Asynchrony

With the highly gifted and geniuses, child development often takes place in time shifted leaps.[3] Some need more time to learn certain skills, e.g. talking, running or drawing. Sometimes their mental development is far ahead of their motor, emotional, or social development.

As a general rule, they later make up for it many times over.

ALBERT EINSTEIN (1879–1955), one of the most important physicists in history was noticeably introverted as a child, and experienced delays in both language and motor skills. He started speaking his first words at the age of three, and only individual words. Even into adolescence, he expressed himself quietly and hesitantly. The housekeeper called him "the fool." He had little contact with peers, behaved in a physically awkward and unsportsmanlike manner and was therefore shamed by his father.[4]

His parents were concerned, and the doctor declared Einstein to be slow. The young boy preferred to work in his uncle's workshop, where he could experiment; his uncle was an electrical engineer. Einstein played his violin for hours and read books. At school, however, he was, as he later writes, "always the last one."[5]

At the age of 15, Einstein dropped out of school due to "nervous breakdowns." He lived with his parents in Italy for a year and worked intensively on philosophy, physics, and politics. His parents let him follow his own path for a time, until he was accepted into a school in Aarau, Switzerland, which embraced liberal principles and promoted independent learning. It was there that Einstein became a motivated student, and his performance improved in all courses. A teacher eventually recognized Einstein's extraordinary talent and later recommended him to the university as a "child prodigy."

As an adult, the quiet and late developed, Einstein not only became an important physicist, but also a great, humorous speaker. He authored numerous eloquent works on physics, politics, philosophy, psychology, and education.

A certain slowness and restraint are often misinterpreted in the highly–profoundly gifted. They have not too little going on in their head, but too much. Their highly active brains absorb vast amounts of information and process it more intensely and complexly than others. They often need more time for this.[6]

Group games or team sports can initially overwhelm the highly gifted because of the multitude of stimuli.

In individual sports such as table tennis, tennis, or fencing they often have far better skills. Sometimes their motor skills are awkward because they think too much about movement sequences. However, once they understand the movements, they can really enjoy exercise. As a child, their undeveloped skills often do not match the perfect picture they have in their heads. Often, they will only participate in an activity when they are certain that they have mastered the activity well enough.[7]

The nuclear physicist LISE MEITNER (1878–1968) was considered stubborn in childhood and "difficult to educate" even by her loving, patient mother. Lise only reads books all day and refuses to help the household. She was the smallest, most delicate, and most sensitive of the seven siblings. At school she was shy and reserved on the one hand, but stubborn and persistent on the other. She showed difficulties with fine motor skills—particularly in handwriting and drawing—and appeared unable to work on activities requiring repetition. In some subjects she seemed to switch off or shut down due to insufficient demands. The teacher did not get along with her and *almost* led the parents to believe that Lise was a "hopeless child."[8]

The parents were not deterred, however. They supported Lise and her siblings in their free time by encouraging the study of foreign languages, providing access to libraries, visiting theaters and museums, and engaging in lively, challenging discussions at the dinner table. After a long struggle, her parents allowed her to graduate so she could start learning physics, mathematics, and philosophy. Lisa Meitner later spoke gratefully of the "intellectually stimulating atmosphere at home" and the patient support of her education by her parents—something highly uncommon for girls at the time. Later, only her male colleague Otto Hahn received the Nobel Prize for the discovery of nuclear fission. Lise Meitner was nominated for the Nobel Prize 48 times, but never received it, despite being recommended several times by renowned colleagues including Albert Einstein and Max Planck.

There are many more brilliant women in history than are commonly known.[9]

Women's achievements are often attributed to men. Other examples include mathematician and computer pioneer, Ada Lovelace; philosopher Émily du Châtelet, and the sculptor Camille Claudel. Still others have been overlooked, forgotten, or not fully recognized for their brilliance, such as Baroque painter, Artemisia Gentileschi; Nobel Prize winners like the writer and publicist Toni Morrison, the geneticist Barbara McClintock, and the first female recipient of the Fields Medal for Mathematics, Maryam Mirzakhani, to name just a few. Winner[10] suspected that the genius traits of independence and exceptional performance challenged traditional female role expectations far more than male ones. Even today, gifted and highly gifted girls are recognized far less often and are less encouraged than boys.

Another striking example of asynchronous development is the painter and sculptor, Pablo Picasso (1881–1973). At the age of four, he painted with enthusiasm and helped his father, also a painter, with commissioned work. In elementary school, Picasso was a loner and dreamer. He didn't want to do anything but paint and stubbornly refused to learn to read, to write, and to do arithmetic. His father finally took him out of school and had a private tutor teach him, to no avail. The father feared that his son would grow up illiterate. However, because of his remarkable talent in painting, Picasso's father sent him to an art academy. There they finally recognized the boy's outstanding talent, and Picasso is allowed to skip two years as a child prodigy. Pablo Picasso also caught up on his development deficiencies. At eleven, Pablo can suddenly read, write, and do arithmetic. Apparently, he learned it on the side and taught himself. As an eleven-year-old Pablo wrote in art magazines, as an adult he wrote poems, essays, and plays.[12]

The inventor, Thomas Alva Edison, also had difficulties in school. At the age of eight, he tearfully declared that he would never return to school because he couldn't follow the lessons properly—and the teacher had called him an "empty head" in front of the entire class. From then on, Edison was tutored at home by his highly educated mother. Edison later said he owed everything he had become to her.[13] The writer Leo Tolstoy often refused to work in school, and his teachers predicted that nothing would come of him. It was only at university that a professor recognized Tolstoy's remarkable intelligence and was inspired by his motivation and love for learning.

The pianist and composer Clara Schumann (1819–1896) did not begin to speak until she was five. Her parents and teachers initially believed that she was hard of hearing. Remarkably, her ear for music and sound was excellent. As a three-year-old, she played the piano very well. Clara Schumann was also considered stubborn and strong-willed. She went to elementary school for a short time but was mostly homeschooled. Her musical talent was intensively developed by her father. Of course, this kind of support by parents is often controversial.

It is important that the child's natural talents and passions are supported and not forced through pressure.

In Clara Schumann's case, the support seemed helpful, and she later commented positively about it. Researchers now suspect that Clara Schumann may have had selective mutism or Asperger's Syndrome.[14] As an adult, she was a celebrated pianist and a mother—productive, successful, lively, and eloquent into old age. This can mean one of two things: either the diagnoses were inaccurate, as is often the case with gifted and highly gifted individuals,[15] or that even non-speaking, autistic children can grow into highly successful adults.

A child who does not speak at age five or who does not learn reading, writing, or arithmetic in school would likely be referred to a psychiatrist or placed in a special education setting today. The child's talent would likely be buried. At that time, however, the school programs were more flexible, and through the help of their parents, Picasso, Schumann, and Edison received individualized guidance that allowed them to pursue their talents and learn at their own pace.

For the highly–profoundly gifted, a strong focus on their dominant talent can be extremely stabilizing.

A child's innate drive to hyper focus on their talent acts as a kind of antidote or relief from internal and external overstimulation. This hyper focus can also apply to highly talented autistsic individuals. Over time, it also helps the children (and adults too, by the way) to gain self-confidence and to develop other academic or social skills.

Sensitivity

Many gifted and highly gifted children and adults have strong sensitivity in one or more areas—emotional or sensory sensitivity.[16] Some react intensely to everyday injustices or dramatic scenes on television, while others are highly sensitive to noise or smells. Some cannot tolerate certain foods, materials, or items of clothing (e.g. tights, scratchy labels, and seams).

If giftedness is based on the nervous system's ability to process information more quickly and in more complex ways, it is entirely possible that sensory and emotional stimuli are processed more intensely.[17]

The physicist and Nobel Prize winner, Pierre Curie was considered "too sensitive for school" and was therefore taught at home. Lise Meitner's parents initially feared that their daughter was too "delicate" to study at university. The writer Franz Kafka was so sensitive to noise that even everyday sounds made it difficult for him to concentrate, often leading to exhaustion and headaches. Albert Einstein, Vincent van Gogh, and Steve Jobs didn't like socks; even as adults they preferred to go barefoot or wear sandals—even in cold weather. They hated wearing restrictive and formal clothing, such as a suit or tuxedo. Picasso and

Einstein were extremely reluctant to visit the hairdresser, as they found it difficult to bear the many touches, smells, and noises.[18]

The natural scientist, Charles Darwin (1809–1882), is known for his pioneering theory of evolution, which he developed after a five-year research expedition aboard a ship that sailed around the world. During his journey, he had endured significant hardships, including excessive alcohol consumption among the crew, cholera outbreaks, extreme heat and cold, and strenuous hikes through the jungle. What is less well known about Darwin, was that as a child and adolescent, he too was particularly sensitive and health prone. He initially studied medicine but could not bear the sight of suffering patients or intensive operations. After all, Darwin's father gave Darwin the option to change subjects.[19] The same applied to the natural scientist Alexander von Humboldt. Driven by an irrepressible thirst for knowledge, he spent half of his life traveling to foreign continents and studying exotic cultures. Alexander von Humboldt was also a sickly, sensitive, and nervous child.[20]

Even as a child, Florence Nightingale (1820–1910), a pioneer of modern healthcare, had a profound reaction to the injustice and suffering of others. She was determined to become a nurse, but this ambition was considered inappropriate in her well-respected aristocratic family. Not allowed to follow her calling, the highly educated and versatile young woman became apathetic and depressed. Nightingale's parents finally gave in to their daughter's will. After completing her training, Nightingale quickly rose through the ranks and took charge of the notorious cholera hospital in London. In 1852, during an unprecedented campaign in the hospitals of the Crimean War, she introduced improved standards of care and hygiene—many of which are still in use today. Later, Nightingale—also gifted in mathematics, statistics, and architecture—advocated politically on behalf of the weak and the sick. For example, she introduced the state of health care and advocated for greater rights for the workers in the Indian colonies.[22]

Nightingale's emotional sensitivity is the foundation of her profound compassion. Her empathy for others served as a powerful drive to improve the situation for those who suffer.

Goertzel et al.[23] suggested that highly gifted children were unhealthy and nervous because they had to take breaks from the overwhelming stimulation present in school and classroom environments. As adults, they learned to deal with their sensitivity better and to have more options for living their lives accordingly. They moved from the big city to more quiet, rural areas. Like Albert Einstein, Vincent van Gogh, and Charles Darwin, they avoided events and the public. Like Marie Curie or Pablo Picasso, they limited contacts to a few close friends. And like Lise Meitner, Simone de Beauvoir, and Ludwig van Beethoven, they longed for extended periods alone in the great outdoors.

Social Contacts

Sometimes, highly gifted individuals feel out of place among their peers because of their unique thinking, perception, and interests.[24]

The writer, philosopher, and Nobel Prize winner Jean Paul Sarte (1905-1980) grew up as an only child and loner. At the age of three, he taught himself to read and learned entire books by heart. He wrote his first novels at seven. His mother tried to slow him down by giving him child-friendly comics. Instead, John Paul combined the content in his own stories with his astute knowledge of German and French literature. It wasn't long before he had adult vocabulary. When it was time to start school at age seven, the teachers held him back a year because he was particularly small and thin and had a malocclusion of the eyes.

His grandfather, a high school teacher, thought John Paul was a genius. John Paul's grandfather taught him at home and developed his talents in a variety of ways. When Sartre went back to the village school, he was afraid of the other students. He's so unusual and different that the other kids won't let him play along. Eventually, Sartre was enrolled in a school for gifted students, but even there, the exceptionally gifted boy stood out—drawing the displeasure of teachers, classmates, and their parents. It wasn't until the age of ten that he completed a full school year at a boarding school for gifted children and made his first good friend, Paul Nizan.[5] The two graduated from high school together at seventeen and went on to attend one of Europe's most prestigious universities, the École Normale Supérieur (ENS). For the first time, Sartre was happy. He studied philosophy, psychology, and Latin to become a teacher. Simultaneously, Sartre attended seminars for filmmaking and jazz music and even learned to box.

Of course, such a special path is not what most parents want for their child.

Sometimes, however, unusual children need unusual solutions.

For the first time, Sartre had the opportunity to develop his talents while being surrounded with like-minded individuals–one of the most important factors for the positive development of profoundly gifted individuals, according to Gross.[26]

When the astrophysicist Stephen Hawking (1942–2018) attended kindergarten for the first time at the age of three, it was a shocking experience. He stood frozen at the edge of the room, overwhelmed and fearful of the many loud, unfamiliar children. Reflecting on the moment, Hawking recalled that his well-educated parents, "had read a lot about the importance of early social contact for children; however, after that terrible morning, they took me out of kindergarten and sent me back a year and a half later." In school and in university, Hawking was considered a shy loner, where he is the youngest of his class. He was given the position of helmsman in the college's sailing club and later stated, "If I could fill a position with clear rules, it was easier for me to be in company… As a helmsman I was unsuccessful, but I made some friends."[27]

Most gifted people approach the world with logic and cannot find their way through the jungle of social rules, expectations, and nuances.

They often think too much and interpret too much in the signals of the other person. Participation in a clearly structured joint activity can be very helpful. As an adult, Hawking led a lively, fulfilling social life (despite significant health restrictions).

Many highly gifted people enjoy being with others but regularly need time for rest and retreat to recover and recharge. That doesn't mean they aren't interested in social issues. Many show a strong sense of justice and an early awareness of world problems.

The physicist and two-time Nobel Prize winner Marie Curie (1867–1934) was known for her cautious nature and avoided the public or social events whenever possible. Surprisingly, however, she was politically active from her youth. Everyone must "strive to take responsibility for humanity. Because it is our human responsibility to help those to whom we can be most useful." During World War I, when she was already a renowned scientist, Curie traveled to the front lines in specially constructed X-ray vehicles to treat the wounded.[28]

Leo Tolstoy, Albert Einstein, Alexander von Humboldt, Florence Nightingale, Vincent van Gogh, the painter Frida Kahlo, and Martin Luther King all engaged with social, ethical, and political issues early in life. The same is true today for highly talented individuals such as publicist Ronan Farrow, the pianist Igor Levit, and climate activist Greta Thunberg. Realizing how unfair the world is can shake the highly gifted to their core both as children and in adulthood. Some need support and comradery to work together with other idealists against injustice.

Underchallenged

The typical symptoms of being underchallenged—such as boredom, difficulty concentrating, restlessness, or loss of motivation—are sometimes less noticeable in the highly gifted than in the moderately gifted.

The highly gifted have a greater tendency to withdraw into themselves or to learn to cover up their otherness and to adapt. Many geniuses have a strong aversion to school.[29]

The computer pioneer, Steve Jobs could already read and do arithmetic when he started school. He learned quickly and got bored in class, even after he skipped a grade. "Usually, he hid in a corner and was busy alone, he didn't want… to have much to do with the rest of the class." Jobs pursued his early, passionate interest in technology rather than playing with his peers.[30]

The theologian and reformer, Martin Luther, was an excellent student, but he described school as "hell and purgatory, in which we were tortured with casus and tempora and yet we learned nothing—absolutely nothing.[31]

Lise Meitner was underchallenged in many subjects and refused to work on boring hard repetitions. Marie Curie went through school in a hurry but still couldn't wait to "finally learn more."[32] The politician and Nobel Prize winner, Winston Churchill, reflected on his school years, describing them as if they were void of everything pleasurable and sensible.[33]

According to Gross[34], the most gifted people have the fewest academic, social, and emotional problems when they are radically accelerated in school and given opportunities to interact with older or equally gifted students at an early age.

Sociologist and civil rights activist, Martin Luther King (1929–1968), grew up in a humble, educated, and warm-hearted home with strong moral values. He was recognized as exceptionally talented early on and started school at the age of five. Even as an adolescent, Martin Luther showed great interest in social issues and at the age of 14, he won a speaker competition on racial segregation. King was allowed to skip high school grades 9 and 12; he was already admitted to the university at the age of 15. King was considered a happy, active, and popular boy and got along well with both his peers and older students.

After completing his sociology and theology studies, he received a doctorate in philosophy.[35]

Radical acceleration was common among many geniuses and highly gifted people who were later successful. Marie Curie graduated from high school at fifteen, the universal genius Johann Wolfgang von Goethe and the physicist Pierre Curie both began their university studies at 16.[36] Stephen Hawking enrolled in the university entrance exam at the age of 16.

Crazy or Declared Crazy?

Extremely gifted people, and geniuses who are not recognized as such and who do not receive support, often have a much more difficult life. For gifted people who are diagnosed with a disorder by untrained doctors, educators, or psychologists, the consequences can be detrimental. Misdiagnoses, such as Asperger's syndrome or social disorders, can lead to completely inappropriate treatment and aggravate symptoms rather than alleviate them.[37] Tragically, over time, the children themselves begin to believe that something is wrong with them. Even highly gifted adults may accept psychological diagnoses, seeking an explanation for their unique nature.

In some cases, overlooked giftedness and the stigmatization resulting from an incorrect diagnosis can have serious consequences.

The painter, Vincent Van Gogh (1853–1890), is still regarded today as a prime example of the "insane genius." He too received numerous diagnoses including bipolar disorder, depression, Asperger's syndrome, epilepsy, and schizophrenia. After a detailed study of the sources, I believe Van Gogh was initially—a completely normal, highly gifted individual with typical peculiarities such as sensitivity, introversion, and intensity. As a child, he seemed "strange" to others, spoke little, drew and read extensively, collected stones and insects, and preferred spending hours alone in nature rather than playing with other children. His parents were concerned, and the doctor suspected, "The boy's cerebellum is probably damaged, nothing will ever come of it."[38] This suspected diagnosis had a profound impact on van Gogh's life, emotional development, and self-assessment.

Like Albert Einstein, van Gogh dropped out of school at the age of 15. At 16, he was sent to London to train to be an art dealer. However, van Gogh turned out to be unsuitable because he could not flatter or lie, and he considered it immoral to sell bad art as good. As a teenager, Van Gogh studied philosophy, social issues, and art. He wrote letters in French and English and devoured novels from world literature. Like many highly gifted people, he was deeply serious about looking for meaning in his life. Van Gogh initially wanted to become a pastor and began studying theology, but after two semesters, he dropped out in disappointment because he could not tolerate the "unbelievable hypocrisy" among theologians. He then worked as an assistant pastor in a Belgian mining village, where he was deeply shocked by the poverty, disease, and hardships miners faced. With a blackened face, Van Gogh hauled sacks of coal through the village alongside the miners, helped the injured after a mine accident; and lived with a miner's family. This was going too far for his superior who fired him. Regarded as a failure by his family, Van Gogh too tormented himself with self-doubt.

The conviction that something was wrong with him was beginning to stick. Van Gogh did not fail due to a lack of intellectual ability, but because he uncompromisingly adhered to his convictions and sought to find his own path. Van Gogh's brother, Theo writes, "he broke all conventions. He is a special person, but people think he's crazy."[40] It wasn't until he was 27 that van Gogh finally decided to paint. Within ten years he created a tremendous artistic oeuvre that was far ahead of its time. Van Gogh established modernism in painting.

More recent research and a comprehensive new edition of his extensive letters have shown that van Gogh was extraordinarily productive intellectually through the last days of his life. The story of his self-severed ear is now considered as controversial among experts as his alleged suicide.[41] No severe depression or delusional disorder was detected. It was certain that van Gogh suffered from epileptiform seizures. He was prone to emotional and sensory overexcitability, common in highly gifted people. In fact, these surges were always followed by phases of complete mental clarity and great productivity. Once it was realized that van Gogh "analyzed his own situation, his own art and the general situation of the art world like no other," these surges of insight were considered innate. "The legend of the manic genius becomes a clever, reflective artist who knew exactly what he was doing."[42]

The long and thorough search for one's own life's work is typical for highly–profoundly gifted individuals; their life paths are often winding.[43] Franz Kafka, Steve Jobs, and Leo Tolstoy each started and dropped out of various courses. For a long time, Marie Curie could not choose between studying literature or physics. For some highly gifted people, this search does not stop for a lifetime. Due to their diverse talents (multipotentiality) and ongoing development, they often change careers more frequently or pursue multiple professions simultaneously.

The artistic talent of the painter and sculptor Camille Claudel (1864–1943) was discovered at the age of twelve. Her father encouraged her talent and sent her to an art academy at an early age. However, her mother was strictly against it. She considered her daughter "not quite right in the head."[44] At that time, a career as a sculptor was unthinkable and offensive for a woman. Claudel received great recognition from renowned professors, and the already famous sculptor Auguste Rodin became her teacher. He called her a "woman of genius." Before long, they have a working relationship and enter a partnership on equal footing. They married, but Rodin did not stick to the agreement and after ten years Claudel separated from him. As a sculptress who lived alone, she fought for her recognition; yet much of her work is attributed to Rodin. Claudel publicly accused Rodin of stealing her ideas and works. Thereupon Claudel was not taken seriously and was accused of paranoia. She received fewer and fewer jobs and fought for her existence. Over time, she became depressed. Claudel's mother eventually arranged for a forced admission to a psychiatric hospital where she spent the rest of her life.

In the case of Camille Claudel, there were many who had a keen interest in questioning her sanity. Her mother feared the reputation of their middle-class family. Auguste Rodin feared his reputation as a unique artist. And society at large feared the disturbance of the ruling order. The bitter irony was that Claudel was mistakenly listed as a man in art encyclopedias until the mid-1970s.

Both van Gogh and Camille Claudel's life paths demonstrate how challenging the life paths of geniuses can be when their unique nature is linked with mental or emotional disorders from an early age. Geniuses are typically unusual people who are way ahead of their time, which is why they are often misunderstood or even declared crazy. They question current rules and authorities. This often also applied to 'normal' highly gifted people. They do not conform, have different views and interests, and are therefore perceived as strange. Of course, even the highly gifted can experience mental health issues, but these must be carefully distinguished from typical personality traits of highly gifted individuals.[45]

Conclusions

The prerequisites under which well-known geniuses could develop their talents:

- Identification of the special talent by parents, relatives, teachers.
- Appreciation and promotion of talent.
- Consideration for peculiarities such as increased sensitivity, introversion, or asynchrony.
- Radical acceleration (acceleration of the school career).
- Attending a special school or homeschooling (if there are severe problems in the traditional school).
- Family characteristics: At least one very ambitious, inquisitive parent; unconventional family dynamics; open and controversial discussions; a high degree of freedom for the children; time spent in the great outdoors; working in the workshop,

> laboratory, or atelier; opportunities for independent discovery and research; access to libraries; the transfer of responsibility; trust in the child's abilities; and a love of truth with clear moral convictions.

According to a recent survey by the German Society for Gifted Children (DGhK), gifted children appeared to benefit mentally and socially-emotionally from homeschooling during the COVID-19 pandemic.[45]

This is not about the question of how to become a genius, but rather what kind of encouragement, guidance, and support can be helpful for the most gifted, especially when facing difficulties.

Restlessness and Resilience

The vast majority of sensitive and introverted highly gifted children described by Goertzel and Hansen, and in the biographies, I have examined[46] become energetic, successful, and tirelessly active adults. This, however, does not mean that they are completely free from social or emotional difficulties.

Due to their highly active nervous system, some highly gifted individuals may be more susceptible to mental or physical health problems into adulthood, such as depression, anxiety, or autoimmune diseases such as allergies and asthma.[47] This seemed to be most evident when an individual's giftedness is not recognized or not appropriately supported.

However, with the highly–profoundly gifted, there is often no either/or: they can be sensitive yet tough shy yet strong-willed, and both sensitive and resilient.

Roeper[48] explains, "From the beginning, the gifted show an even greater awareness of the complexities of the world, a greater desire to make sense of it all. They need to overcome the anxiety that results from this awareness by trying to bring order into the apparent chaos around them. They also have greater skills to deal with the task (p. 153)." Due to their high intelligence and creativity, highly gifted individuals develop powerful strategies throughout their lives to manage the complexity and intensity of their thinking. Often, through this innate process, they gain experience. High intelligence often goes hand in hand with a high degree of resilience.[49]

The ingenious brain is almost always in problem-solving mode.

Geniuses usually have an ideal in their head that far exceeds the real world. This can relate to one's own person and abilities, as well as artistic and/or academic performance or social and political conditions. Any deviation from this ideal causes discontent, unrest, and discomfort in the highly gifted and geniuses. Once they have recognized an error or a problem, they must take action to achieve the best possible state.

Outstanding performance is therefore often the result of what I refer to as "productive restlessness." The excessive mental activity and heightened perceptual abilities of extremely gifted individuals are most effectively channeled through a strong focus on one or two specialties. Long, intensive work on a topic is an important prerequisite for groundbreaking achievements.

The universal genius Leonardo da Vinci was a restless, passionate, and driven spirit who rushes restlessly from one project to another. His thirst for knowledge in all areas is insatiable… Only when painting does he pause and calm down.[50]

The mathematician, Ada Lovelace described her strict and intensive application of scientific studies as a way to positively nurture her overflowing imagination.[51] The natural scientist, Alexander von Humboldt reported a restlessness that was calmed through the enjoyment of physical work.[52] The pianist, Hélène Grimaud writes about a sense of an enormous inner energy that she was able to transfer-to playing the piano. Hélène is now considered to be one of the best pianists of our time worldwide.[53]

The musician and composer, Wolfgang Amadeus Mozart, depicted his composing as less work than resting.[54] Mozart's enormously versatile, intense, and erratic personality only found peace when he was challenged to the maximum when composing, and he was able to direct his enormous energies into productive paths.

Albert Einstein sums it up most clearly: He believed that the creative person tried to create a simplified, clear version to substitute for the often, swirling personal experience in order to seek calm and stability. The painter, the poet, the philosopher, and the natural scientist all do this, each in their own way.[55]

References

[1] Rost, Detlev. *Hochbegabte und hochleistende Jugendliche*. Münster: Waxmann, 2000; Terman, Lewis M. *Genetic Studies of Genius*: Vol. 1, "Mental and Physical Traits of a thousand Gifted Children". Stanford: Stanford Universitiy Press, 1925.

[2 15 37] Webb, James T. *Doppeldiagnosen und Fehldiagnosen bei Hochbegabung*. Bern: Huber, 2015.

[3] Brackmann, Andrea. *Extrem begabt. Die Persönlichkeitsstruktur von Höchstbegabten und Genies*. Stuttgart: Klett-Cotta, 2020; Lovecky, Deidre V. "Exceptionally gifted Children: Different minds". *Roeper Review*, Vol. 17 (2) (1994): 116-120.

[4 38] Goertzel, Mildred G. et al. *300 Eminent Personalities: A psychological analysis of the famous*. San Francisco, CA: Joey-Bass, 1978.

[5] Winkler, Daniel & Voight, Adam. "Giftedness and Overexcitability: Investigating the Relationship Using Meta Analysis". *Gifted Child Quarterly*, 60 (4) (2016): 243-257.

[6 7] Lovecky, Deidre V. "Exceptionally gifted Children: Different minds". *Roeper Review*, Vol. 17 (2) (1994): 116-120.

[8] Rennert, David &Traxler, Tanja. *Lise Meitner: Pionierin des Atomzeitalters*. Salzburg: Residenz, 2018.

[9] Jaffé, Deborah. *Geniale Frauen. Berühmte Erfinderinnen von Melitta Bentz bis Marie Curie*. München: Piper, 2014.

[10] Winner, Ellen. *Hochbegabt*. Stuttgart: Klett-Cotta, 2004.

[11] Fietze, Katharina. *Kluge Mädchen. Frauen entdecken ihre Hochbegabung*. Berlin: Orlanda, 2010.

[12 23 25 29 35] Goertzel, Ted G. & Hansen, Ariel M. *Cradles of Eminence*. Scottsdale: Great Potential Press, 2004.

[13 31 33 36] Prause, Gerhard. *Genies in der Schule*. Münster: LIT, 2006.

[14] Reich, Nancy B. *Clara Schumann. Eine Biographie*. Wunderlich: Hamburg, 1991.

[16] Winkler, Daniel & Voight, Adam. "Giftedness and Overexcitability: Investigating the Relationship Using Meta Analysis". *Gifted Child Quarterly*, 60 (4) (2016): 243-257.; [Gere], Douglas R. et al. "Sensory sensitivities of gifted children". *American Journal of Occupational Therapy*, 63 (2009): 288-295.

[17] Brackmann, Andrea. *Jenseits der Norm: Hochbegabt und hoch sensibel? Die seelischen und sozialen Aspekte der Hochbegabung bei Kindern und Erwachsenen.* Stuttgart: Klett-Cotta, 2005.

[18] Prause, Gerhard. *Genies ganz privat.* München: dtv, 1998.

[19] Stone, Irving. *Der Schöpfung wunderbare Wege. Das Leben des Charles Darwin.* Hamburg: Rowohlt, 2005.

[20 52] Wulf, Andrea. *Alexander von Humboldt und die Erfindung der Natur.* München: C.Bertelsmann, 2016.

[21] Genschorek, Wolfgang. *Schwester Florence Nightingale.* Leipzig: Hirtel/Teubner, 1990.

[22] Strachey, Lytton. *Florence Nightingale. Eine Biographie.* München: Penguin, 1980.

[24] Hollingworth, Leta. *Children above 180 IQ: Their origin and development.* New York: World Book, 1942; Winner, Ellen. *Hochbegabt.* Stuttgart: Klett-Cotta, 2004.

[26 34] Gross, Marica. *Exceptionally Gifted Children.* London: Routledge, 2003.

[27] Hawking, Stephen. *Meine kurze Geschichte.* Hamburg: Rowolth, 2015.

[28 32] Wimbauer, Tobias (Hrsg.). *Marie Curie. Selbstbiographie.* Nimmertal 75, 2016.

[30] Isaacson, Walter. *Steve Jobs. Die autorisierte Biografie des Apple-Gründers.* München: BtB, 2012.

[39] Plachta, Bodo (Hrsg.). *Vincent van Gogh.* Briefe. Ditzingen: Reclam, 2011.

[40 41] Naifeh, Steven & White Smith, Gregory. *Van Gogh—Sein Leben.* Frankfurt/M: S. Fischer, 2012.

[42] Koldehoff, Stefan. *Ein rationales Genie.* Hamburg: Die Zeit, No 47. 2009.

[43] Schwiebert, Andrea. *Kluge Köpfe, krumme Wege? Wie Hochbegabte den passenden Berufsweg finden.* Paderborn: Junfermann, 2015.

[44] Duda, Sibylle & Pusch, Luise F. *WahnsinnsFrauen.* Frankfurt/M: Suhrkamp, 1994.

[45] Brackmann, Andrea. *Jenseits der Norm: Hochbegabt und hoch sensibel? Die seelischen und sozialen Aspekte der Hochbegabung bei Kindern und Erwachsenen.* Stuttgart: Klett-Cotta, 2005; Schmider, Silvera. "Corona: Die beste Schulzeit des Lebens?" *Labyrinth* 143, Deutsche Gesellschaft für das hochbegabte Kind (DGhK), 2020; Webb, James T. *Doppeldiagnosen und Fehldiagnosen bei Hochbegabung.* Bern: Huber, 2015.

[46] Brackmann, Andrea. *Extrem begabt. Die Persönlichkeitsstruktur von Höchstbegabten und Genies.* Stuttgart: Klett-Cotta, 2020.; Goertzel, Ted G. & Hansen, Ariel M. *Cradles of Eminence.* Scottsdale: Great Potential Press, 2004.; Goertzel, Mildred G. et al. *300 Eminent Personalities: A psychological analysis of the famous.* San Francisco, CA: Joey-Bass, 1978.

[47] Karpinski, Ruth I. et al. "High intelligence: A risk factor for psychological and physiological overexcitabilities". Elsevier: *Intelligence 66* (2018): 8-23.

[48] Roeper, Annemarie. "The "I" of the beholder: An essay on the Self, it´s exsistence and it´s power". *Roeper Review*, 20 (3) (1998): 144-149.

[49] Daniels, Susan & Piechowski, M. Michael. (Hrgs.). *Living with Intensitiy.* Tucson: Great Potential Press, 2009.

[50] Isaacson, Walter. *Leonardo da Vinci: Die Biographie.* Berlin: Propyläen, 2018.

[51] Krämer, Sybille (Hrsg.). *Ada Lovelace. Die Pionierin der Computertechnik und ihre Nachfolgerinnen.* München: Wilhelm Fink, 2015.

[53] Grimaud, Hélène. *Wolfssonate.* München: Blanvalet, 2006.

[54] Hildesheimer, Wolfgang. *Mozart.* Frankfurt/M: Suhrkamp, 1993.

[55] Wickert, Johannes. *Albert Einstein.* Hamburg: Rowohlt, 2010.

Chapter 5

Socio-Cultural Context of Highly–Profoundly Gifted

Roland Persson, Ph.D.

As far as I know, no scholar, teacher, parent, or citizen of any country has ever disputed the fact that some individuals excel in ways that surpass most others, regardless of the context. While different societies may place varying levels of value on this group, few are likely to question their existence or exceptional abilities. Contentions emerge, however, when we try to explain why such differences in skills and abilities exist. It becomes even more contentious when attempting to accommodate and implement these differences in education, society, and professional life. The reason for this diversity of opinion and practice is easy to explain.

Individual prowess, particularly when extreme, presents a challenge to society—unless it somehow strengthens the collective identity or helps the majority of society feel good about themselves.

Sports heroes, world-famous actors, authors, or other celebrities are examples of such individuals. We admire these individuals, often look up to them for various reasons, and take great pride in acknowledging their national origin, as it reflects well on everyone. However, the same recognition is not usually extended to individuals with extreme intellectual abilities, social skills, or understanding. These extremes are often perceived as threatening to the self-esteem of those who are not equally skilled and may pose a threat to leadership—especially when brilliant insights and an unwavering sense of fairness risk exposing injustice and corruption. This is precisely what American psychologist, Leta Hollingworth discovered decades ago, long before the term *gifted education* existed. She studied a small group of exceptionally gifted children and followed their development for over twenty years. Hollingworth concluded that:

> *a lesson which many gifted persons never learn as long as they live is that human beings in general are inherently very different from themselves in thought, in action, in general intention, and in interests. Many a reformer has died at the hands of a mob, which he was trying to improve in the belief that other human beings can and should enjoy what he enjoys. This is one of the most painful and difficult lessons that each gifted child must learn if personal development is to proceed successfully.*[2]

While this might not apply to everyone—after all, Hollingworth studied a small group of individuals—history is full of examples of how individuals with extraordinary abilities, profound understanding, and remarkable deeds have remained unrecognized or entirely unknown. The ones who somehow reached the public eye often found themselves ridiculed by their contemporary society. Sometimes they simply vanished because they were too difficult to understand or too inconvenient for established social structures and their leaders to tolerate. Art and music historians are well aware of this phenomenon. Few creatively gifted individuals have been recognized and valued during their own lifetime. Only after their demise, were they recognized as ground-breaking geniuses and as heralds of something new, valuable, and unique. Their only "problem" during their lives was that their ideas and insights often challenged established conventions. Recipients of the so-called Genius Grant; the American MacArthur Foundation Fellowship—given to individuals as an investment in their originality—similarly reported how difficult it was for most of them to be creative and pursue something that had never been done before.

While pursuing something unique, unconventional, and unknown can be intrinsically rewarding, it is often also a very lonely endeavor.

Denise Shekerjian[3], an American science journalist, interviewed 40 of these MacArthur Fellows. Her concluding observation hardly reflected the success, the recognition, and the motivating glory that today's world often projects onto unique individuals. She found that society indeed tends to "shun its heretics." Apparently, being too unique is a social problem, and the reason for this lies in the biologically determined social dynamics that govern our reactions to deviations from what most perceive as normal. We rarely reject those who break social convention by choice; we do so automatically if we perceive that the integrity of the social fabric with which we identify is at risk.

The single most important reason for this reaction is the human need for social cohesion.

We are a social species and, as such, we are generally constituted by collectives. This need to maintain in both large and small groups of humans creates *function*, and few are more effective in operationalizing that function than the extremely gifted and talented.

One might think of such socio-functional behaviors in terms of our general need for *heroes* to look up to and "nerds" to seek help from when complex issues arise. However, there are also the less fortunate *martyrs* among us. They are the exceedingly knowledgeable who have great insight and an unwavering sense of fairness, motivating them to intervene on behalf of others. With the very noblest and most selfless of intentions, they confront leaders and authorities in an effort to achieve justice. Unfortunately, as history has repeatedly shown, such interventions are rarely successful or taken seriously. Instead, these martyrs are often seen as divisive troublemakers and tend to simply disappear from view—either silenced or unfairly discredited, ensuring that no one believes what they are saying. In evolutionary terms, no matter how correct or justified their actions may be, they are frequently perceived as a threat to social cohesion and its leadership.

To better understand these labels—such as hero, nerd, or martyr—one must recognize which social evolutionary function they represent: maintenance, entertainment, and change respectively (see Table 1 for an overview of these functions, their skills, abilities, knowledge domains, and the typical social response). We value and reward maintenance behavior, we depend on entertainment, and we are generally intimidated by the thought of change.

Table 1. Taxonomy of Gifted and Talented Behavior

A taxonomy of gifted or talented behavior, their social function, and the common response of mainstream society to this behavior (adapted from Persson, 2009; 2020)[4]

Primary social function	Skills, abilities and knowledge domains (Examples)	A probable universal social response
Maintenance	• Medicine • Technology • Practical skills • Problem-solving and creativity within social acceptance	Acceptance and encouragement (Supports social cohesion)
Entertainment	• Music • Theatre and drama • Literature • Art • Sports	Acceptance and encouragement (Supports social cohesion)
Change	• Intellectual skills • Understanding causality • Acting on perceived injustice • Problem-solving and creativity beyond social acceptance	Resistance and challenge (Has the potential to threaten social cohesion)

Facts Not Always the Result of Research

We must not overlook the fact that when the exceedingly gifted and talented share knowledge and insight in a context where illusion and wishful thinking take precedence over fact, they are likely to be ignored and are more likely to become martyrs than heroes. This is more common than most of us are aware of, even though our high-tech society prides itself on being science oriented. We tend to seek and accept illusion in order to maintain a positive self-image, believing that the world is always just and that we are more superior than we objectively are. Our brain is programmed by evolution to favor that which is experienced as positive and hopeful. This inclination increases our species' chances of survival over time. Social psychologists have known about this quirky human phenomenon and recognize it as one of many *cognitive biases.* Evolutionary psychiatrists view this tendency as an unconscious survival instinct, where, under adversity, we are motivated to seek escape—even if such an escape is unavailable.

The result of these biological drives prompt us to be selective about which facts to accept and which to ignore. In this context, there is little difference between scholars and non-scholars. We are all born with biased thinking and reasoning. Biases pose a challenge to any scientific endeavor.

Scholars are always assumed to be neutral in relation to what they choose to study or at least make their utmost effort to be as objective as possible. With the emergence of feminist science in the 1970s, one of the first issues addressed was the claim that no scientific process can be pursued without bias—a well-established truth now echoed in society's increasing reliance on computer algorithms and artificial intelligence. Engineered and programmed by people, they too have been recognized as heavily biased.

Humans are inherently biased because, in some way or another, all behavior must ultimately serve the survival of the species. To reduce the impact of bias, for the sake of reasonably correct science, one first needs to be aware of the problem. Next, we must recognize the existence and understanding of human nature and the biology on which it is based. For most social scientists—and for scholars in education and high ability in particular—this is knowledge is either entirely unfamiliar or has intentionally been ignored. Understanding society as shaped by a biological legacy is viewed as controversial and therefore contrary to current political ideologies. As a result, advocating for such knowledge can present significant obstacles to many academic career possibilities. After all, who would vote for a politician who argues that not everyone can succeed? Who would employ a professor of education who argues that not everyone can learn everything? It matters little that there is well-established and uncontroversial scientific evidence for both. Science always gives way when there is a need for illusion and positive thinking. London School of Economics scholar, Satosho Kanazawa, stated when interviewed in *The Guardian* in November 2010, "nature is simply not politically correct." Stephen Pinker[5] of Harvard University has made the same point. He strongly advises against ignoring human biology when attempting to understand society, its social dynamics, or when drawing conclusions from research findings. In his words, this would have a "corrupting influence." Indeed, it has had a corrupting influence.

This relative ignorance has been particularly devastating for the study of giftedness and talent. The research field has a political origin and largely reflects American values rarely valid elsewhere in the World. The more systematic study began with a fascination with how the gifted and talented functioned and what were their socio-emotional needs. Scholars were genuinely motivated not only to understand who they were but also to identify suitable ways to support their development. With the beginning of the Cold War of the 1950s, however, this focus changed drastically into, what these individuals could do for society. Americans wanted an edge over what was then the Soviet Union. But the Soviets also wanted an edge over the United States. During the Communist era, intellectually gifted and talented individuals in Russia were routinely drafted into the military to support efforts toward military dominance.

Cultural bias is unfortunately ripe in giftedness and talent scholarship. Even though this bias is well known, few are willing to abandon utility for need. Maintaining ideological research orientations aligns with the ideals of the global knowledge economy, which remains continuously engaged in a "war for talent."

Notions of Giftedness

After almost a century of study, it is not surprising that the notions of giftedness and talent have generated a wide range of views, agendas, and opinions. This diversity is reflected not only in academic theories, ideologies, schools of thought, and educational practices, but also in the terminology used— terms such as genius, high-achiever, eminent, cash-cow, A-player, stars, high-potentials, highly able, extreme, expert, excellence, elite, brilliance, high ability, giftedness, and/or talented. The latest and perhaps most politically opportune term to emerge from this hotchpotch of labels is transformational giftedness. Depending on the context, gifted and talented individuals have also been described with less flattering designations like rebels, dissidents, free-thinkers, mavericks, and non-conformists. We should also not forget that there have also been gifted and talented criminals. Within any group of humans, there can also live a darker side.

This extreme stems not from science, but from the diverse vested interests in high ability—many of which are driven by wishful thinking. Adding to the complexity, there is no agreement on whether this group of remarkable children and adults are few or many. Some argue that only a few in any population are truly gifted, while others contend that anyone can become highly able through a decade of deliberate practice, skilled instruction, and support from those around them.

One example of how absurd this variety of positions has become is found in talent management. For a productive, ever-growing national economy focused on innovation, the prevailing view is that everyone can become a creative high achiever— given the right motivation and guidance from clever, well-educated teachers. Surprisingly, this was also the conviction of the European Union, during the Hungarian EU Presidential Conference on Talent Support in 2011, a position in which the European Council for High Ability (ECHA) played a key role. In summary, ECHA acknowledged that there are different terminologies and definitions related to talent development, we see a broader consensus. Everyone may be able—at something. Talented people can perform at a high level in any walk of life. To find gifted people and develop their talents is in the direct interest, common task, and common responsibility of governments, local communities, businesses, and nongovernmental organizations.

Several scholars invited to the conference as consulting experts protested this rendition of the declaration. However, their criticism was brushed aside and ignored. Instead, the final declaration was publicly read aloud—in front of press, media, and several EU Commissioners—by a deeply moved Hungarian Minister for Education, unaware that not all of the experts supported the declaration.

If everyone is indeed talented at something, why do markets so often reflect the belief that brilliant leadership is not accessible to everyone? Great leadership is commonly construed as something rare and difficult to come by. Excellent leaders must be carefully selected to ensure that the right woman or man is chosen to guide large companies and organizations into the future. This constitutes a paradox. It is scientifically impossible to have one type of talent applying to all and another type of talent pertaining only to a select few. It contradicts well-established and widely accepted principles of physical and social life that follow a normal statistical distribution.

It has long been known that most human abilities and characteristics follow a normal distribution—meaning the majority of individuals are similar, while fewer differ significantly at either end of the spectrum. Sleep is a good example. Most people need around 7-8 hours of sleep; that is 68% of the population, but a few can manage quite well on only 5 hours or less. A few have the opposite need and require more hours of sleep than the average individual. Our need for sleep—like many other human characteristics and numerous other physical and biological phenomena —is normally distributed in terms of frequency, occurrence, and intensity.

While living in a democracy grants equal responsibilities and opportunities to all, it does not mean we are alike in our characteristics, needs, abilities, looks, preferences and so on. We inevitably vary on every aspect of being human. This variation is inescapably normally distributed. This also means that not everything is possible for everyone—no matter how much we want it, how much we try or practice, and no matter how supportive and skilled our teachers and instructors may be.

Human Desire to Be Similar

One of the unconscious drives of human nature is to be like everyone else, or at least not to be too dissimilar. Construing someone as a gifted or talented, therefore poses a problem. The extremely gifted and talented individual stands out in school, at university, in the workplace, and in society—if they decide to make use of their abilities. High ability scholars have been puzzled that extremely gifted individuals often seek to hide their skills and knowledge. It has been suggested that their self-esteem is lacking. Perhaps, this is true of some. However, considering evolutionary human nature, hiding one's uniqueness is easy to understand. Gifted and talented individuals who do not want to show their prodigiousness are unconsciously trying to fit in socially. They are doing what everyone else would also do if they perceived themselves as too different from the group that they wished to identify with. They want to be like everyone else, be part of the group, and fulfill their need to relate to and identify with others in a social context.

It is a very Western characteristic, to insist that being different is always something positive and therefore should be encouraged. To say that you must "think outside the box" to be successful has become a mantra in the global knowledge economy and in all institutions driving it. However, this is contrary to how Homo Sapiens functions socially. This is how gifted and talented individuals naturally think, they cannot help themselves. They will think differently, in directions other than what social conventions expect, no matter what. They will do this without anyone telling them to.

Since non-conformity is often their defining trait, it is nearly impossible for them to be universally accepted by a society that is unconsciously bound together unconsciously by similarity.

He or she may well be a hero to like-minded individuals, and an appreciated "nerd" to many others—both of whom due to the nature of normal distribution, will always represent a small portion of the population. But it is highly unlikely that such a non-conformist will become a nationally and politically celebrated figure, let alone a transformative world leader. More often, they risk becoming martyrs.

This argument has, in fact, been used to justify calls for increased investment in supporting the highly able at all levels of education. While understandable, such advocacy borders on wishful thinking—driven more by ideological fervor and enthusiasm than by scientific fact. Pamela Clinkenbeard[6] of the University of Wisconsin, for example, urges us to "advocate the significance of the highly able for future prosperity" as do several of her American colleagues. April Bleske-Rechek, David Lubinsky, and Camilla Benbow[7] view these individuals as "extraordinary human capital for society at large".

No one argues against the prodigiousness of this remarkable group of individuals. They are very likely to be able to resolve a great many of the World's problems. However, the important question is, will they be allowed to by the society in which they exist?

Human nature sets the rules of what is possible, and normal distribution defines the non-negotiable boundaries—not politicians, not educators, and certainly not scholars, no matter how well-intended they may be. Few have phrased it better than the London-based psychologist, Joan Freeman,[8] the highly able need *permission* to be gifted.

Consequences of Limitations

Given the boundaries that human social dynamics inevitably imposes on all of us, the question becomes: how should we raise, educate, and support the extremely gifted and talented? Clearly, instilling in them the belief that they are "destined for greatness" or that they should "transform society" is a highly questionable practice—more likely rooted in the hopes and illusions of others than in the genuine well-being of the gifted individuals themselves.

In all my years of working with and advising these individuals—despite their differences, whether they are secondary school students, university students, or adult professionals—they seem to share a few common characteristics:

- They tend to believe that something is wrong with *them* because no one else they have encountered is like they are. They often feel, and often are, socially excluded and blame themselves for it.
- When presented with reasonably reliable research on highly gifted and talented individuals, they almost invariably refuse to see themselves as part of that group. This is not difficult to understand. They have spent a long time pretending to be like everyone else hoping that this could eventually be achieved. Like all of us, they too live by hope and illusion when it serves a purpose of satisfying basic needs.

In my experience, when highly gifted individuals finally embrace who they are and come to terms with the fact that they cannot be like everyone else, they express profound gratitude. Above all, for finally understanding who they are and why so many find it difficult to take them seriously and to include them socially.

Understanding gives these individuals a long sought-after revelation, allowing coping mechanisms to function. They are then better able to rebuild a more meaningful social existence—because they can also accept the limitations that come with their uniqueness.

These common denominators have been observed in individuals from diverse regions, including Canada, Britain, Bosnia, Scandinavia, and South Africa. This is important information, because few fields of study and practice are as culturally biased as the study of the gifted and talented. The vast majority of research, theories, and practices are either directly American or heavily influenced by American findings and values. In the natural sciences, this has little significance. In the social sciences however—of which both education and psychology are part—it matters a great deal. It has been known since the 1970s that research findings and ideas about human social behavior cannot be successfully transferred across cultures without careful consideration. However, this has been largely ignored leaving the idea that someone who is gifted and talented is superhuman. This concept, rooted in American research, has generally been adopted by the global knowledge, economy, and its architects. From the outside, it appears that the gifted and talented in the United States are often attributed "superhero status." While extreme human abilities and the personal characteristics they inspire exist in every culture and population, their expression varies across social contexts. It seems, this notion does not exist elsewhere. The notion of leadership provides an enlightening example. In American culture, great leaders are often viewed as individual superheroes—expected to achieve anything they set their minds to, while being self-reliant, strong, brave, noble, and deeply invested in preserving their reputation, image, identity, and sense of purpose. Leadership in Scandinavia, on the other hand, is construed in the completely opposite way. A formidable leader in Norway or Sweden is never a charismatic star. He or she is perceived as socially equal. Even when knowledgeable, eminent, and well-suited for the role, the leader empowers others, remains modest, and strives to stay relatable to everyone else.

Therefore, to truly understand the needs of the extremely gifted and talented, we must not focus solely on their personal needs—or what they can do or achieve for society—but we must also consider their social context and cultural legacy. While commonalities may exist across cultures, important differences are inevitable.

Adding to this significance is the reality of normal distribution: the number of extremely gifted and talent individuals is small. If IQ is used as a hypothetical criterion for intellectual giftedness, then by statistical distribution, only 0.1% or less of a population with an IQ of 145 or higher would qualify. In the European Union, with 550 million citizens in 27 member states, that equates to 550,000 individuals who would be considered extremely intelligent. Why have we not heard more about half a million exceedingly intellectual people?

There are many reasons, but the most significant reason, in Europe—as in other parts of the world, the evolutionary social dynamics of human differences are poorly understood by social scientists and the architects of modern society. In light of these dynamics, it is also likely that this knowledge is viewed as unimportant, even though it has been well established in the natural sciences for a long time.

To prepare extremely gifted and talented children and young adults for their future professional and social lives, the single most important aspect of their education is helping them understand of themselves—what human nature is, and how the social world functions in relation to being exceptionally gifted and talented, regardless of their field. With this knowledge, they will be better equipped to make sense of their own existence, understand their social position, and identify a path forward that feels both possible and meaningful.

This small group of individuals is indeed remarkable, but they are *not* superhuman. For the sake of their own happiness and well-being, they too must follow and understand the dictates of human nature—and the very real boundaries imposed on everyone in every society.

References

[1, 2] Hollingworth, Leta. S. 1942. *Children above IQ 180: Their Origin and Development.* New York: World Books.

[3] Shekerjian, Denise. 1990. *Uncommon Genius: How Great Ideas are Born.* New York: Viking Penguin.

[4] Persson, Roland S. 2009. "The Unwanted Gifted and Talented: A Sociobiological Perspective of the Social Functions of Giftedness." In *International Handbook of Giftedness*, edited by Larissa V. Shavinina, 913–24. Dordrecht, NL: Springer-Science.

Persson, Roland S. 2021. "On Psychoses, Conspiracies, Creative Flow and the Absent- Mindedness of Genius: An Evolutionary Function-Dysfunction Taxonomy of the Multiple Subjective Realities of the Human Mind." *International Journal of Talent Development and Creativity* 9 (1 & 2): 55–80.

[5] Pinker, Stephen. 2002. *The Blank Slate: The Modern Denial of Human Nature.* London: Penguin Books.

[6] Clinkenbeard, Pamela R. 2007. "Economic Arguments for Gifted Education." *Gifted Children* 2 (1): 5–9.

[7] Bleske-Rechek, April, David Lubinski, and Camilla P. Benbow. 2004. "Meeting the Educational Needs of Special Populations: Advanced Placement's Role in Developing Exceptional Human Capital." *Psychological Science* 15 (4): 217–24.

[8] Freeman, Joan. 2005. "Permission to Be Gifted: How Conceptions of Giftedness Can Change Lives." In *Conceptions of Giftedness*, 2nd ed., edited by Robert J. Sternberg and Janet E. Davidson, 80–97. New York: Cambridge University Press.

Part 3
Highly–Profoundly Gifted

Chapter 6

Gifted Grown-ups in Confucian Heritage Culture: Creative Achievers or Fade-Aways?

Seokhee Cho[1], Juah Kim[2], Doehee Ahn[3], Els De Wit[4]

[1] *St. John's University, Department. Of Education, New York, USA*

[2] *Korean Educational Development Institute, Sejong, Korea*

[3] *ChungAng University, Seoul, Korea*

[4] *Els De Wit*

**Corresponding author, e-mail: chos1@stjohns.edu*

Predicting Achievement: What Do We Know?

Stories of eminent adults affirm they were superior to their peers when they were young. However, stories of prodigies also tell us that not all high IQ children grow up and achieve at a higher level.

Since the 1960s, many studies have confirmed that while IQ is a necessary condition for creative achievement, it is not sufficient on its own.

Once an IQ threshold has been met, other factors have been found to be more critical for predicting creative achievement. Subotnik, Olszewski-Kubilius, and Worrell[1] developed the Mega Model of Talent Development, which outlines the trajectories of talent growth and, the critical factors required at each developmental stage. According to the Mega Model, key factors for creative achievement include the recognition of interest or talents by parents and family, as well as a rich learning environment at home in the initial stage of development. Recognition of talents by others is also essential.

In the middle stage, the acquisition of knowledge and skill development through education, meaningful experiences, dedicated teachers, and engagement with intellectual peers becomes crucial. In the later stage, opportunities to explore or deepen one's interest through mentorship and creative discovery play a vital role.

In terms of educational factors, Tannenbaum[2] emphasized the importance of appropriately differentiated enrichment and acceleration, tailored to gifted students' abilities and roles, along with the influence of teachers and intellectual peers. Bloom[3] identified challenging educational opportunities and the role of teachers at each developmental stage as the most critical factors in nurturing young talent.

In his Differentiated Model of Gifted and Talented, Gagné[4] highlighted education, experience, and domain-specific training as essential catalysts for talent development. Similarly, Subotnik and Jarvin[5] found that the most important factors in developing musician talent were exceptional teachers, an appropriate learning pace, high-level of instruction, and a strong teacher-student relationship.

Several longitudinal studies have examined the characteristics and developmental paths of the gifted. For instance, Subotnik, Kassan, Summers, and Wasser[6] traced 210 elementary-school graduates from 1948 to 1960 and found results similar to those in Terman's study. Although the study participants had not participated in gifted education programs, they became productive professionals who were mentally and physically healthy and maintained stable interpersonal relationships.

The focus on high achievers in most of the longitudinal studies may have led to the neglect of the full spectrum of gifted development—including the existence of the under-achieving gifted child. Only a few studies followed up on gifted students who did not experience a gifted education program. Hollingworth's study7 of 12 gifted children with a mean IQ of 187 found that many of the children experienced significant difficulties due to a lack of intellectual challenge and inadequate treatment by adults. At that time, and still today, people believed that "the bright can take care of themselves." In another ten-year study, Gross[8] followed 60 gifted Australian youngsters ages 5 to 13 with IQ scores of 160 or greater. These youngsters showed precocity in reading and numeracy and were copious readers. Many were inappropriately treated at schools and were provided with few educational interventions. There were achievers and underachievers among them.

As part of Terman's longitudinal study of children in California with IQs of 140 or greater, two groups were compared: the A's (the most successful 150 adults) and the C's (the least successful 150 adults)

The children appeared similar in academic achievement until high school, but the "C group" demonstrated greater self-confident, read more frequently, and showed stronger motivation toward goals than the "A group."

The A's succeeded in such fields as engineering, law, medicine, and academia. The effects of accumulated advantages or disadvantages from early experiences were not clearly evident.

What distinguished the A's from the C's was the socioeconomic status (SES) of their homes.

Half of the fathers of the A's had college degrees or beyond. However, one third of the C's dropped out of school before 8th grade. The A's could have enjoyed the benefit of a higher SES than the C's, and they had families that encouraged their success.

In another study, Freeman[9] compared 210 British children, between the ages of 5–14 who were identified as gifted or non-labeled gifted. Additionally, Freeman randomly selected peers based on their personal characteristics, academic experiences, and environments. Some of the children were followed for 10 and 27 years. The gifted children exhibited more emotional difficulties; however, the life outcomes of the gifted and non-labeled were not significantly different.

Most of these longitudinal studies were conducted in Western countries, potentially leading to a biased understanding of giftedness. How do other cultures perceive giftedness? And what can we learn from this? It remains unclear which findings are generalizable to gifted children in the Confucian Heritage Culture and which are not. It would be valuable to identify the critical factors for talent development and creativity at each developmental stage, particularly within the context of the Confucian Heritage Cultures. It has been known that not just one factor, but the confluence of several factors is needed for talent development. This is especially true of creativity. Studies looking at the development of creativity and the factors influencing it in gifted individuals are rare. This chapter presents two retrospective studies of gifted individuals who did not participate in public gifted education during their elementary and middle school years.

Confucian Influence on Korean Gifted Education System

Differentiated by knowledge but not differentiated by learning ability. Confucius distinguishes between different classes of individuals based on their acquisition of knowledge: those who possess knowledge innately, those who learn it easily, those who learn at a slower pace, and those who do not—or cannot—learn it at all.

Those who are born with the possession of knowledge are the highest class of men. Those who learn and obtain the possession of knowledge, are the next. Those who are dull and stupid and learn slowly are the next class. Those who are dull and stupid and who do not learn; they are the lowest of the people (*Analects* 16, 9).[10]

Those who are born with the possession of knowledge are referred to as *Tien cai* (天才)[11], meaning heavenly talent. This type of talent is easily recognizable when the individual's knowledge and ability are so exceptional that they cannot be compared to others. Those who learn and readily gain the possession of knowledge are called 秀才(high achiever). If Western criteria of gifted identification are to be applied, these two groups of people might be recognized as the gifted. However, the *Analects* say that there should be no distinction in the education among different classes "('*you jiao wulei*' (有教無類) (*Analects* 15, 38)." This concept suggests that the same knowledge can be acquired by individuals of all classes through the learning process and through the sincere efforts of both students and teachers. This system of education can lead to "positive intellectual progress."[12]

Current educational practices and policies in Confucian Heritage Cultures have been shaped by principles such as the "joy of learning and practice of learned," "belief in growth," "obedience and conformity," and the "imperial examination (or Keju)."

Joy of learning: In *Analects*, the Confucius articulated the joy of learning and the practice of the learned. Yu and Suen[13] cited "all pursuits are of low value; only studying books is high". Confucius teaching on the "joy of learning" has helped children become highly motivated and develop the knowledge and skills needed for high achievement and creativity.

Belief in the growth of the human being: Confucian heritage long embraced a growth mindset similar to Dweck concept, based on the ideal of cultivating the perfect human being. Dweck's concept of growth mindset has often been misunderstood as "you can become anything you want if only you have the right mindset." Based on this philosophy, children work hard to get the best scores on exams. They believe that effort, not ability, can make differences in their achievement. Because of this mindset, there was no concept of special education for brighter children since anybody can do well by working hard. This belief—centered on the possibility of intellectual progress through the efforts of both students and teachers—has fostered values such as diligence, perseverance through hardship, sustained effort, persistence, focus, hard study, and a sense of shame for not working hard."[14]

Obedience and conformity: Confucius said "I transmit but do not create knowledge. I believe in and love the ancients" (Analects 7:1). It implies that the essential qualification for teaching anything is to review the old, to find new meaning (Analects 2:11). Instead of creating novelty, the understanding was that the old was more valued. In a very broad terms, Confucian philosophy is rooted in the established social order and the maintenance of strict hierarchies in social relationships. Further, the acceptance of a clear code of moral conduct was expected. Fairbank[15] wrote that parents were superior to children, men to women, and rulers to subjects. "If we take this Confucian view of life in its social and political context, we will see its esteem for age over youth, the past over the present, and established authority over innovation. This is one of the greatest historic answers to the problem of relatively lower scores on creativity test (p.53)." While this philosophy may have positively influenced high achievement, it has also hindered the development of creativity for many years.

Chinese Imperial Exam System, Keju, and Education Fever for Success: Keju was a civil service examination system in Imperial China that began in 587 AD to select candidates for the state offices. The system became dominant during the Song Dynasty when it was opened to the public until it was abolished in the late Qing Dynasty reforms in 1905. Its influence can be found by the amplified parental education fever for success on the exam to secure high social prestige. Education fever is defined as "parents' desire and motivation to help their children to be successful in their lives"[16]

Since the 1980s, Korea has developed a gifted education system aimed at nurturing creativity within the context of Confucian Heritage Culture. Gifted education in STEM began with the establishment of the first specialized residential science high schools (SHSs) established in 1983, under the Elementary and Secondary Education Act. This initiative recognized the need to free talented STEM students from the pressure of the university entrance exam.

After completing two years of accelerated learning at SHSs, students could enter one of the national universities without taking an entrance examination. The removal of this exam was to protect students from excessive test preparation, allowing them to focus on developing creativity rather than practicing test-taking skills.

However, until the enactment of the Gifted Education Promotion Act in 2000, gifted identification and gifted education programs were not implemented in elementary and middle schools. The government had been hesitant, fearing that early identification would lead to excessive private tutoring by parents eager to prepare their children.

In 1997, acceleration policies—such as early school entrance, grade skipping, and early graduation—were introduced. However, these policies were not widely practiced due to parental concerns that their children might struggle to maintain top rankings when studying alongside older peers. In 1987, an after-school private gifted education center was established for children ages five to eleven.

Even with the enactment of the Gifted Education Promotion Act in 2000, only after-school gifted education centers affiliated with school districts and universities were permitted. Gifted education in public elementary and middle schools was not permitted. Again, this was to prevent excessive private tutoring for gifted identification exams. Gifted education centers identified domain-specific talents for students in grades three or higher.

Two retrospective longitudinal studies are presented on the following page. Participants in the first study were identified as gifted in 1985-1987 when they were ages 3-8. Participants of the second study were also born in the 1980s, attended SHSs, and were recommended by the schools or alumni offices. While the study participants in the studies were in elementary and middle school, no public gifted education programs were available, and most did not experience gifted education within the school system. Only a few experienced after-school gifted education programming at a few private gifted education centers.

Blooming or Fading Away: Possible Causes

Study 1: Development of Academic Talent of Gifted Children

Cho and Han[17] followed children who were identified as gifted over an 18-year period, examining their academic achievement as well as their behavioral and emotional characteristics throughout elementary school, middle school, high school, and college. Developmental patterns were analyzed to address how and when giftedness thrived or faded-away.

The sixty-three study participants were young adults, ages 20 to 24 years old, mostly attending colleges and a few were college graduates. They were identified as gifted between the ages of two to six, during 1985-1987, through two different channels: National Initiative Cohort (NIC) and Parental Initiative Cohort (PIC). Fifty-nine of their parents participated in the study and four parents elected not to participate.

In 1985, NIC was identified by the Ministry of Education of South Korea. Pre-school children recognized as highly bright were recommended by community members to local elementary school principals across the nation. Based on their reading levels of Korean and Chinese, as well as Arithmetic skills, these children were screened by principals, then recommended to school districts, and ultimately to the Ministry of Education. The finalists were narrowed to 144 children. The finalists were assessed using a non-standardized intelligence test and categorized into three levels of giftedness: "profoundly gifted" (equivalent to IQ scores of 150 and above), "highly gifted" (IQ scores of 141–150), and "mildly gifted" (IQ scores of 131–140).

Out of the 57 participants in the NIC group, only 35 agreed to participate in the study. Of the participants, 23 attended top-tier colleges and 12 attended 2nd or 3rd tier colleges.

Table 2. Tiers of Colleges Attended and Family SES of the Gifted Identified at Ages, 3-8

College		Top-tier college (23)	2nd & 3rd tier colleges (34)
High school attended	Science HS	3(13.0%)	0(0.0%)
	Regular HS	20(87.0%)	34(100.0%)
Gifted Ed Experience	Yes	3(13.0%)	0(0.0%)
	No	20(87.0%)	34(100.0%)
Family income	High ($60K+)	5(21.7%)	4(11.8%)
	Middle($40K-59K)	13(56.5%)	18(52.9%)
	Low (-$39K)	5(21.7%)	12(35.3%)
Mother's education	College or more	9(39.1%)	9(26.5%)
	High school	9(39.1%)	17(50.0%)
	Middle school	5(21.7%)	8(23.5%)
Mother's occupation	Home maker	11(47.8%)	20(58.8%)
	Teacher	5(21.7%)	1(2.9%)
	Small business	1(4.3%)	6(17.6%0
	Farmer/Laborer	3(13.0%)	4(11.8%)
	White collar	3(13.0%)	3(8.8%)

A parent-initiated cohort (PIC) was identified in 1987. Parents brought their children to a private gifted education center for identification. Of the 116 children who scored above 130 on the KEDI Wechsler Intelligence Test, 59 were invited to participate, but only 28 gifted children (20 males and 8 females) and 25 of their parents agreed to take part in the study. The PIC participants' average IQ score was 137.64. The study participants were reclassified into three groups—profoundly gifted, highly gifted, and mildly gifted—based on their IQ scores. A total of 63 participants were composed of 34 profoundly gifted, 15 highly gifted, and 14 mildly gifted individuals.

Effects of Social Economic Status (SES), GPA, and College Attendance

The first cluster, the Full-Bloomers, consisted of 35 gifted individuals. The Full-Bloomers' maintained consistently high GPAs elementary through high school, with 40.5% gaining admission to top-tier colleges or medical schools—compared to 25% of the overall study participants. A common characteristic among the Full-Bloomers was the highest average IQ score. However, not all the Full-Bloomers had parents with a high SES. SES was determined by education level and income level.

> *Jinu (pseudonym) was raised by his grandmother in a rural area where his mother ran a small grocery store, and his father worked as a barber. His mother was busy, but interacted with Jinu's school teachers by visiting his school regularly. In middle school, Jinu's teacher informed his parents about a residential SHS in his province that he could apply to. He attended the SHS, where his talents in math and science were nurtured. Jinu was accepted to MIT with a major in mathematics.*

The second cluster, the Good-Achievers, consisted of 15 gifted individuals. The Good-Achievers' maintained stable GPAs that were slightly lower than those of the Full-Bloomers throughout their education, with 37.5% gaining admission to top-tier colleges. The chosen majors were diverse, including science, mechanics, design, engineering, and literature. Their average IQ score fell below the Full-Bloomers and the SES of their families was at or above middle class.

The third cluster, the Fade-Aways, consisted of 8 gifted individuals. The GPAs of the Fade-Aways declined consistently from elementary to high school. These gifted individuals entered low ranking colleges, such as junior colleges. One of the key characteristics of this group was that all participants came from lower SES families compared to the Full-Bloomers and the Good-Achievers.

> *Rae (pseudonym) recalled that her parents were happy to see her enter elementary school. In her first year, Rae's teacher told her parents that she was very bright and that she was doing well in school. However, Rae had learned nothing at all; she had already learned everything that was being taught three years ago.*

The fourth cluster, the Late-Bloomers, consisted of five gifted individuals. The GPAs of the Late-Bloomers were low in elementary school but improved gradually from middle to high school. They entered the top- or 2nd-tier colleges. The average IQ score was in line with the Good-Achievers and Fade-Aways. The SES of the Late-Bloomers' families were either very high or very low.

> *Soori (Pseudonym) recalled that he played on the street until it was dark, and his parents were returning from work. In grade five, Soori's eyesight became weak due to a lack of proper nutrition. In grade eight, his mother enrolled him in a neighborhood cram school, where his exceptional mathematical talent was recognized, and he was encouraged to apply to a residential SHS. Soori was admitted to one of the prestigious national colleges.*

> *Woojin (Pseudonym) is from a high SES family and both of his parents, with doctoral degrees, were too busy with their own works to advocate for his needs. In elementary school, Woojin was not given any challenging activities, and no meaningful learning opportunities were provided at home. Only in middle school did Woojin realize that all his friends were studying hard. He started paying attention to his schoolwork, but he realized he did not know how to organize his work, take notes, manage his time, or prepare for exams. He was admitted to a 2nd-tier college.*

Effects of Reading and Self-Study

Number of Books Read: The Full-Bloomers consistently read significantly more books than the other study participants throughout elementary, middle, and high school. All the clusters of students showed a decline in the amount of reading as they grew older. However, the difference between the Full-Bloomers and the other three clusters was significant. These declines may have been caused by the increased difficulty level of the books and the time required to read each book. Additionally, this may have left less time for the children to read for leisure.

Self-Study Hours: Self-study hours increased over time from elementary, to middle, to high school. However, there was no significant difference among the students' groups in terms of self-study hours.

During the interviews, Fade-Aways and Late-Bloomers recalled they were able to maintain good grades with little effort in elementary school. This was thanks to their excellent memory and ease of understanding.

However, due to unchallenging schoolwork, they did not develop persistence, note taking abilities, or time management skills. The lack of good study habits became a barrier to their overall learning at school and affected their later stage development.

Table 3. Numbers of Books Read per Month

Clusters	N	Elementary		Middle		High	
		M	SD	M	SD	M	SD
Full-Bloomers	34	3.38	.78	2.71	.94	2.35	.81
Good-Achievers	14	2.79	1.12	2.43	.94	2.14	.67
Fade-Aways	8	2.88	.85	2.25	.89	2.00	.76
Late-Bloomers	5	1.80	.45	2.00	1.24	2.00	.00
Total	61	3.05	.96	3.05	.96	2.52	.96

How to Develop Creativity Across the Life Span

Using a retrospective method, this study examined how the STEM talents of graduates from specialized residential SHS were identified and how their creativity developed over the course of their lives.

Twenty-three alumni from eight of the regional specialized residential Science High Schools were interviewed. The participating students were either recommended by their respective alumni offices or identified as creative achievers. The first regional SHS was established in South Korea in 1983. Following the enactment of the Gifted Education Promotion Act, the number of regional SHSs steadily increased from 2003 to 2014, and their official designation was changed to national science high schools. As of 2021, there are 20 regional and 8 national specialized residential science high schools in South Korea.

While attending high school, most SHS graduates completed the compacted three-year curriculum in just one year, took college-level courses, and then advanced to the Korean Advanced Institute of Science and Technology (KAIST). No entrance examination was required of these students. Those few who chose to apply to other colleges, beyond KAIST, studied the high school curriculum in three years.

The study participants ranged in age from 31 to 51 years in 2020 and entered SHSs between 1984 and 2004. Their educational degree earned ranged from Bachelor (6), Master (1), to Doctorate (16). Their majors included Math (1), Science (4), Engineering (12), Music (1), and Industrial Design (2).

The study participants held various occupations, including college professors (12), CEO of companies they established (3), Executive of Corporations (3), Designer (1), Finance (1), Engineer (1), and Social Activist (1) as shown in Table 4.

Table 4: Participants: Creative Alumni of Science High Schools

Cases	Class of SHS by admission year	Gender	Final Degree	Major	Occupation
A1	1991	Male	Ph.D.	• Electronic Engineering • Computer music	Professor
A2	1991	Male	Ph.D.	• Industrial Management	CEO of his own company
A3	1991	Male	BS	• Electronic engineering	Freelancer Designer
A4	1991	Male	BS	• Industrial design	US company executive
A5	2003	Male	BS	• Industrial engineering	CEO of his company
A6	2004	Male	Ph.D.	• Mathematics	Professor
A7	1984	Male	MS	• Industrial design	Executive of a Corporate
A8	1987	Male	Ph.D.	• Physics (BS, MS, Ph.D.) • Business Management (Ph.D.)	Professor (in US)
A9	1987	Male	Ph.D.	• Material Engineering	Professor
A10	1994	Male	Ph.D.	• Bioscience	Professor
A11	1994	Male	Ph.D.	• Electronics	Executive of a Corporate
A12	1996	Male	Ph.D.	• Atomic Nuclear Engineering	Professor
A13	1999	Male	Ph.D.	• Chemistry (BS) • Physics (MS, Ph.D.)	Professor
A14	1986	Male	Ph.D.	• Physics(BS)	Professor
				• Material Science and Engineering (MS)	Professor
				• Material Engineering (Ph.D.)	Professor

Cases	Class of SHS by admission year	Gender	Final Degree	Major	Occupation
A15	1990	Male	Ph.D.	• Mechanic Engineering	Professor
A16	1991	Male	Ph.D.	• Business management	Professor
A17	1991	Male	BS	• Physics	Activist
A18	1995	Male	Ph.D.	• Environmental engineering	Professor
A19	1995	Male	BS	• Industrial design	CEO of his company
A20	2000	Male	Ph.D.	• Industrial design	Professor
A21	1991	Male	Ph.D.	• Engineering	Financier
A22	1997	Male	Ph.D.	• Electronic engineering	Engineer

Regarding talent recognition, alumni were asked about their talent domain, when their abilities were first recognized, and any notable experiences related to that recognition. For educational experiences, they were asked about their learning speed, concentration, early entrance or graduation, classroom experiences, research activities, extracurricular involvement, and relationship with peers and teachers. In terms of creative achievement, alumni were asked about their achievement in their career.

Preschool: Freedom to Explore

During the preschool period, several common themes emerged from the study, including the opportunity for free exploration of diverse activities. Parents recognized their children's talent when they were young.

Parents respected and supported their children's choices of activities and decisions. Parents observed their children's interests and allowed them to choose related activities, rather than pre-determining what was meaningful or valuable.

> *"My parents encouraged me to pursue what I was interested in and what I wanted to do. If I express my dislike about certain activities, they said 'Let us think about alternatives (A6).'"*

Another common theme included a home environment which allowed and encouraged intellectual exploration. Parents generally supported their children's choices by providing many books at home. This allowed the children to choose and to read books whenever they want to. A wide selection of books was provided, including fiction, non-fiction, biographies, and encyclopedias. Because of the parents' own interest and jobs, they were exposed to books in specific field such as history, language, and computer science. Those with older siblings were also exposed to higher-grade textbooks and, in some cases, college-level fiction and philosophy.

"Since all my older brothers read books extensively, I started thinking early on those reading books is what everybody does. My brother was much older than me and read many advanced books. So, I thought it is just an ordinary thing to read such advanced books. (A14)"

Among the study participants, it was common that their diverse talents were recognized when at a young age.

They attended SHSs as talented individuals in math and science. However, in their early years, their talents emerged across a wide range of areas, including math, science, the arts, liberal arts, and social sciences.

Most of them were "Jack of all trades", displaying interest in math and science, as well as in music, art, and the liberal arts. These diverse talents were again realized in their broad range of careers in design, business, and acoustics.

Elementary and Middle School: Boredom

Common themes among the participants during the elementary and middle school years are discussed next. During the elementary and middle school period, they did not get enough intellectual challenges in school. School offered no enjoyment, no new learning, and little engagement, leading them to seek challenges instead through non-academic interests.

They were not given differentiated materials or instruction, even when teachers recognized that they had a more advanced understanding of math and science than what was being taught. They read other books in class, slept, or engaged in off-task behaviors.

> *"I remember I used to sleep during class (A12.)"*

> *"There was no fun after I entered elementary school. What was given by teachers was all what I have already had known for some years. I did not get any other homework or tutoring. In retrospect, it could have been better if I learned something meaningful. But there was neither guidance nor teaching for me (A 4)."*

Math and science contests provided external recognition of their talents and offered intellectually stimulating challenges. Participating in math and science contests provided a great momentum for talent development. These contests offered an alternative to the otherwise unenjoyable and unchallenging school learning environment. Solving challenging problems to win contests stimulated them intellectually. In addition, when they won awards, , teachers, parents, and others provided affirmation of the students' talents in math and science. Contests were also a great channel for developing creativity.

> *"I got a gold medal at the School Science Contest. Then I got a gold medal again at the City Science Contest. Then, I realized that 'I am quite good at science.' This was how I got into science (A9.)"*

Additional opportunities for advanced contests, enriched content, and stimulation from like-minded peers were included through participation in after-school Gifted Education Centers. Gifted individuals' intellectual curiosity was satisfied at the after-school private gifted education center. The Gifted Education Center provided an enrichment program for these students. Their interest in math and science grew stronger when they were introduced to appropriately challenging content and new experiments not available in their traditional school curriculum.

Interaction with intellectual peers at the private gifted education center provided them with meaningful intellectual stimulation. However, it was not affordable for many parents.

> *"School life was not much meaningful to me, since all what I was interested in and curious about was taken care of at the gifted education center (A18)."*

Science High School: Acceleration

In high school, several themes emerged, including curriculum acceleration through compacting and early graduation. The gifted individuals reported feeling motivated by the extremely fast-paced curriculum at the SHSs, compared to the very slow-paced instruction they had experienced at the elementary and middle school. Most of them completed the three-year curriculum by the end of their 1st year through curriculum compacting. Then, in the 2nd year, they took college level course electives. After two years of science high school, most of them graduated early to go to college.

> *"The pace of the curriculum at the high school was very fast. I felt the learning speed at the high school was 5-6 times faster than at the elementary and middle schools. We were crazy to catch up and speed to go to college after just two years of high school (A4)."*

Among the study participants, acceleration was identified as the greatest benefit during this ideal period of career development. The alumni spoke positively about acceleration for two reasons. First, it saved time by reducing unnecessary preparation for university entrance examinations. Second, acceleration allowed them to begin their professional careers in their early 20s—an ideal time for entering STEM fields. Due to the two to three years of compulsory military service, Korean males are typically delayed in starting their STEM careers compared to their international peers. Acceleration helped these talented students compensate for the time lost during military service.

> *"Considering global competition, acceleration saves time for career development, since Chinese and Americans do not have to serve the compulsory military service. For example, at the Google company, you can find many high positioned people who are still young and whose brains run fast (A19)."*

In addition to acceleration, the opportunity to study alongside intellectually talented STEM peers was another key strength of the SHSs. This environment fostered healthy competition, which proved to be a double-edged sword—motivating high achievement in some students while causing frustration in others.

They had frequent heated discussions, exchanged bright ideas, and stimulated each other. In this environment, some students fully realized their potential and achieved at a high level, while others experienced intense frustration upon discovering they were no longer "the best."

Students who performed at or below average in high school experienced frustration due to the overwhelmingly fast-paced curriculum and the large volume of information they were expected to absorb.

> *"It was good to be with bright students, since intellectual stimulation was available. However, that was a source of frustration for some students (A21)."*

College Period: Learning to Cope with Challenge and Frustration

Up to high school, graduates were running predetermined tracks. At college, they needed to choose one of many tracks or create their own track. Autonomy was fully allowed, and no specific guidelines were provided about the direction they needed to pursue.

They spent a lot of time seriously speculating about meaningful purposes of life and about choosing a specific field to study for a career.

"I wandered around not knowing what my area is or should be. I was very good at studying, but …. (A3)."

"I started questioning what it really meant. I was not sure which area I was really interested and talented in. There was no support system for me to understand the meaning of life and study…. I could not find my role models except for my older colleagues who were either working at the school or were professors (A1)." A1 later invented electronic music instruments.

During college and graduate school, these individuals began to pursue careers that had been unclear or undefined during their younger years. A1 dreamed of integrating science and music. He studied electronic engineering and took some courses at the college of music. After college, he worked for a piano manufacturing company, held a position as a software engineer, and pursued studies in music technology. Currently, he is a professor in the Graduate School of Culture Technology in one of the prestigious universities in Korea.

Another example is A8, who was very interested in social sciences in addition to physics. He got a doctoral degree in physics but was not sure whether physics would be his best life-time work. He gained work experience at a consulting firm and then studied business administration. He is currently a professor of business administration in one of the most prestigious universities in the United States.

Critical Encounter: Persistent Hard Work and Continued Training

---

During their college and graduate school period, they learned to cope with challenges and frustrations through persistent effort. Throughout this rigorous training period, key experiences and encounters played a pivotal role in leading them to creative achievements.

A10 switched his profession from law to science researcher by meeting a professor in Neuroscience. He studied under a Nobel Laureate in

Neuroscience. Currently, he is a professor in brain engineering at one of the prestigious universities in Korea. Another alumni got an unexpected invitation to study at MIT after asking a question to a MIT professor through email while working on his undergraduate project. He is currently a professor in Nuclear and Quantum Engineering in Korea.

Summary

So, what is the difference between a Fade-Away and a Full-Bloomer according to these studies? These two studies supported the Mega model of talent development. Subotnik, Kubilius-Olszewski, and Worrell[18] suggested that:

- the abilities of individuals do matter especially in specific talent domains
- opportunities provided by society are crucial at every point in the development process
- individuals with talent also have responsibility for their own growth and development
- fulfilling one's talents lead to high levels of personal satisfaction and self-actualization

---

In this study, beneficial psychosocial traits—such as perseverance and curiosity—were either nurtured or hindered by the opportunities available in society, particularly during the early stages of talent development.

Study one revealed that extensive early reading was a key accumulated advantage among the Full-Bloomers.[19] Even in the face of inadequate education in schools and limited opportunities for talent recognition and development, these individuals cultivated their abilities through the compounded benefits of early reading. Another noticeable finding was that some high achievers—students attending top-tier colleges—came from low SES backgrounds, with mothers who were not highly educated and families with limited income. This was a rare finding from other studies.

The Confucian Heritage Culture's emphasis on growth likely contributed to the recognition and support of these gifted individuals from low SES families, both at home and at school. Additionally, the community's collective growth mindset may have helped offset the negative effects of poverty on academic achievement. Even if parents were not educated at a high level, they placed high priority on education and sought information from teachers or schools. In this way, gifted from low SES families found opportunities to develop their children's talents. However, it is important to note that many talented individuals from low-SES families either became Fade-Aways due to a lack of school support or declined to participate in the study. Unchallenging school environments and limited opportunities during the early developmental stages created significant disadvantages—particularly those from low-SES backgrounds—which hindered the full development of their potential. From the 1980s to 1990s, many gifted Korean individuals were placed in disadvantaged situations because of the accumulation of disadvantages, such as low SES.

However, if their talents had been recognized and appropriately challenged through gifted education, they would likely have achieved at levels comparable to those of students in other studies who had participated in acceleration and/or gifted education programs.

Fade-Aways and Late-Bloomers prevailed among those who were not followed and/or those who declined to participate in the study. This is important to keep in mind when interpreting the findings.

Study two showed that, even in the absence of formal support systems like gifted education programs, winning contests provided the students with valuable external recognition. This validation boosted their confidence and motivated them to seek out additional opportunities to further develop their talents.

In some Confucian Heritage Culture countries, governments attempted to eliminate gifted education programs due to concerns over excessive private tutoring. There was a belief that identifying gifted children contributed to achievement gaps, as affluent parents could afford intensive tutoring to prepare their children for selection. With the elimination of gifted education programs, gifted students from low SES had a hard time finding opportunities. Without a gifted education system specially designed to support low-SES families, gifted students from these backgrounds struggled to find opportunities to develop their talents.

The study found that the math and science competitions, after-school gifted education centers, and specialized SHSs each served as unique channels for nurturing the creativity of STEM-talented students. Competitions helped to affirm the individual's talents. Acceleration contributed to the development of perseverance, while university admission without entrance examinations allowed students to take risks without hinderance. Gifted individuals from low-SES backgrounds should be given the same opportunities to develop their talent in diverse ways—especially during early childhood.

When interpreting the findings of the study, two limitations need to be considered. First, some of the data was self-reported and retrieved from the memory of the individual. A second limitation was the higher attrition rate of underachievers compared to high achievers. For example, in Study 1—those who achieved less than their potential—were harder to trace, as they were more likely to remain hidden compared to the high achievers. Even after they were traced, more of the underachievers compared to the high achievers declined to participate in the study. This was likely due to the psychological difficulties these individuals faced related to self-esteem and underdeveloped high potential. In study two, those students who did not achieve at a high level were less recommended by the schools or alumni offices.

No emotional problems such as depression or maladjustment were reported in study one or study two. In interviews with gifted individuals, some reported negative relationships with teachers due to their exceptional abilities. This may have stemmed from the Confucian Heritage Culture, which places a high value on learning and expects all students to achieve high levels.

References

[1] Subotnik, Rena F., Paula Olszewski-Kubilius, and Frank C. Worrell. 2011. "Rethinking Giftedness and Gifted Education." *Psychological Science in the Public Interest* 12: 3– 54. https://doi.org/10.1177/1529100611418056.

[2] Tannenbaum, Abraham J. 1983. *Gifted Children: Psychological and Educational Perspectives*. Macmillan College.

[3] Bloom, Benjamin S. 1985. *Developing Talent in Young People*. New York, NY: Ballantine.

[4] Gagné, Françoys. 2005. "From Gifts to Talents: The DMGT as a Developmental Model." In *Conceptions of Giftedness*, edited by R. J. Sternberg and J. E. Davidson, 98–119. 2nd ed. New York, NY: Cambridge University Press.

[5] Subotnik, Rena F., and Linda Jarvin. 2005. "Beyond Expertise: Conceptions of Giftedness as Great Performance." In *Conceptions of Giftedness*, edited by R. J. Sternberg and J. E. Davidson, 343–57. 2nd ed. New York, NY: Cambridge University Press.

[6] Subotnik, Rena F., Lee Kassan, Ellen Summers, and Alan Wasser. 1993. *Genius Revisited: High IQ Children Grown Up*. Norwood, NJ: Ablex.

[7] Hollingworth, Leta S. 1942. *Children Above 180 IQ Stanford-Binet: Origin and Development*. Yonkers-on-Hudson, NY: World Book Company.

[8] Gross, Miraca U. M. 1993. *Exceptionally Gifted Children*. New York: Routledge.

[9] Freeman, Joan. 2001. *Gifted Children Grown Up*. London: David Fulton.

[10] Waley, Arthur, and Confucius. 1938. *The Analects of Confucius*. London: George Allen & Unwin Ltd.

[11] Chan, Jimmy. 2007. "Giftedness and China's Confucian Heritage." In *Conceptions of Giftedness: Sociocultural Perspectives*, edited by Mary T. McCann and Norman Shane, 38. Mahwah, NJ: Lawrence Erlbaum Associates.

[12] Park, Jae. 2017. "Sociocultural Concept of High Ability and Heart-Mind Epistemology in Confucian Societies." *International Studies in Sociology of Education* 26, no. 4: 382. https://doi.org/10.1080/09620214.2016.1187078.

[13] Lan, Yu, and Hoi K. Suen. 2005. "Historical and Contemporary Exam-Driven Education Fever in China." *KEDI Journal of Education Policy* 2, no. 1: 17–33.

[14] Li, Jin. 2002. "A Cultural Model of Learning: Chinese 'Heart and Mind for Wanting to Learn'." *Journal of Cross-Cultural Psychology* 33: 284. https://doi.org/10.1177/0022022102033003003.

[15] Fairbank, John King. 1992. *China: A New History*. Cambridge: Harvard University Press.

[16] Kim, Tack-ho, Sang Min Lee, Kum-lan Yu, Seungkook Lee, and Ana Puig. 2005. "Hope and the Meaning of Life as Influences on Korean Adolescents' Resilience: Implications for Counselors." *Asia Pacific Education Review* 6, no. 2: 11.

[17] Cho, Seok-hee, Doehee Ahn, Suk Sil Han, and Hye-Jin Park. 2008. "Academic Developmental Patterns of the Korean Gifted during the 18 Years after Identification." *Personality and Individual Differences* 45: 784–89.

[18] Subotnik, Rena F., Paula Olszewski-Kubilius, and Frank C. Worrell. 2011. "Rethinking Giftedness and Gifted Education." *Psychological Science in the Public Interest* 12: 3– 54. https://doi.org/10.1177/1529100611418056.

[19] Merton, Robert K. 1968. "The Matthew Effect in Science." *Science* 159: 56–63.

Chapter 7

Social-Emotional Needs

Peers

Els De Wit, M.A.

> *"The exceptionally gifted child has one of the most difficult problems of social adjustment that any human being is ever called upon to meet."*
>
> *–Burks, Williams, and Terman, 1930*[1]

For decades, giftedness and friendship have been a heavily discussed topic. Leta Hollingworth (1942)2 recognized that "the more intelligent a person is, regardless of age, the less often he can find a truly congenial companion." Highly–profoundly gifted individuals are not inherently loners, as they are often perceived to be, but they may struggle to find genuine friendship in a world that feels so different from themselves. I refer to Roland Persson's chapter on social acceptance.

While most young children seek playmates, highly–profoundly gifted children often look for close friendships—friends they can fully trust and connect with on a deeper level. Gross[3] described the highly–profoundly gifted as feeling the social pressure to conform or dumb down. Wood & Laycraft[4] described these children as intentionally "dumbing down" or "masking" in an effort to fit in with peers their own age. The same thing can be seen in highly-profoundly gifted adults, dumbing down has become a go-to style when trying to be socially accepted.

Typically developing children often prefer to avoid conflict or deep discussion in friendships, whereas highly–profoundly gifted girls tend to competitive discussion with friends.[5] For these individuals, the discussion centers on content and self-challenging thought process—though it is often misunderstood by others. Holding philosophical sessions can support these thought-provoking processes and serve as a meaningful outlet for in-depth discussions.[6]

Successful, highly–profoundly gifted women have shared that during adolescence, they experienced social isolation, deliberately performed poorly on tests, and intentionally failed to submit assignments. Gifted adolescents often report avoiding "geeky" clubs—such as chess, debate, or computer clubs—to avoid the undesirable social labels.[7] However, highly–profoundly gifted individuals can truly enjoy working with others when they feel their contributions are valued by both teachers and peers.[8]

Finding peer groups can also be a great relief for children. Bringing together groups of children with shared interests creates a positive environment for gifted children. In general, this alignment provides opportunities for their social-emotional development. Peers play a critical role in the social, behavioral, emotional, and cognitive development.[9]

The like-minded peer-relationship differs from the adult-child relationship. For example, what is expected in terms of affection, intimacy, personal support, and how they resolve conflicts.[10]

It is also not unusual for highly–profoundly gifted children to spend time with older people. It is common for preschoolers to hang out with older playmates.[11] While the relationship may not appear to be a friendship to outsiders, the child often experiences it as a meaningful connection. Authentic friendship can be considered a rare find. Some highly–profoundly gifted children may need to learn that one friend cannot meet all the requirements of what they perceive to be a genuine friendship. One friend can be a good discussion partner, another can have a similar interest in astronomy, and another friend can be a good tennis partner.

A great antidote for peer pressure is a positive home environment; one where demonstrating talent and emotions is encouraged and valued. Parents can support their children by affirming that the competitiveness and drive for popularity are only temporary. More mature relationships often develop later, particularly in university, and tend to center around shared interests rather than popularity.[12] It's also important to distinguish popularity from true friendship. It has been reported that once in university, problems with making friends usually resolve. Gifted adolescents in university reported that forming friendships became easier, as they found peers with similar interests and shared expectations—such as openness to discussions and the ability to "agree to disagree."

Mentors

Mentorship appears to be as hard to define as giftedness. It has led to many definitions, which mostly serve just the author themself. Definitions vary from long-distance, time-delayed group mentoring to one-on-one personal, intensive training. In an ideal situation, mentorship involves a personal, dyadic, hierarchical relationship in which the mentor provides supervision to support the mentee's learning, development, and progress.[13]

The idea of mentoring has been around for a long time and was a very common way to pass on knowledge and abilities. Good mentorship can be based on admiration. Admiration is achieved when someone else you look up to is better at something than you are. Both admiration and envy can trigger motivation.[14] Admiration is a powerful tool to achieve the formation of both personal and collective values, ideals, and identities. This is precisely why mentoring is such a powerful tool for fostering motivation, perseverance, and the development of executive functioning skills. Good mentorship can thus achieve change in attitudes, values, qualities of character and more.

Mentors can effectively tailor learning content not only to specific goals but also to the developmental level of the highly–profoundly gifted individual. These individuals often develop asynchronously. For example, a highly–profoundly gifted child may be capable of understanding strategic concepts of warfare or the philosophical themes in George Orwell's ***1984*** *yet may not be emotionally prepared to process the more graphic or disturbing aspects of war or totalitarianism depicted in the book.*

Ziegler[15] mentions four big conditions for the optimal mentorship of gifted children:

1. **Improvement-oriented learning**—just experiencing something is not enough. A mentor should make sure that a mentee does not stand still but keeps on improving.

2. **Individualization**—a mentor should concentrate on a single learner, focusing on the learning and the progress of the mentee. Every achieved goal calls for a next, more demanding goal.

3. **Feedback**—appropriate feedback is necessary. To prevent the gifted mentee from becoming easily satisfied with their progress, specific and frequent feedback is essential to keep them moving forward.

4. **Practice tasks with minimal transfer**—practice makes perfect. Tasks that require minimal transfer—those that do not involve understanding of higher-order steps—are necessary to ensure full comprehension of newly learned material. This is the part that the gifted often find overwhelming, not seeing the learning steps in between.

The mentor and mentee ideally serve as an interactive system, i.e. not controlled one-sidedly by the mentor. The mentee plays an important role in influencing the mentor as well. Research shows that during parent-child or mentor-mentee interactions, the adult often imitates the child or mentee more frequently that the reverse. Mentees tend to prefer mentors who are similar to themselves suggesting that similarity plays an important role in fostering empathy. While there is no one-size-fits-all approach to mentoring, effective mentoring should be adapted to fit the specific discipline and goals of the relationship.

In 1977, Vaillant[16] demonstrated that the most successful Americans had experienced personal mentorship in their lives. Similarly, Bloom found that individuals who had achieved excellence were often raised in individually tailored learning environments. Mentoring can be highly effective for achieving clear goals, such as improving of academic performance, work habits, and self-confidence. For some, individual mentoring is the "gold standard." It is, however, not clear to what extent this applies to gifted education; there are not enough studies conducted on the topic. Brackmann[17] notes that personal mentoring—often in the form of homeschooling—was more common in the past and that identifying and supporting talent is especially crucial for the highly–profoundly gifted. Grassinger[18] rightly points out that while mentoring can be highly effective and perhaps the most pedagogically sound intervention, its impact has often been limited due to weak implementation.

Mentoring is a brilliant solution for those whose needs have not been met by traditional education.[19] Although academic self-concept tends to be higher among the gifted, many have struggled to develop their skills due to the absence of a mentor to guide and support them. In addition to guidance, gifted individuals need mentors to serve as role models and counselors. Gifted individuals also need help navigating through life experiences that they find difficult.

Highly–profoundly gifted individuals need a mentor who can handle their intensity. As Jacobson[20] stated, the gifted know the answer to question; the highly–profoundly gifted question the answer. The highly–profoundly gifted are very capable of putting on a façade and often develop strategies to look as "normal" as possible. It takes an attuned mentor to waltz through these strategies.

Because highly–profoundly gifted individuals can often teach themselves and grasp concepts quickly, scaffolding is an effective tool to use in mentorship. Starting from the foreknowledge of the mentee, you provide support as a mentor up until the point he or she can do it independently. This means that, in the beginning, the mentee needs more support than at the end. As a mentor, you guide your mentee step by step toward taking ownership of their own learning process by gradually retracting your own level of support. During this process, the mentor provides the child with clear-cut instructions and detailed feedback on how to improve. For instance, instead of saying "write more clearly", a mentor might say "next time, try and write your loops a bit smaller. I'll show you one more time, then you try it."

Besides needing a mentor for specific courses, the highly–profoundly gifted also need a "mentor of life". A person they can look up to (admire), someone who can relate to them (i.e. highly–profoundly gifted) and who is willing to experience together. Mentors can help them ponder the things that they are thinking or questioning. They lead with an open mind to the questions the mentee has and often question their own thought process along the way. In my experience, most highly–profoundly gifted individuals struggle to find a trusted advisor with whom they can explore their questions and thought processes. The highly–profoundly gifted have advanced metacognition and introspection capabilities. They spend a lot of time evaluating and strategizing about one's own thinking in order to improve it. Many gifted people suffer from internal conflicts because of their emotional sensitivity. They have an acute perception of what is and what ought to be. Dabrowski suggested that instead of viewing these internal conflicts as something negative, we see them as positive indicators of development potential. Moreover, academic self-concept tends to be higher within the gifted.

One great tool to allow for these thoughts to be processed is holding philosophical sessions. For children, this is also known as philosophy for children (P4C)[21,22]. In a "community of inquiry" with peers, children learn to express their thoughts and collaboratively reflect on a particular theme or question. Though the results of a preliminary study on the effects of philosophy should be analyzed with care, both teachers and students reported that the children developed greater confidence in speaking, improved listening skills, higher self-esteem, and a stronger sense of judgment.[23]

In the next chapter, Peter Visser will tell us more about this tool and the link with metacognition.

References

[1 3] Gross, M. U. M. 2004. *Exceptionally Gifted Children.* 2nd ed. New York, NY: Routledge Falmer.

[2] Hollingworth, L. S. 1942. *Children Above 180 IQ (Stanford-Binet): Origin and Development.* Yonkers-on-Hudson, NY: World Book Company.

[4] Wood, V. R., and K. C. Laycraft. 2020. "How Can We Better Understand, Identify, and Support Highly Gifted and Profoundly Gifted Students? A Literature Review of the Psychological Development of Highly–Profoundly Gifted Individuals and Overexcitabilities." *Annals of Cognitive Science* 4 (1).

[5 10]Neihart, M., S. Reis, N. Robinson, and S. Moon. 2002. *The Social and Emotional Development of Gifted Children: What Do We Know?* Sourcebooks, Inc.

[6 21] Worley, Emma, and Peter Worley. 2019. "Teaching Critical Thinking and Metacognitive Skills through Philosophical Enquiry: A Practitioner's Report on Experiments in the Classroom." *Childhood & Philosophy.*

[7 11 12] Rimm, S. 2022. "Social Adjustment and Peer Pressure for Gifted Children." *Davidson Gifted Blog.* Last modified 2022. https://www.davidsongifted.org/gifted-blog/social- adjustment-and-peer-pressures-for-gifted-children/.

[8] French, Lisa, Cheryl Walker, and Bruce Shore. 2011. "Do Gifted Students Really Prefer to Work Alone?" *Roeper Review*33: 145–59.

[9 17] Brackmann, A. 2020. *Extrem Begabt: Die Persönlichkeitsstruktur von Höchstbegabten und Genies.* Stuttgart: Klett-Cotta.

[13 18] Grassinger, Robert, Marion Porath, and Albert Ziegler. 2010. "Mentoring the Gifted: A Conceptual Analysis." *High Ability Studies* 21: 27–46.

[14] Van de Ven, Niels. 2017. "Envy and Admiration: Emotion and Motivation Following Upward Social Comparison." *Cognition and Emotion* 31, no. 1: 193–200.

[15] Grassinger, Robert, Marion Porath, and Albert Ziegler. 2010. "Mentoring the Gifted: A Conceptual Analysis." *High Ability Studies* 21, no. 1: 27–46.

[16] Mammadov, S., and A. Topçu. 2014. "The Role of E-Mentoring in Mathematically Gifted Students' Academic Life: A Case Study." *Journal for the Education of the Gifted* 37 (3): 220–44.

[19] Cakir, L., and I. Kocabas. 2016. "Mentoring in Gifted Student's Education and a Model Suggestion." *Educational Process: International Journal* 5 (1): 76–90.

[20] Jacobsen, M.-E. 1999. *The Gifted Adult.* New York: Ballantine Books.

[22] The Global Metacognition Institute. 2022. "Why P4C (Philosophy for Children) Is Important for Metacognition." Last modified 2022. https://www.globalmetacognition.com/post/why-p4c-philosophy-for-children-is- important-for-metacognition.

[25] Colom, R., F. G. Moriyón, C. Magro, and E. Morilla. 2014. "The Long-term Impact of Philosophy for Children: A Longitudinal Study (Preliminary Results)."

Chapter 8

Philosophizing and Highly–Profoundly Gifted

Dr. Peter Visser

UNESCO and Matthew Lipman: the (re)birth of Philosophical Dialogue

Philosophizing with children (and young adults) is now known worldwide as Philosophy for Children (P4C).[1] Inspired by the democratic climate of political and pedagogical revolution during "the roaring sixties," Matthew Lipman[2] developed the P4C approach. His colleagues and students at the Institute for the Advancement of Philosophy for Children (IAPC) at Montclair State University in New Jersey later propelled this participative model of intensive philosophical dialogue onto the global stage.[3] This approach stood in stark contrast to the traditional view of philosophy as a dry academic subject focused on memorizing historical ideas, facts, and figures for exams.

On the contrary, by the turn of the millennium, P4C and several other related approaches had been integrated into various school curricula.[4] They also appeared on many wish lists from a wide range of stakeholders advocating for support of highly–profoundly gifted children identified by IQ.[5] P4C tools emerged as a widely embraced pedagogical innovation, contributing to the ongoing process of differentiation and individualization in education.

In 1946, the United Nations Educational, Scientific and Cultural Organization (UNESCO), was built on a solid philosophical foundation after the disaster of World War II. Its emergence brought new energy to a wave of P4C initiatives, including the *Paris Declaration for Philosophy* in 1995.[6] At that time, the UNESCO participants considered:

> *"...that the practice of philosophy, which does not exclude any idea from free discussion, and which endeavors to establish the exact definition of concepts used, to verify the validity of lines of reasoning and to scrutinize closely the arguments of others, enables each individual to learn to think independently..."*

From the nineties until the very beginning of the 21st century, that in a nutshell represented what P4C was all about. Today, we see a large amount of newly published manuals and other useful didactical materials. Various initiators have organized master classes and courses reflecting a remarkable diversity of philosophical practices—each offering its own emphasis and modifications of the original P4C concept developed by Lipman.[7] Significantly, a growing global network of P4C groups has emerged, supported by members with significant educational and political interest—an encouraging sign for the future of this movement.

P4C Guidelines

There are several steps to initiate an approach of philosophizing in a real dialogical setting. Depending on the chosen topics, participants' starting competencies, and their learning progress, certain steps in the process can be combined, extended, or occasionally skipped. These are the common guidelines we see in many P4C- sessions:[8]

1. Give a short example as a motivational starting point from a well-chosen story, poem, video scene, photo, news topic, song ... or dive-in with a topic or theme that is appealing or interesting to the participants.

2. The chosen topic(s) to explore and experienced together should be spontaneously raised and immediately open some philosophical questions formulated by the participants. Here are some examples from different philosophical fields picked at random. They can be significant from a certain point of view and revisited at different ages:
    - Is telling the truth always obliged?
    - When are people far too old to learn something new?
    - What is 'zero'?
    - Could you think without using language?
    - Why are we so fascinated when we look upon a starry night?
3. With the group, gather all these nominative questions in detail and make them visible for all.

4. Choose (in a democratic way) with a focus on the content, one starting question.

5. Summarize some answers to the chosen problem.

6. Give the participants another question that dives deeper into the current research.

7. Try to analyze just one concept that is the main part of the larger question.

8. When it seems the inquiry has reached a dead end, try to give a new angle or another perspective.

9. When a strong argument or position is taken by one participant, ask for more examples or something that claims the opposite (play devil's advocate).

10. Try to conclude, if possible, with a (temporarily) consensus. Or give the members a last chance to talk about what went (very) good or (extremely) wrong during the session.

P4C through Time and Space

Matthew Lipman was not the first philosopher to recognize and describe the immense potential of philosophy in an educational context. Many philosophers have viewed philosophy as an interactive and dynamic discipline—far removed from the stereotype of a dry academic subject filled with unreadable texts. Amongst others, we can draw a constant philosophical/pedagogical line. Throughout history and across cultures philosophers have championed the educational power of philosophy—from Socrates to Rousseau, Pestalozzi, Fröbel, Alcott, Mann, Dewey, Tagore, and ultimately Lipman and his P4C colleagues. In 2016, the publisher of Martha C. Nussbaum's described her Socratic pedagogy in her manifesto *Not for Profit: Why Democracy Needs the Humanities* as "… a rallying cry for anyone who cares about the deepest purpose of education."[9] As a result, many P4C-practitioners adapted their approaches, especially in the early stages of organizing philosophical dialogue for different age groups. These adaptations were typically designed for school settings, with enough flexibility to be used in settings with both five and six-year-olds and lifelong adult learners.

The democratic principle of generating the discussion topics from participants' own interests has a strong motivational effect. The ongoing exploration, of one of the questions in a group, where every voice counts is an important principle. First, the questions should be carefully evaluated. Then selected in a democratic process and elaborated on in a continuing philosophical dialogue. The teacher or parent plays the role of a "not knowing wizard." Their role is to ask questions at the right time, to deepen and extend as much as possible the actual thoughts and arguments from the participants. This art of questioning, as described by Oscar Brenifier, can only be developed through repeated practice—not by following a fixed list of standard questions. Who will take the initiative to carefully lead a group on the long and winding thinking road into a Community of Philosophical Inquiry (CoPi)? Catherine C. McCall cautioned that the facilitator should avoid delivering a lecture on the topic or adopting the role of the "all-knowing teacher."

The Importance of Metacognition

Focusing on meta-cognitive questions *can be especially helpful in the careful (re)emergence of old ideas—suddenly experienced in the moment as astonishingly new. The repeated 'wonder why' is the engine of this extraordinary type of conversation and investigation.*

At times, there are remarkable moments when someone articulates an idea with exceptional clarity and receives immediate recognition for their "great thinking." To better understand meta-cognitive questions, here is a brief and inspiring list:

- How do you know that your answer is a better one than the alternatives?
- How strong is the evidence on which that claim is based?
- Are you certain, or is there room for doubt in that statement?
- How can you challenge that idea you just heard?
- Why might other people claim the opposite is true?

When possible, a philosophical dialogue may conclude with a consensus, reached after all possible answers have been thoroughly explored. However, a dead end may also happen. There may be confusion about alternatives or not enough alternatives examined. It may also happen that participants become so fascinated and engaged by the various issues that they continue the debate long after the official conversation has ended. This sense of (temporary) uncertainty is a hallmark of philosophical inquiry—and an important experience that participants must learn to navigate.

Philosophizing and Cognitive Research

Matthew Lipman made an extended list of *thinking skills* that can be trained during a series of P4C sessions. Lipman noted that the "key features of higher-order thinking" closely parallel the thinking skills outlined by Lauren B. Resnick in *The Child as Thinker.*[10] This view is supported not by philosophers advocating for the steady growth of insight skills, but by cognitive researchers in the field of intelligence. Robert J. Sternberg,[11] emphasized that significant new understandings of major works in literature, philosophy, and related fields almost always require deep intellectual insight and unentrenched thinking.

A general theory of giftedness extends beyond any single content domain. Mathematical problems should certainly be explored, but verbal talents must also be recognized, nurtured, and developed through a variety of language courses. Sternberg was an early critic of STEM, as was Nussbaum (see also Chapter 8). The cognitive outcomes and positive impacts of P4C practices have been documented in numerous research P4C projects across various domains.

While the interpretation of results should be approached with caution, there is strong evidence of positive effects across a wide range of academic and developmental domains—including reading comprehension and learning, mathematics, logic, cognitive abilities, philosophical inquiry, language, listening, social and communicative skills, behavior and personal growth, emotional intelligence, moral reasoning, democratic attitudes, and skills.[12]

Explore Philosophical Talent

It's not enough to introduce a new P4C practice or specific track for the highly–profoundly gifted. One should always be aware of the long-term goal for implementing and anchoring P4C in the curriculum for the most beneficial effects.

We can only hope that the value of philosophizing and its powerful impact in Socratic education is not merely a thing of the past or a relic confined to history books. Thecla Rondhuis[13] believed that everyone should have the opportunity to explore their own philosophical potential—with the gentle guidance of a supportive hand. Try practicing with a small group of teachers or parents by exploring this philosophical question: is a low, average, or high IQ a curse or a blessing? Thinking pleasure guaranteed!

References

[1] *Philosophy for Children (P4C): A Dialogic Pedagogy for Creative Conversations.* n.d. https://mon.uvic.cat/grell/philosophy-for-children-p4c-a-dialogic-pedagogy-for- creative-conversations/.

[2] Lipman, Matthew. 2003. *Thinking in Education.* Cambridge, MA: Harvard University Press.

[3] *Transforming Thinking: Philosophical Inquiry in the Primary and Secondary Classroom.* n.d. https://www.routledge.com/Transforming-Thinking-Philosophical-Inquiry-in-the-Primary-and-Secondary/McCall/p/book/9780415476683.

[4] Trickey, S., and K. J. Topping. 2004. "Philosophy for Children: A Systematic Review." *Research Papers in Education* 19 (3): 365–80.

[5] Yan,Sijin,LynneMaselWalters,ZhuoyingWang,andChia-ChiangWang. 2018."Meta- Analysis of the Effectiveness of Philosophy for Children Programs on Students' Cognitive Outcomes." *Analytic Teaching and Philosophical Praxis* 39: 13–33.

[6] *DéclarationdeParispourlaphilosophie.* 1995.https://graines-de-philo-d- ascq.nursit.com/IMG/pdf/declaration-de-paris-pour-la-philosophie-fev-95-unesco.pdf.

[7] *TheArtofPhilosophicalPractice.* n.d. https://www.academia.edu/33840499/The_Art_of_Philosophical_Practice.

[8] *KlassevolFilosoferen:HandboekvoorLeerkrachten.* n.d. https://vefonieuw.filosofieonderwijs.be/klassevol-filosoferen-handboek-voor-leerkrachten/.

[9] Nussbaum,MarthaC. 1997. *Not forProfit:Why Democracy Needs the Humanities.* https://archive.org/details/notforprofitwhyd0000nuss_w9e1.

[10] Meadows, Sarah, and Geoffrey Meadows. *The Child as Thinker: The Development and Acquisition of Cognition in Childhood.* n.d. https://www.routledge.com/The-Child as Thinker The-Development-and-Acquisition-of-Cognition-in-Childhood/Meadows-Meadows/p/book/9781841695129.

[11] Sternberg, Robert J. *Beyond IQ: A Triarchic Theory of Human Intelligence.* n.d. https://www.cambridge.org/be/academic/subjects/life- sciences/neuroscience/beyond-iq-triarchic-theory-human- intelligence?format=PB&isbn=9780521278911#contentsTabAnchor.

[12] *Artikel School en Klaspraktijk VEFO.* n.d. https://filosofieonderwijs.be/wp-content/uploads/2022/02/Artikel-School-en-Klaspraktijk-VEFO.pdf.

[13] *Dspace Library UU: Handle1874/7311.*https://dspace.library.uu.nl/h

Chapter 9

STEM Disciplines Favored over Gifted and Talented Programs:

Parents' Perception and Choices to Support Their Child's Talents

Hyeseong Lee, Ph.D.
Min Jung Lee, Ph.D.

There is an international trend toward creating effective STEM (science, technology, engineering, and math) education programs to prepare and advance the future.[1] However, even in the United States, students often enter STEM fields lacking foundational knowledge of STEM approaches. The need to grow a strong domestic STEM workforce in the U.S. is clear.[2] In reviewing the *National Science Board's* (NSB's) *Vision 2030*, the National Science Foundation (NSF) noted that the United States still has a long way to go to meet its goals.

Current trends and demographic shifts in U.S. science and engineering fields are not promising. Our nation's youth lack interest in research STEM careers, and progress is slow in reversing these concerning trends. Women, individuals with disabilities, and other underrepresented groups among the innovation ecosystems are at risk; the U.S. is at risk of surrendering its global leadership in technological innovation. Urgent action and sustained investment in STEM education and workforce development research are essential for building a modernized infrastructure. The United States needs to be able to attract, retain, and develop diverse STEM talent for its future needs.[3]

Due to these concerns, STEM education is viewed as a critical pathway to increasing the number of skilled individuals in the STEM fields. Programs that promote the integration of STEM disciplines are currently a major focus in educational research and practice.[4] When STEM education is combined with gifted education, it can also create meaningful opportunities for talent development.[5]

So, who are scientifically gifted and talented students? According to the National Association for Gifted Children (NAGC), as of 2023, gifted students are defined as "students with gifts and talents who perform—or have the capability to perform—at higher levels compared to others of the same age, experience, and environment in one or more domains." They require modification(s) to their educational experience(s) to learn and realize their potential."[6]

Kaufman and Sternberg argued that while giftedness is a broad concept that varies across time and cultures, it is ultimately more domain-specific.[7] Reflecting current trends in STEM education, the STEM Network under the NAGC aligned its mission accordingly, "to strengthen STEM education research in these areas, enhance recognition for the gifted, talented, promising, and creative students, and increase opportunities for these students inside and outside of school."[8]

As such, universal calls have been made to recruit and retain talented students in STEM to meet the growing need for STEM professionals. Recently, Ülger and Çepni examined 72 studies to explore recommendations for integrating scientific giftedness and STEM education.[9] They coded and categorized the suggestions from the articles, identifying the top five as follows: (1) offer a rich variety of STEM educational opportunities and activities (15.06%), (2) provide experiences focused on scientific investigation and inquiry (12.32%), (3) restructure gifted schools and programs (10.96%), (4) conduct further research on STEM talent development (10.96%), and (5) provide supportive and challenging educational environments (8.22%).

The results underscore the importance of providing challenging STEM educational opportunities for future generations. In this context, this chapter explores why STEM enrichment programs are both popular and well-supported in gifted education, the need to cultivate talent across diverse domains, and the factors that influence parents' decisions to enroll their children in out-of-school enrichment programs—since parents are often the primary decision-makers in these choices.

Need for STEM and Developing Talent

Nationwide calls have been made to retain and recruit talented students in STEM fields. STEM is recognized as the foundation of the economies motivating and retaining the students worldwide. To support the growing need for STEM professions, it is estimated that over one million STEM graduates are needed over the next decade. However, the supply of STEM graduates is insufficient to meet these needs.

STEM Disciplines Over Gifted and Talented Education

The stereotypes and rigor of STEM disciplines might explain the shortage of STEM labor. Research specific to the lack of participation and retention highlights negative STEM stereotypes. A common misperception is that STEM is reserved for those with individuals with innate talent and intelligence. This perception is deterring individuals from considering a career or college major in the STEM fields. Studies also suggest that students who struggle in STEM subjects often reject them. entirely, concluding that these students lack the innate intelligence they believe is necessary for success in those fields. This arduousness perception of STEM caused students to withdraw from academic careers in STEM.

Whalen and Shelley found that students with high American College Testing (ACT) scores often started their majors in STEM fields but later switched to non-STEM majors.[10] Among students who initially enrolled in STEM programs, those who changed to non-STEM had lower ACT scores than peers remaining in STEM. More critically, a decline in student motivation was high for STEM majors. Chen reported that approximately 48% of students changed from a STEM major to a non-STEM major or dropped out of college altogether.[11]

Similarly, Whalen and Shelley found that 73% of students who began in STEM majors continued their studies in those fields, compared to 92% of students in non-STEM majors who remained in their chosen disciplines.[12] This disparity contributed to the perception of STEM fields as more demanding. As a result, parents of gifted students encouraged their children to take more STEM courses to better prepare for STEM careers. Although post-secondary education and STEM fields experienced low participation rates in mainstream education, the opposite trend emerged in gifted education—where more STEM classes and programs were offered, and student participation was notable higher.

To support STEM talents, a variety of programs exist, including specialized STEM high schools, out-of-school enrichment programs, internships, mentoring opportunities, competitions, and early college entrance. Olszewski-Kubilius found that residential schools for gifted students, compared to mainstream schools, allocated a larger proportion of resources to STEM.[13] Lee and Desmet reported that 71.75% of university-based enrichment programs offered STEM courses alongside gifted education graduate programs.[14] They also reported that non-STEM courses were often canceled due to low enrollment, suggesting that stakeholders favored STEM offerings. These conclusions aligned with earlier findings by Olszewski-Kubilius and Lee, who reported that mathematics enrichment programs were the most frequently attended among academic offerings.[15] Additionally, 63.5% of participants regularly engaged in independent science learning, whereas only 35% pursued independent language arts.

In addition to the disproportionate emphasis on STEM subjects in gifted education, research in the field is also heavily skewed toward investigating STEM-related programs.

Lee and Gentry reviewed doctoral dissertations (*N*=683) in gifted education from 2006 to 2016 and found that 51% focused on STEM subjects, 34% on non-STEM subjects, and 15% addressed both (e.g., mathematics and reading).[16] As of 2021, the National Association for Gifted Children (NAGC) had 16 networks exploring various topics in the field. While the "Curriculum Studies" was among them, networks such as "STEM" and "Computer and Technology" also represented educators' interests. "Arts" had its own network and represented all non-STEM disciplines such as language arts, humanities, and social studies. In terms of empirical research, little to no research explored the impact of non-STEM programs.

A Call for STEM Talent Development to Support Diverse Talents

As described earlier, nations called for action to advance the STEM frontier. The emphasis was even more significant in gifted and talented education. The NSB (2010) reported that the current STEM education system "too frequently fails to identify and develop our most talented and motivated students who will become the next generation of innovators."[17] The U.S. is not alone—many other nations have emphasized talent development and innovation as essential global and central strategies to sustain long-term prosperity. More specifically, Atkinson and Mayo argued for the "All STEM for Some" framework in contrast to the prevailing "Some STEM for All."[18] The former prioritizes delivering high- quality opportunities to capable, motivated students who are interested in pursuing STEM, while the latter emphasizes broad STEM exposure for all students. Students with gifts and talents deserve rigorous, domain-specific learning experiences to help them realize their full potential—beginning with early exposure to STEM. This "All STEM for Some" approach is favorably embraced by some experts as cost-effective.

But what exactly is talent development? Informally, talent development refers to the deliberate cultivation of giftedness and capability within a specific domain. More familiarly, it serves as a theoretical framework within gifted education. In recent years, there has been an ongoing paradigm shift towards a broader psychological understanding of giftedness—one that emphasizes nurturing students' talents rather than simply identifying them as gifted. This concept of talent development marks a departure from the traditional view of giftedness, which focused primarily on static intelligence.

Talent development recognizes a broader range of giftedness, including non-cognitive traits, and places specific emphasis on potential and development. From this perspective, ability is seen as dynamic and malleable throughout the developmental process.

The development of talent varies based on the domain and psychosocial variables. Based on multiple intelligence theory, which emphasizes innate capacity, Dai postulated five foundational domains of human effectivities shaped through dynamic person-environment interaction.[19] He identified the domains as: "*expressive* (expressing oneself through imaginative play and artistic means, such as writing, drawing, acting, singing, dancing), *technical* (making tools and gadgets to enhance effectiveness and efficiency), *intellectual* (reasoning, understanding, explaining, theorizing using mathematics, logic, visual-spatial imaging, or literary means), *social* (achieving practical purposes through effective communication, negotiation, collaboration, and leadership), and *psychomotor* (executing and coordinating body movements to accomplish complex physical tasks as in the case of most competitive and extreme sports and complex surgical operations) (p. 173)."

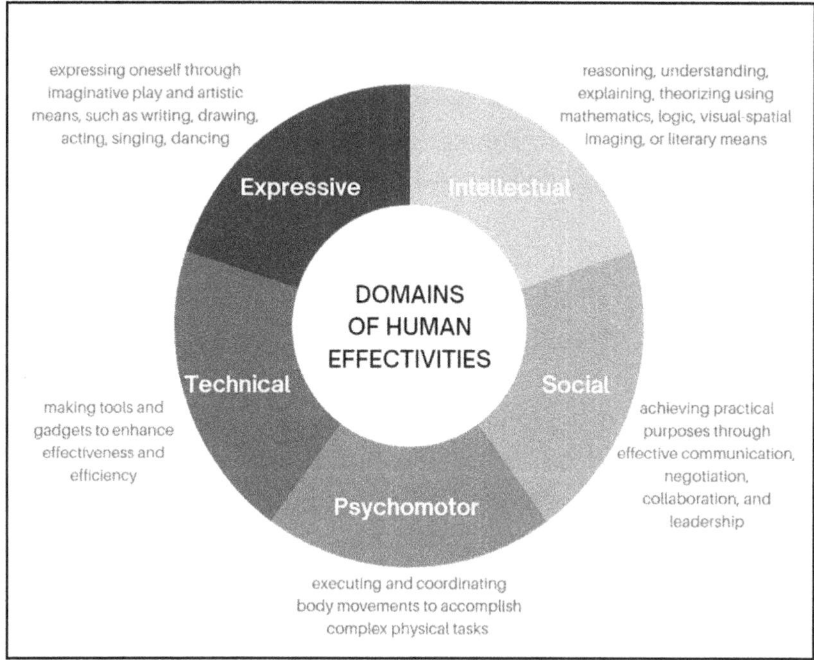

Figure 1. Five foundational domains of human effectivities addressed in Dai's (2017) study

Talent development researchers have conducted study-based domains or specific interests.

Some researchers in gifted and talented education have not only categorized specific domains of talent but also identified the unique developmental trajectories associated with each. According to Olszewski-Kubilius et al., interest and ability in certain areas—such as mathematics, music, and art—can be observed as early as preschool.[20] They suggest that assessment and enrichment in these domains may begin early, with accelerated studies in mathematics and private lessons in music and art serving as effective supports.

They also argued that early interest and potential may be evident in other domains, such as science and writing, however, assessment and nurturing for these domains may begin later. Even within domains, developmental trajectories—including the optimal age, to begin training and the timeline for peak talent performance—vary significantly. For example, tennis and gymnastics, instruments and voice, and mathematics and history all follow different developmental paths. Regarding such, Olszewski-Kubilius and Thomson (2015) noted: "in sports, age of initial instruction is affected by physical attributes such as size and strength, as is length of participation (e.g., diminishing speed with age). In music, instruction in many instruments can start very early, while voice lessons typically do not begin until late adolescence or early adulthood. Children begin to study some academic areas, such as mathematics, at the start of school or even earlier, but other subjects are not studied until college (e.g., psychology). Furthermore, individuals can make major contributions to some fields, such as mathematics, at a relatively young age, while other fields require long years of preparation and accumulation of knowledge and expertise (Subotnik et al., 2011)."[21]

Likewise, each domain follows a unique developmental trajectory, which influences the appropriate for identifying and nurturing specific talents. Figure 2 synthesizes the different trajectories per subject areas from the current literatures.

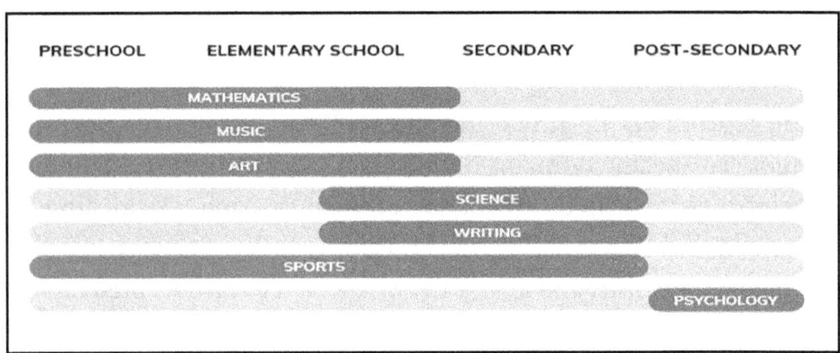

Figure 2. Approximate optimal age to initiate training and nurturing by subject areas

To support individual talent development, experts recommend several key practices: (a) In the early stages, general intelligence is important as a foundational base for the development of domain-specific abilities; (b) Multiple types of domain-specific assessments should be conducted by middle school at the latest; (c) Programs and services should be available through various pathways and at different stages of development—such as exposure, acceleration, and enrichment, mentorships, and apprenticeships—in chronicle order. Students' unique talents should be fully supported across domains, including both STEM and non-STEM fields, with equal attention given to each. Talent development is shaped not only by formal education but also by parental support, including early exposure and enrichment opportunities. Therefore, understanding how parents perceive subject areas—particularly the preference toward STEM—and how they support their children's talents is a critical area of study.

Factors Affecting Parents' Choice for Enrichment Programs

Parents play a pivotal role in the development of their children. Often, parents are crucial in identifying giftedness and providing talent-nurturing environments. For example, Daglioglu and Suveren found that families were significantly more accurate than teachers in identifying gifted children and evaluating their performances; parents were more effective observers of their children's cognitive and social abilities.[22] Similarly, Bicknell emphasized the parent's multifaceted role in nurturing giftedness—as motivator, resource provider, monitor, content adviser, and counselor.[23]

However, few studies have explored how parents create opportunities for their gifted child or how they influence the developmental trajectories.

Next, we discuss the factors affecting parents' choice when selecting gifted programs.

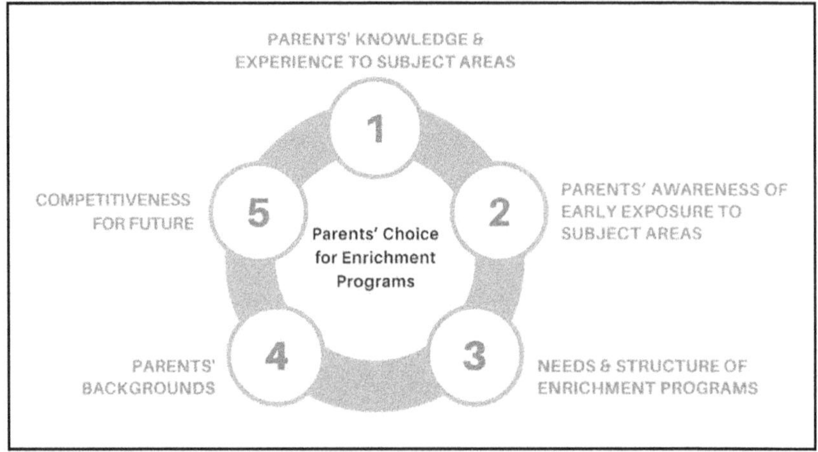

Figure 3. Factors Affecting Parents' Choice for Enrichment Programs

How Parents Identify Talent

A parent's ability to identify talent in their child is vital for providing developmentally appropriate opportunities to nurture that talent. To do so effectively, parents need to understand the signs and traits of giftedness. In STEM subjects, resources such as objective assessments and clear indicators—like solving advanced mathematical problems—can help parents recognize giftedness. For instance, parents know that multiplication is typically introduced in elementary school after addition and subtraction. If their preschool age child is independently solving and explaining multiplication problems, it quickly becomes clear that the child may be gifted in mathematics. Because many parents are more familiar with STEM content, they are often better equipped to identify giftedness in those areas.

However, what does it mean to be advanced or show talents in non-STEM subjects, such as music, arts, and humanities? Does memorizing all the historical facts indicate a child is talented in humanities?

Also, the child's talent in music may not always be expressed obviously or be obvious to the parents. Adding codes for dissonance or playing rhythm uniquely or unexpectedly, may be harder for parents to identify. It can be difficult for parents to recognize giftedness in non-STEM subject areas unless the signs are obvious (e.g., playing tunes by ear) or the parents have a background in those fields. As a result, they may have a limited understanding of learning progressions or developmental trajectories in non-STEM disciplines making it more difficult to recognize and identify their child's talent in these areas. Because parents' recognition and understanding of their children's abilities influence decisions about educational options—such as schools, programs, and curricula—it is important to explore how parents perceive and understand giftedness.

Criteria for Choosing Enrichment Programs

For gifted students to thrive, the enrichment programs selected by parents should align with their children's individual characteristics, such as cognitive profile, areas of strength, and personality.[24] However, it is important to realize that while a child's interest and ability are important factors in program selection, parents may also be influenced by societal pressures, their own interests, or their own aspirations for their child's future career. For example, some parents may choose STEM programs with the hope that their child will pursue a socially prestigious profession, such as becoming a medical doctor. Parental decision-making is complex, "involving a mixture of rationalities related to values, preferences, child-rearing practices, social networks, and aspirations for their children."[25] This study explored the factors that influenced parents' preference for STEM disciplines when selecting enrichment programs for their children.

The Importance of Early Exposure to STEM

The United States needs talented scientists and engineers to meet the demands of the high-tech global economy. Studies have shown that the early exposure to STEM is a significant factor in students' continued engagement with STEM beyond high school, as it helps spark and sustain their interest. As a result, educators increasingly promote out-of-school enrichment programs for K-12 students as a means of fostering interest and engagement in STEM fields. The benefits of exposing children to STEM early is recognized by educational experts and parents alike. For instance, according to Tay et al. parents of preschool and kindergarten-aged children expressed strong interest in STEM, noting that it helped their child discover new interests, explore diverse topics, and begin to think about their future education and career paths.[26] This awareness and enthusiasm for STEM continued throughout the elementary and secondary school years. Notably, their STEM interest peaked in high school given the increased registration rate for advanced STEM courses and enrollment in Advanced Placement (AP) programs during the pre-college period.

The Structure of Enrichment Programs

Each subject area employs unique methods for teaching and learning. Non-STEM subjects, such as music and the arts, are typically taught through private lessons or apprenticeship involving one-on-one interaction with a teacher. In contrast, STEM subjects are often taught through "public" education (as opposed to private education). Engagement may include attending STEM camps or enrichment programs, visiting science museums, and watching STEM-related videos and documentaries. When choosing public educational options—such as specialized schools or enrichment programs—parents often selected STEM subjects because they envisioned them being taught within a group setting. In contrast, parent sought private lessons to support their children's talent in non-STEM areas.

In addition, parents often chose out-of-school enrichment opportunities that offered content that not readily available through their child's school. In Lee and Desmet's (2020,443-444) study, one parent who works as a science teacher in a public school shared her opinion.

> *"It clicked for me why there were so many (students) going into STEM programs and not language arts. In my opinion, STEM programs are chosen because they are not offered in school. As a science teacher, I am telling you that there is not a whole lot of hands-on focus on science. The school curriculum is focused on what is being tested.*

> *I taught 6th-grade science a couple of years ago. That was something tested, but I still did not have many resources."*[27]

Due to limited resources and funding in public schools, students often lacked sufficient opportunities to engage in STEM, which may have motivated parents to enroll their children in supplemental out-of-school STEM programs.

Parents' Background

Parents' backgrounds—including their values, beliefs, culture, education, and careers—influence how they supported their child's talent development. A parent's career, particularly in STEM can significantly shape the choice of enrichment programs for a gifted child. Parents who worked in STEM fields were more likely to select and encourage their STEM programs, often placing greater value on these subjects enthusiastically fostering their child's interest in the sciences. While many parents stated that their child's interest is the primary factor in selecting an enrichment program, parent's career in STEM may influence this preference by naturally exposing the child to the field and sparking an interest.

Studies have found that parents' education level influenced their choice of STEM-related enrichment programs. This pattern can be explained in multiple ways. Simpkins et al.'s study showed that parents with higher educational degrees were more likely to have children with increased interest in science fields.[28] Similarly, according to Almarode et al. parents' academic level affected the resources and opportunities they provided to foster their children's interest in STEM.[29] This conclusion aligned with earlier findings that exposure to STEM is a key factor in developing interest in the field. Moreover, Raty and Karkkainen found that parents with higher levels of education accurately perceived their child's competence in mathematics.[30] Mathematics is one of the most common indicators used to place children in STEM educational programs, and parents' education levels are linked to a preference for STEM enrichment.

Parents' cultural backgrounds, including race and ethnicity, are well-known factors influencing their preference for STEM fields, as these preferences are closely tied to their perceptions of and trust in STEM disciplines.

In Lee and Desmet's study, the authors indicated that while most parents viewed STEM subjects and non-STEM subjects as equally important, they believed their child would obtain more benefits by pursuing a STEM major.[31] Such perceptions were particularly noted among families of Latino and Asian heritage; these parents saw STEM careers as stable, lucrative, and respected, and believed they could provide dependable support for the family. As a result, parents who prioritized family were more likely to choose STEM-related enrichment programs, viewing STEM as a path to social success and family stability.

Market Competitiveness—The Pursuit of STEM

According to the Harris Interactive survey, slightly more than half of participating parents believed that a STEM education should be prioritized in schools. The survey found that 53% held this view because they wanted to ensure the U.S. remains competitive in the global marketplace, while 51% of parents believed a focus on STEM would produce the next generation of innovators.[32] These findings reflect how parents perceived the STEM fields—as a pathway to national competitiveness. This belief may have motivated some parents to choose STEM subjects over non-STEM subjects when selecting enrichment programs, viewing them as a means to ensure their children's leadership roles and future competitiveness in the job market.

However, it is essential to note that some parents prioritized STEM simply due to the societal pressure associated with STEM disciplines. According to Lee and Desmet's survey, which asked parents about the abundance of STEM course offerings in enrichment programs, 26.92% of parents acknowledged the societal emphasis on STEM, and 25.38% cited anticipated job opportunities in STEM fields as a motivating factor.[33] Notable shared comments (Lee & Desmet, 2020, p. 439) included:

> *"There is a big culture push to increase the number of STEM activities and courses to make Americans more competitive with other developed countries.*[34] *That is what gets the media focus including advertising."*

> *"Perhaps the current emphasis placed on STEM fields in education in general—at the local, state, and national levels. Children and parents may be getting the message that STEM fields are the key to future professional success and economic well-being."*

> *"While we recognize the need for a balanced education, all signs point to a need and demand for STEM staff now and into the future. Our world is driven by technology and requires all students to be STEM proficient to contribute."*

Summary

In conclusion, this chapter explored the state of STEM disciplines within gifted and talented education through the lens of talent development and explored the various factors that influence parents' decisions when selecting enrichment programs for their gifted children. Parental choice is not a straightforward process governed solely by a child's interests; rather, it is shaped by a complex interplay of social influences, cultural expectations, and deeply held personal values and beliefs. While acknowledging the imbalance in enriched opportunities that favor STEM, it is important for educational researchers and policymakers to pursue greater equity by expanding access and support for both STEM and non-STEM programs. This includes generating evidence and resources that inform and support parental decision-making in enrichment program selection.

References

[1] National Science Board (NSB). 2020.*Vision 2030*. Alexandria, VA: National Science Foundation. https://www.nsf.gov/nsb/publications/2020/nsb202015.pdf..

[2] National Science Board (NSB). 2020. *STEM Education for the Future: A Visioning Report*. Alexandria, VA: National Science Foundation. https://www.nsf.gov/edu/Materials/STEM%20Education%20for%20the%20Fu ture%20-%20 2020%20Visioning%20Report.pdf.

[3] NSB. 2020. *Vision 2030*, 29.

[4] Ulger, Bestami B., and Salih Çepni. 2020. "Gifted Education and STEM: A Thematic Review." *Journal of Turkish Science Education* 17 (3): 443–66.

[5] Ulger and Çepni. 2020. "Gifted Education and STEM."

6 National Association of Gifted Children (NAGC). n.d. "What is Giftedness?" https://nagc.org/page/what-is- giftedness#:~:text=Students%20with%20 gifts%20and%20talents,learn%20and%20realize% 20their%20potential.

[7] Kaufman, Scott B., and Robert J. Sternberg. 2008. "Conceptions of Giftedness." In *Handbook of Giftedness in Children: Psychoeducational Theory, Research, and Best Practices*, edited by Steven I. Pfeiffer, 71–92. New York: Springer. https://doi.org/10.1007/978-0-387-74401-8.

[8] National Association of Gifted Children (NAGC). n.d. "Networks – STEM." http://www.nagc.org.442elmp01.blackmesh.com/get-involved/nagc-networks- and-special-interest-groups/networks-stem.

[9] Ulger and Çepni. 2020. "Gifted Education and STEM."

[10] Whalen, Donald F., and Mack C. Shelley. 2010. "Academic Success for STEM and Non-STEM Majors." *Journal of STEM Education: Innovations and Research* 11 (1-2): 45–60.

[11] Chen, Xianglei. 2013. *STEM Attrition: College Students' Paths into and out of STEM Fields. Statistical Analysis Report*. Washington, DC: National Center for Education Statistics.

[12] Whalen and Shelley. 2010. "Academic Success for STEM and Non-STEM Majors."

[13] Olszewski-Kubilius, Paula. 2009. "Special Schools and Other Options for Gifted STEM Students." *Roeper Review* 32 (1): 61–70. https://doi.org/10.1080/02783190903386892.

[14] Lee, Hyeseong, and Ophelie Desmet. 2020. "Parent Perceptions of Enrichment Program Course Offerings: What about Non-STEM Courses?" *Journal of Gifted/Talented Education* 30 (3): 427–51. https://doi.org/10.9722/JGTE.2020.30.3.427.

[15] Olszewski-Kubilius, Paula, and Seon-Young Lee. 2004. "The Role of Participation in In- school and Outside-of-school Activities in the Talent Development of Gifted Students." *Journal of Secondary Gifted Education* 15 (3): 107– 23. https://doi.org/10.4219/jsge-2004-454.

[16] Lee, Hyeseong, and Marcia Gentry. 2019. "The Major Characteristics and Trends of Gifted Education Doctoral Dissertation Research from 2006 through 2016." Paper presented at the World Conference for the Gifted and Talented Children, Nashville, TN.

[17] National Science Foundation. 2010. *Preparing the Next Generation of STEM Innovators: Identifying and Developing Our Nation's Human Capital.* Alexandria, VA: National Science Foundation.

[18] Atkinson, Robert D., and Michael J. Mayo. 2010. *Refueling the US Innovation Economy: Fresh Approaches to Science, Technology, Engineering and Mathematics (STEM) Education.* Washington, DC: Information Technology and Innovation Foundation.

[19] Dai, David Y. 2017. "Envisioning a New Foundation for Gifted Education: Evolving Complexity Theory (ECT) of Talent Development." *Gifted Child Quarterly* 61 (3): 173. https://doi.org/10.1177/0016986217701837.

[20] Olszewski-Kubilius, Paula, Lisa Limburg-Weber, and Steven Pfeiffer. 2003. *Early Gifts: Recognizing and Nurturing Children's Talent.* Waco, TX: Prufrock Press.

[21] Subotnik, Rena F., Paula Olszewski-Kubilius, and Frank C. Worrell. 2011. "Rethinking Giftedness and Gifted Education: A Proposed Direction Forward Based on Psychological Science." *Psychological Science in the Public Interest*12 (1): 53. https://doi.org/10.1177/1529100611418056.

[22] Daglioglu, H. Elif, and Senem Suveren. 2013. "The Role of Teacher and Family Opinions in Identifying Gifted Kindergarten Children and the Consistence of These Views with Children's Actual Performance." *Educational Sciences: Theory and Practice* 13 (1): 444–53.

[23] Bicknell, Brenda. 2014. "Parental Roles in the Education of Mathematically Gifted and Talented Children." *Gifted Child Today* 37 (2): 83– 93. https://doi.org/10.1177/1076217513497576.

[24] Rogers, Karen B. 2002. *Re-forming Gifted Education: Matching the Program to the Child.* Tucson, AZ: Great Potential Press.

[25] Bosetti, Laura, and Mary C. Pyryt. 2007. "Parental Motivation in School Choice: Seeking the Competitive Edge." *Journal of School Choice* 1 (4): 107. https://doi.org/10.1300/15582150802098795.

[26] Tay, Juliana, Alissa Salazar, and Hyeseong Lee. 2018. "Parental Perceptions of STEM Enrichment for Young Children." *Journal for the Education of the Gifted* 41 (1): 5–23. https://doi.org/10.1177/0162353217745159.

[27] Lee and Desmet. 2020. "Parent Perceptions of Enrichment Program Course Offerings," 443–44.

[28] Simpkins, Sandra D., Pamela E. Davis-Kean, and Jacquelynne S. Eccles. 2006. "Math and Science Motivation: A Longitudinal Examination of the Links Between Choices and Beliefs." *Developmental Psychology* 42 (1): 70–83.

[29] Almarode, John T., et al. 2017. "Parent or Guardian Characteristics and Talented Students' Persistence in STEM." In *Teaching Gifted Learners in STEM Subjects: Developing Talent in Science, Technology, Engineering and Mathematics*, edited by Keith S. Taber, Manabu Sumida, and Lynne McClure, 46–64. New York: Routledge. https://doi.org/10.4324/9781315697147.

[30] Räty, Hannu, and Riitta Kärkkäinen. 2011. "Talent or Effort? Parents' Explanations of Their Children's Mathematical Performance in Relation to Mathematical Competence." *Social Behavior and Personality: An International Journal* 39 (5): 691– 99. https://doi.org/10.2224/sbp.2011.39.5.691.

[31] Lee and Desmet. 2020. "Parent Perceptions of Enrichment Program Course Offerings."

[32] Harris Interactive. 2016. *STEM Perceptions: Student & Parent Study: Parents and Students Weigh in on How to Inspire the Next Generation of Doctors, Scientists, Software Developers and Engineers*. Microsoft Corp. https://news.microsoft.com/download/archived/presskits/citizenship/docs/STEMPe rceptionsReport.pdf.

[33] [34] Lee and Desmet. 2020. "Parent Perceptions of Enrichment Program Course Offerings."

Chapter 10

Checklist for Parents of Highly–Profoundly Gifted

Els De Wit, M.A.

Taking care of your child's or your own high-profound giftedness is not always easy. Knowing what you need and how to translate it to the world, standing your ground in all of this, can be a very hard task. Over the years, I have developed some guidelines that can be a guide to life.

Adapt and Cope

Asynchronous development, overexcitabilities, and the experience of standing apart in life are important considerations every step of the journey. It can be difficult to know when to endure and when to adapt. Adapt where you can. Find the quiet place and the quiet people at a party, agree on a code word when the tension gets too high, carry ear plugs, consider wobbly cushions, wear comfortable clothes, allow doodling, read a book or newspaper, learn something by yourself when assignments are done.

However, sometimes there is just no way out and you must deal with boredom, slowness, and environments that are just "too much." Learning how to cope is an important skill you will need for the rest of your life. Sometimes it is what it is. A hard lesson to learn for some people who just don't accept things like that, but life cannot always be explained by clear-cut rules.

Redefine Your Normal

It should be clear by now that normal is a very relative concept. Philosophy is a great tool for discussing this. Try this with yourself: an alien comes to earth and asks you what a person looks like. Can you explain this? What is the normal hair color, the normal color of eyes, the normal height, the normal biological sex, the normal way of walking, talking, eating, sleeping, learning, or working. "Normal" is where you grew up or what you grew up with.

Normal cannot be easily defined, no matter how hard we want to. We all want to be normal, but no one can really say what that is. Because you are reading this book, it means that your household, or the household of one of the people you are close to, is by no means normal. So why bother trying? Redefine your own norms and values. What is important to you? Having friends you can really get along with or fitting in? Following the pace of your own brain, or not standing out too much? Be the mentor in this, led by example and by trial and error.

Find friends for you and/or your child. Loneliness and having no peers can be a genuine issue among the highly–profoundly gifted. Friendship can easily be misunderstood as "the ones you see every day." This is not necessarily the case. In adult life, we rarely see our real friends on a day-to-day basis. Yet, this is how we define friendship when we talk about children. Friendship can be the one you keep talking to long after astronomy class on Saturday has ended. A friend can be someone you only see during the holidays because they live so far away, but every time you meet it feels like yesterday. A friend can be an online gaming partner. No matter how old or young you are, normalize these types of friendships in your household.

Be the Mentor and the Advocate

Mentors can be very important in a child's and an adult's life. Someone who guides you along the way. As you get older, you can become your own mentor in life, but younger ones need the guidance by someone else. Someone who guides you when your environment doesn't fully understand your needs, isn't like you, and doesn't always comprehend your actions or words. A mentor is someone you fully trust, who gets you, and provides you with the help you need.

Being the fighter for your child is just as important. If not you, then who? Do not expect things to turn out for the best. Do not expect other people to know what to do. Ask, plan, talk. Remember, for the typical developing child, there is a path already paved. From the age you go to kindergarten to the age you graduate from elementary school, high school, and university. For the typically developing child, there are plans for what you learn at each age. None of these chronological plans work for the highly–profoundly gifted. None of these age-restricted paths were meant for the highly–profoundly gifted. The path for the highly–profoundly gifted child needs to be re-established over and over again. The plans must flex with asynchronous development, overexcitabilities, and the child's learning preferences. The plans must be created, tried, adjusted, expanded, expanded, expanded, and completely re-figured.

Ask for Help

Guiding a highly–profoundly gifted child is very demanding. It can easily become a lot to handle on your own. There are no clear-cut solutions, there is little information, and the people you would usually go to for advice, don't know either. It takes a village to raise a child, but it takes a city to raise a highly–profoundly gifted one. This help is unfortunately not easy to find. Counselors, teachers, psychologists, or family who get it, are spread thinly.

Be critical of who you allow in your life, but do not be afraid to say, I don't know what to do. It is okay to feel overwhelmed, exhausted, frustrated, and tired. Stepping away from the clear-cut path can be very frightening. Too often, I've found that stepping away from the traditional choice invites scrutiny—and when the initial plan doesn't work out, the environment is quick to assign blame. It is okay to not have all the answers and to look for someone who does.

More Hobbies are Not Enough

When your nine-to-five job is painfully dull, it is hard to make up for it by going to the bowling alley every evening. You are counting down the hours until you can do something more rewarding, but when the time comes, it no longer interests you. Yet, it is often what is expected of the highly–profoundly gifted. Most others don't understand the problem of "a little boredom." What they fail to realize is that day after day, that boredom can become profoundly overwhelming. The brain just won't tolerate it anymore. I often become tired myself when I hear of the number of hobbies the child has, just to cope with the dreadfulness of the school day.

Many studies have explored the benefits of acceleration, curriculum enrichment, pull-out classes, and homeschooling. Online resources and books also recognize the benefits and provide guidance through the process. Even so, parents still need to fight for these learning choices for their child. Supplementing a child's boredom at school with numerous hobbies can become a dangerous, vicious circle—one in which there is neither enough time for meaningful work nor adequate time for rest.

Keep Your Goal in Sight

When the world seems to be at loss with you or your child, keep your eye on the end-goal. Usually, that is happiness. Keeping your goal in sight helps you stay motivated. By keeping your focus, you maintain clarity. Define for yourself how you want to achieve your goal. What you need, who you need, how you need it, and why you need it. Map out when you want to achieve your goal and define what questions need to be answered. Never forget to include your child in the process. We can easily speak over the heads of our children. They are often well-spoken, may be able to talk fluently about their feelings and know what they want, but they may not know what they need or how to get there. They may have it already planned out for you, but this shouldn't be the expectation.

In times of hardship, it helps to have a plan. For students who have difficulty staying motivated, I highly recommend keeping the plan in front of their desk. Keep goals top of mind. No matter how big or small, you should have a goal. Your goal may be to make it through the end of the year, to ensure your child passes the test, or gets into the pull-out class. Or maybe your goal is to help your child accomplish their goal of becoming a pilot.

It is Not Because You Can, That You Should

No one is at the top of their game all the time including the highly–profoundly gifted. Expectations can be high for our highly–profoundly gifted. Some expect them to always be at the top of their class for every single course. Some expect them to be a typical child and to play with toys. Some expect them to be well-spoken in all situations, assertive when needed and compliant when needed. Some expect them to be enthusiastic about every enrichment activity that is being offered.

Highly–profoundly gifted individuals can feel these expectations all too well. They will try to adapt or defiantly step away. Be their mentor and their advocate. If your child is interested in languages and someone gives them math enrichment, they should not suffer in silence and do it anyway. Instead, ask for a Spanish course. If you are well-spoken, but do not feel comfortable, then don't do it. If someone asks you to take the leadership role when you already have enough on your plate, then say so, and offer to be part of the team instead. This all has to do with setting boundaries; it is not because you can, that you should. Highly–profoundly gifted may be served with more traits than others, but this does not mean they owe the world. It does not mean they have to do something because they can.

References

Colangelo, N., and G. A. Davis. 1991. *Handbook of Gifted Education*. Boston, MA: Allyn & Bacon.

Daniels, S., and M. M. Piechowski. 2009. *Living with Intensity*. Scottsdale, AZ: Great Potential Press.

De Wit, Els. 2020. *Slapende leeuwen: Uitzonderlijk hoogbegaafd. Is dat nu écht zo anders?*

Gross, M. U. M. 2004. *Exceptionally Gifted Children*. 2nd ed. New York: Routledge Falmer.

Hollingworth, L. S. 1942. *Children Above 180 IQ (Stanford-Binet): Origin and Development*. Yonkers-on-Hudson, NY: World Book Company.

Neville, C., M. Piechowski, and S. Tolan. 2017. *Off the Charts*. New York: Royal Fireworks Press.

Webb, J. 2008. "Dabrowski's Theory and Existential Depression in Gifted Children and Adults."

Webb, J. 2013. *Searching for Meaning: Idealism, Bright Minds, Disillusionment, and Hope*. Scottsdale, AZ: Great Potential Press.

Webb, J. 2016. "When Bright Kids Become Disillusioned." *Teaching for High Potential.*

Wood, V. R., and K. C. Laycraft. 2020. "How Can We Better Understand, Identify, and Support Highly Gifted and Profoundly Gifted Students? A Literature Review of the Psychological Development of Highly–Profoundly Gifted Individuals and Overexcitabilities." *Annals of Cognitive Science* 4 (1).

Part 4
Testimonials

Chapter 11

Testimonials From Around the World

France

Christine de Kersaint-Gill and Branka Boskov, School for the Gifted Ecole Arborescences

As to giftedness, the country is still divided about this issue. Some —such as our school—have deep knowledge of giftedness, others think giftedness is a figment of the mind. National education, for example, provides a one-hour workshop per week for these children or additional work. In my opinion, that is not enough. Schools can also set up a PAP (personalized support plan) that will help them to learn and concentrate. However, these children are often seen as spoiled children with "bad" behavior. Recently, there has been a growing movement advocating for nationwide school acceleration as an enrichment strategy for gifted children.

When it comes to the highly–profoundly gifted, people know the names of famous people but nothing more. Most of the time, these people are genius, so people think giftedness means being a genius and being more intelligent than other people.

Currently, specialized schools do exist, but they operate outside the traditional system and are not funded by the French State. These private schools are often very expensive so most of the people think these schools are only for rich people. Fortunately, there are some associations that provide donations, allowing private schools to offer scholarships.

I don't know about the other schools, but in our school, we have a holistic approach to our gifted classes. We work with our pupils on the management of emotions which can be very difficult. We focus on living together and on the development of precocious children. For those who need to be stimulated academically, we increase the level of learning. Of course, there are also children who first need to acquire study techniques. They need to learn "how to learn."

South Korea

Dr. Seokhee Cho, St. John's University, USA

Under the influence of the Confucian Heritage Culture for many centuries, South Koreans have placed a high value on learning and scholarship. Only profoundly gifted children were considered truly gifted, as Confucian beliefs hold that everyone can achieve at high levels through rigorous study, perseverance, and dedicated practice.

There has been a great change in public perception of, and provisions for exceptionally and profoundly gifted from the 1960s to the 2000s. In the 1960s, parents had to hide their prodigy child from the public to protect them. There were no means for schools and teachers to support them. In the 2000s, after the enactment of Gifted Education Promotion Act (GEPA), parents gained the right to seek appropriate education for their exceptionally and profoundly gifted child. The Act made it possible to implement acceleration, dual enrollment, and the provision of counselling services for gifted children.

Examples of a prodigy in the 1960s and 2000s is described below. 'K' was born in the early 1960s with an IQ of 210, as reported in the Guinness World Records. At age five, K was on TV shows solving differential equations and integral calculus problems. Afterward, he did not appear in public for 13 years. Then, K was seen at one provincial university entrance examination site. He was admitted and studied like any typical college students. K eventually obtained a doctoral degree in civil engineering and became a professor at one of the regional universities in Korea.

'S' was born in 1997. He skipped several grades and graduated high school at age eight. In addition, while he was attending elementary school, he was also enrolled in college as well. Psychological counselling services were also provided. S obtained his high school diploma through the Korean General Education Development (GED) Testing System, and a bachelor's degree at age 11. At age 12, he started a graduate program with a major in physics. His colleges customized their curricula to meet his educational needs. However, he did not earn a doctoral degree because he could not defend his dissertation successfully. Dissertation Committee failed him due to a plagiarism issue and his weak academic foundation.

In South Korea, the legal framework for gifted education is established separately from that of general education, with the exception for acceleration. The Elementary and Secondary Education Act permits acceleration without restrictions related to age or the number of years, allowing for grade skipping, early entrance, and early graduation. In general, it is neither preferred nor practiced often by parents and schools. Based on the GEPA, which emphasizes enrichment with the goal of nurturing creativity, there are eight specialized science high schools, as well as 200 gifted education centers affiliated with school districts and 85 universities. These GECs provide after-school enrichment programs in specific domains for talented and gifted students in elementary and middle schools. However, the GEPA does not permit self-contained schools or self-contained classes at the elementary and middle school levels. Differentiation is minimally implemented in both general education schools and gifted education centers in South Korea.

The GEPA outlines two primary goals for gifted education: the actualization of gifted students' potential and the cultivation of future leaders who can contribute to the advancement of Korean society. Therefore, these gifted education programs are more holistic than cognitive. Student selection for gifted education institutions—such as specialized high schools or GECs—is based on demonstrated creative problem-solving abilities in specific domains, along with an evaluation of the student's personality through interviews and observation of problem-solving processes. Specialized residential science high schools follow a unique curriculum that includes introductory subjects, research courses, and creative activities. Fifty percent (50%) of the total curriculum is filled with math and science and many elective courses. A wide variety of elective courses are offered, including research courses, advance placement (AP) courses, commissioned education courses at universities, and international credit exchange courses. Out of 180 required course credits, 30 credits are allocated to research courses. Some high school students publish articles in prestigious international journals listed in the Science Citation Index, the Science Citation Index Expanded, and the Korea Citation Index. As residential science high school students, they also participate in a variety of extra-curricular activities on campus. Additionally, these schools require students to complete non-credit volunteer activities as part of their graduation requirements.

Sweden

Roland S. Persson, PhD

Sweden, like all other countries, has individuals within its population who are extremely gifted and talented. However, it is by no means a given, to be formally recognized as such by society and its educational system. While children talented in sports, music, and the arts have often been fully endorsed and well supported by the education system since World War II, intellectually gifted individuals have been largely overlooked. Frequently, the intellectually gifted are viewed as too privileged to warrant special attention or accommodations at any education level. Both teachers and educational authorities have often assumed that these students are self-sufficient and do not require support. As a result, school resources have been prioritized for students with learning difficulties and neuropsychiatric disorders. To include gifted and talented students in a group with special needs was seen as undemocratic and even unethical.

With growing awareness across Europe of the potential contributions of intellectual prowess—particularly in gaining an edge in an increasingly competitive global economy—Sweden has finally begun to take notice. They became open to the idea that this group of individuals also required attention from the Swedish school system. Otherwise, the country risked becoming economically disadvantaged in a highly competitive world—one in which the war for talented individuals has been raging since the mid-1980s.

Historically, Sweden has been ignorant as to what gifted education represented. They first heard of the term when joining the European Union in 1994. While other European ministers of education had at least some understanding of what gifted education entailed, the Swedish minister of education at the time had none. This lack of knowledge within the Swedish educational system became a political embarrassment and led to a lengthy article in the national press in 2002, in which the minister for education publicly acknowledged the importance of supporting highly able students. The article marked the beginning of a political endeavor that set the needs of individual intellectual excellence against a long-standing, cross-party political ideology—one that prioritized collective equality at all costs. The pursuit of both individual excellence and strict collective equality, especially in relation to ability, has been proven to be an unachievable goal.

While some initiated efforts to refocus attention on high achievers in the Swedish school system, in wasn't until 2010 that the legislative framework for education was changed. Individual schools were granted the autonomy to develop solutions for stimulating and supporting their gifted and talented students. However, this change did not guarantee implementation. What followed was a period of experimentation.

The National Agency for Education introduced national programs across various subjects to allow particularly brilliant students to excel beyond the standard curriculum. Yet, selection into these programs was based largely on student interest and parent consultation, with little or no emphasis on demonstrable academic achievement.

Susanne Dodillet[1] at Göteborg University undertook critical review of these new practices and concluded that Swedish excellence programs were fraught with contradictions— failing to fulfill the elitist aims suggested in their official policies while also falling short of the egalitarian ideals held by many educators.

Political and educational experimentation has continued. The cabinet in power at the time responded by assigning the National Agency for Education the responsibility of equipping all Swedish teachers with tools and resources to support highly able students in their everyday teaching. Nearly 20 experts from a variety of fields and about the same number of educational consultants were summoned. The end result was the development of national curriculum materials that included examples of how to stimulate gifted and talented pupils, while still maintaining responsibility for delivering the national curriculum within a classroom of diverse abilities.

Several participating experts had no idea what giftedness was. Only a few had such expertise, one of which was quickly dismissed by the

Agency and declared unwanted. The provided knowledge—though scientifically uncontroversial and well-accepted elsewhere—was not received well by the Agency, as it was perceived to challenge the ideological foundations of Swedish education. The material was finally published in 2014 and made available to every teacher who desired. This effort had similar results to the effort to promote previous excellence programs. It was not a great success, and it did not make Swedish teachers more accepting and more knowledgeable of their gifted and talented pupils. It is not difficult to understand why.

Teachers largely remained unaware of what constitutes a gifted and talent pupil or what their specific needs are. When it was suggested to the National Agency for Education that such an effort *must* begin by amending the content of teacher education at universities, the idea was rejected on the grounds that teacher training was not part of the cabinet's original directive. One study evaluated Swedish teachers' understanding of giftedness and how they identified a student as being "very clever" in the classroom. Alarmingly, giftedness was often equated with being an "ideal and trouble-free pupil." Since the psychology of ability has been absent in Swedish teacher training since the late 1970s—and no effort has been made to integrate gifted education into that training—this flawed perception of high ability largely persists.

There is one notable exception: gifted education has found a platform within mathematics education and has been surprisingly well received. This success is due in large part to the political acumen Inger Wistedt of Stockholm University, an early and passionate advocate for the gifted and talented in mathematics. When presented through the lens of mathematics education, giftedness became more politically acceptable. As a result, this area now enjoys thriving research and widespread teacher support, with educators regularly praised for enthusiastically embracing this knowledge.

Unfortunately, the same cannot be said for other areas of gifted education in Swedish schools. Despite the new legal framework, gifted education in a broader sense continues to clash with cultural traditions and collective values held by many Swedish teachers. Even with access to curriculum materials provided by the National Education Agency, most teachers remain uninformed.

The political turnaround in the early 2000s brought a general legitimacy to the discourse on gifted and talented now regularly addressed in the media. Books have been written, some research is underway, and a growing number of psychologists have made this field their area of special interest. However, within the educational system, the brilliance of individual students has not been reconciled with the prevailing ideology. The fundamental incompatibility between the pursuit of individual excellence and the political demand for collective equality persists. Public discourse on gifted education has allowed the political establishment to maintain the appearance of addressing the needs of the gifted and talented, but in reality, very little has changed since the new legislation was enacted in 2010.

The initiatives taken thus far amount to little more than a symbolic gesture—a nod to the business world's interest in talent investment—while the Swedish political ideological commitment to absolute equality remains firmly entrenched in both schools and society at large. There are, of course, individual schools and teachers who make sincere efforts to support gifted students, despite the prevailing cultural resistance. Some succeed more than others. These efforts are driven by personal commitment rather than by systemic accountability or institutional responsibility. More than a decade after the legislation was introduced, reluctance persists, and gifted education continues to be a low priority.

Are schools, teachers, and others in Sweden acquainted with the notion of someone being not only gifted, but *exceptionally* and *profoundly* gifted? Sadly, no. Although the recognition of high achievement in education was eventually acknowledged, it was arbitrarily decided that 20% of all pupils could be categorized as performing beyond average. Among these, 5% were to be labeled as gifted. No distinction was made regarding degrees of giftedness, despite longstanding recommendations from international scholars in educational psychology.

The National Agency for Education even dismissed one Swedish scholar from its task force for insisting that the concept of normal distribution must apply, regardless of how gifted or talented is defined in the school system. The Agency instead maintained that *all* pupils must be regarded as "gifted"—a position from which no deviation is permitted. Under this policy, and despite the Agency's claim that Swedish schools must be based on "science and tested experience," the result has been a paradox: an astoundingly 120% of all Swedish pupils are considered at least high achievers—100% as students, plus 15% as high achievers, and an additional 5% as gifted.

Such numbers highlight the disconnect. The Swedish school system remains highly politicized, clinging to values that often cannot be defended as functional in either real life or scientific practice.

Any effort to support students who excel well beyond average achievement levels remains largely dependent on individual teachers and school leaders—some of whom have taken genuine interest in these exceptional students. However, such efforts are the exception rather than the norm. Grade-skipping as a form of acceleration has been practiced for some time, but homeschooling is largely prohibited and is only permitted under exceptional circumstances. Families who choose to homeschool their gifted children often face significant challenges, including legal battles or even emigration to countries with more accommodating educational systems. On occasion, thanks to the initiative of particular educators, arrangements have been made for highly advanced students to engage with university scholars. Still, there is no system-wide consensus that such actions are appropriate or necessary.

Singling out individuals from the diverse ability classroom is legally reserved for special educational assistance, and only in cases where cognitive abilities are deemed to be on such a level that the student cannot successfully progress through standard instruction. Such students are typically placed in special classes within special schools, where they follow an adapted national curriculum. The reverse, however, is not permitted. Special classes and schools for the intellectually gifted do not exist and would be considered contrary to the foundational principals of the Swedish school system. The inclusive classroom—comprising students of varying abilities, socio-economic backgrounds, and ethnicities—a legally enshrined principle that is unlikely to change. Any attention to gifted and talented students must therefore occur within this framework, provided that teachers and school leaders have a clear understanding of what giftedness truly is, and how these exceptional individuals experience the world.

References

[1] Dodillet, Susanne. "Inclusive Elite Education in Sweden: Insights from Implementing Excellence Programs into an Egalitarian School Culture". *Scandinavian Journal of Educational Research* 63, no.2 (2019) 258-71.

Finland

Professor Kirsi Tirri, University of Helsinki

In Finland, the word "gifted" is considered taboo, making it more acceptable to discuss talent development than giftedness.[1] The Finnish educational system is best described as highly egalitarian. Since the 1970s, equality has been the core principle, reflected in the strong emphasis placed on supporting the most vulnerable students, such as those with learning difficulties.[2] Teachers are expected to tailor their teaching instruction practices to address each student's unique characteristics, needs, and interests.[3] Child development is a central focus, and personalized support is provided through multi-professional teams.[4] However, this growth mindset pedagogy has not been extended to gifted students, who have been largely overlooked when it comes to opportunities for advanced learning and development through challenging tasks.[5]

In Finland, gifted education has largely depended on individual teachers, as the topic has not been addressed within the national educational system teacher preparation programs.[6] American policy experts, Finn and Wright[7] also described a "Finnish mindset," in which standing out—except in music and sports—is considered unfashionable, reinforcing a cultural emphasis on inclusion and uniformity in education.

Individualized values became concrete in Finnish education with the publication of the National Core Curriculum in Basic Education 2004.[8] For the first time, it explicitly stated that each student is entitled to instruction that corresponds to his or her personal abilities, special needs, and the development of those abilities. The emphasis on individual needs has been further strengthened in subsequent revisions of the Finnish core curriculum. The most recent national core curriculum identifies differentiation as the pedagogical foundation of instruction.[9] Accordingly, all students—including the gifted—should receive an education tailored to their individual needs. In this respect, the system is highly developed in its approach to gifted education.

For the first time in the history of Finnish curricula, the 2014 curriculum explicitly mentions talented students and acknowledges their learning needs. This marks a significant step forward and may gradually broaden the scope of Finnish education to more fully include gifted and talented learners. As this development progresses, the role of teacher education in transforming current school practices and advancing gifted education should be emphasized.[10]

Teachers are the key agents in identifying and nurturing all types of talent. In Finland, teachers are ethical professionals who have the autonomy to design classroom curricula and shape their students' learning environments.[11] When teachers gain an understanding of and commitment to the goals of gifted education, meaningful changes can occur in schools. Realizing this change, however, requires targeted intervention studies that equip teachers with a clear understanding of the purpose and desired outcomes of gifted education. Researchers and scholars in the field must embrace this mission and actively engage in collaboration with schools.

References

[1] Tirri, Kirsi. 2022. "Giftedness in the Finnish Educational Culture." *Gifted Education International* 38, no. 3: 445–48. https://doi.org/10.1177/02614294211054204.

[2] Tirri, Kirsi, and Elina Kuusisto. 2013. "How Finland Serves Gifted and Talented Pupils." *Journal for the Education of the Gifted* 36, no. 1: 84–96. https://doi.org/10.1177/0162353212468066.

[3] Tirri, Kirsi, and Sonja Laine. 2017. "Teacher Education in Inclusive Education." In *The SAGE Handbook of Research on Teacher Education* (Vol. 2), edited by D. J. Clandinin and J. Husu, 761–76. SAGE Reference. https://doi.org/10.4135/9781526402042.n44.

[4] Laine, Sonja, Risto Hotulainen, and Kirsi Tirri. 2019. "Finnish Elementary School Teachers' Attitudes Toward Gifted Education." *Roeper Review* 41, no. 2: 76–87. https://doi.org/10.1080/02783193.2019.1592794.

[5] Rissanen, Inkeri, Elina Kuusisto, Moona Tuominen, and Kirsi Tirri. 2019. "In Search of a Growth Mindset Pedagogy: A Case Study of One Teacher's Classroom Practices in a Finnish Elementary School." *Teaching and Teacher Education* 77: 204–13. https://doi.org/10.1016/j.tate.2018.10.002.

[6] Tirri, Kirsi, and Kari Uusikylä. 1994. "How Teachers Perceive Differentiation of Education among the Gifted and Talented." *Gifted and Talented International* 9, no. 2: 69–73. Laine, Sonja, and Kirsi Tirri. 2016. "How Finnish Elementary School Teachers Meet the Needs of Their Gifted Students." *High Ability Studies* 27, no. 2: 149–64. https://doi.org/10.1080/13598139.2015.1108185.

[7] Finn, Cester E., and L. Brandon Wright. 2015. *Failing Our Brightest Kids: The Global Challenge of Educating High-Ability Students*. Cambridge, MA: Harvard Education Press.

[8] Finnish National Agency for Education (FNAE). 2004. *National Core Curriculum for Basic Education*. Helsinki, Finland: Finnish National Agency for Education.

[9] Finnish National Agency for Education (FNAE). 2014. *National Core Curriculum for Basic Education*. Helsinki, Finland: Finnish National Agency for Education. http://www.oph.fi/ops2016.

[10 12] Tirri, Kirsi. 2017. "Teacher Education Is the Key to Changing the Identification and Teaching of the Gifted." *Roeper Review* 39, no. 3: 210-12. https://doi.org/10.1080/02783193.2017.1318996.

[11] Tirri, Kirsi. 2014. "The Last 40 Years in Finnish Teacher Education." *Journal of Education for Teaching* 40, no. 5: 600–09. https://doi.org/10.1080/02607476.2014.956545.

Belgium

Kathleen Hellinx, *Parents of Exceptionally Gifted Children Flanders and Community Peer Support of the Exceptionally Gifted*

The general perception of giftedness in Flanders is similar to the one prevalent within the other European countries. Giftedness is mainly viewed from a cognitive perspective. Although other forms of talent—such as creative, artistic, or athletic—are accepted and supported, in Flanders, the concept of giftedness remains primarily associated with IQ. Generally, a high IQ is still considered the primary trait of giftedness. Within education, giftedness is often linked to high performance. High achievement in the areas of learning and school performance are the most easily recognized by teachers and therefore viewed as the most obvious indicator of intellectual giftedness.

Slowly but surely, it is becoming more widely accepted that intelligence alone does not define giftedness; multiple factors contribute to whether someone is considered gifted. Increasingly, teachers report that gifted students not only exhibit overexcitabilities but also tend to think differently. There is also growing recognition that gifted children who are underachieving may have distinct needs related to their giftedness.

Without "proof" of intelligence—typically demonstrated through IQ tests—giftedness, is not formally recognized in Flanders. Identification is necessary for educational adjustments and support. However, this creates a challenge for children or adolescents who do not score high enough on an IQ test. Trauma, psychological problems, long-term cognitive deprivation, or underachievement can all contribute to an inaccurately low IQ score, particularly in highly–profoundly gifted children. If they do not score in the 145+ range, they are not identified as highly–profoundly gifted by the evaluator.

The concept of EG and PG, known in English literature, is still far from familiar in Flanders. This is partly because, in Flanders, there is no official use of language to indicate the differences within the 145+ category. Even the term *UHB* (in Flemish Uitzonderlijk HoogBegaafd translated to: Exceptionally Gifted) was not used for a long time. Until more recently, this group within the gifted population was barely discussed. The distinct characteristics or needs associated with exceptional giftedness were not recognized or understood by counselors or teachers.

Until very recently, IQ tests in Flemish (Dutch) could only test up to a ceiling score of 145. As a result, all children who reached the ceiling score were classified as 145+, without any distinction among the higher levels of giftedness. Until a few years ago, these children were simply called *gifted* in Flanders. The term *UHB*, or exceptionally gifted, only emerged in Flanders after some parents of these children began independently researching this topic. They sought out literature and substantiated research—which, to until recently, originated exclusively from abroad. Flanders had no research on UHB or the highly–profoundly gifted (until the 2024 study by the International Gifted Consortium (IGC), Research Center for Highly–Profoundly Gifted, in collaboration with the University of Antwerp, which included children and adolescents residing in Belgium). Drawing from their self-constructed expertise, parents of these children from Flanders started spreading the term and united in 2018-2019 as the association, Parents of Exceptionally Gifted Children Flanders. The term UHB was still largely unknown.

Meanwhile, the concept of exceptional giftedness is gradually becoming more familiar—particularly within communities already knowledgeable about giftedness. Unfortunately, awareness is spreading very slowly within the broader landscape of Flemish education and counseling. Moreover, the understanding of the varying levels within this category remains virtually nonexistent. The fact that there can be a significant difference between high giftedness (HG), exceptional giftedness (EG) and profound giftedness (PG) is typically only known to those who interact directly with exceptionally gifted individuals—, most often parents who conduct their own research, are referred by someone with expertise, or connect with the association Parents of Exceptionally Gifted Children Flanders. Occasionally, we see emerging awareness among those involved in the lives of these children, such as teachers, caregivers, giftedness coaches, and psychologists.

However, the road is still very long. It is necessary that the knowledge about UHB and the different categories within UHB is spread throughout Flanders. In fact, Flemish governmental and educational institutions should prioritize this need by increasing both awareness and scientific research on exceptional giftedness. Knowledge and expertise primarily come from parents and, increasingly, from a few private coaches and psychological practices that are beginning to specialize in this matter.

Within the broad Flemish society, the term UHB is not very well received. A distinction made within giftedness is for many one step too far even for people who are already familiar with giftedness. The term *exceptional* is often perceived as snobbish or elitist, as though these exceptional children are somehow "better" or "more" gifted than others. When talking about UHB children—and especially PG children—people still seem to have very stereotypical ideas. People with no knowledge of giftedness often equate gifted children with "nerds" or "little professors," making the idea of a highly gifted category completely unrealistic to them. The prejudices about these children are widespread.

As an association of parents of exceptionally gifted children, we sometimes observe that parents of gifted children express discomfort when the topic of UHB (exceptionally giftedness) is discussed. This reaction is often due not only to the term "exceptional," but also to the belief that the broader challenges faced by gifted children in the Flemish educational system should be addressed before focusing on the needs of the exceptionally gifted. In recent years, exceptional giftedness has been in the Flemish press several times. For example, when the association filed a complaint with the Children's Rights Commissioner regarding the lack of appropriate education for UHB children, the response was not universally positive. As an association, we advocate for attention to exceptional giftedness based on the belief that attention to exceptional giftedness also promotes broader attention for giftedness in general. We are firmly convinced that any educational measures taken on behalf of UHB children will ultimately benefit all gifted children—particularly in the long term. Nevertheless, we are sometimes accused of creating "division" and are often advised—to simply include our children under the general category of giftedness. This would, however, be doing the children within the UHB category a disservice.

For some years now, there has been more attention to giftedness in Flemish education. Since the most recent coalition agreement in September 2019, attention to gifted students has been officially included in the educational agenda, with a dedicated budget allocated for measures specifically targeting their needs.

In 2019, Prodia published a *Specific Diagnostic Protocol for Cognitively Strong* Functioning, to support the needs of gifted students. However, the protocol intentionally avoids using the term "giftedness," opting instead for "cognitively strong functioning." The reasons cited for this preference include:

> *"First, cognitive functioning has the most impact on school learning. Consequently, this is where the focus is specific to educational practice and student guidance.*
>
> *Second, strong cognitive skills can be measured more validly than, say, strong social or creative skills.*
>
> *Cognitive functioning is a broader term than intelligence or broad cognitive skills. The term includes a student's school-based skills as well."*

As a result, the protocol makes no mention of *giftedness*—let alone of the different categories within it—nor does it address the specific learning or functional needs of these students.

In this protocol, the measures recommended for supporting "cognitively high-functioning children" included: compacting, enrichment, deepening, broadening, peer group education, and acceleration.

Compacting appears to be a widely used measure for gifted students in Flanders, especially in elementary schools. Yet, we see that compacting is mostly applied step by step and it is limited. Material is compacted, for example, by chapter, which means that testing must be done repeatedly, and the student is dependent on the teacher's direction.

Enrichment appears to be the most commonly and most widely recognized measure within the Flemish educational field, and it is gradually becoming more established due to the increasing awareness of giftedness. However, we observe that standard differentiation for gifted students is most often applied. "Relevant academic enrichment," which is more engaging and effective for UHB children, is still rarely implemented. This type of enrichment requires teachers and schools to relinquish rigid instructional patterns and allow for greater autonomy in the child's learning process—an adjustment that remains a significant challenge for many educators.

In early 2020, the Parents of UHB Children Flanders association conducted a survey among its members regarding the educational experiences of UHB children in Flemish schools. This survey showed that:

- Approximately 60% of students surveyed were offered enrichment materials
- Extra-curricular enrichment material represented approximately 25%. Examples included chess lessons and foreign languages such as Chinese and Spanish
- One fifth of the students receive enrichment in languages (Dutch, French, English)
- The percentage of students who received enrichment in mathematics was lower than the percentage of students who experienced subject acceleration in the subject

The surveys also found that:

- 83% of the pupils who were accelerated were still receiving enrichment for mathematics
- 21.6% of students who were accelerated for two years, or more were still receiving enrichment
- Children who had been accelerated for two years or more all still received enrichment

Plus classes are a popular way for schools to meet the additional needs of gifted or highly functioning students. Since the 2020-2021 school year, the Flemish government (Cabinet of Education) has been running a project in which schools with established programs for gifted or cognitively strong students serve as "model schools" for others. A budget of € 500,000 was allocated for this initiative, divided between the participating schools and an external organization responsible for overseeing and supporting the project. Many of the schools that applied for this project turned out to have a "Plus class" with a specific opportunity for gifted pupils. The government also requested that these schools specifically consider the needs of UHB pupils. The project has not yet been evaluated.

Acceleration in school is gradually being freed from its stigma in Flanders, although this shift is occurring more slowly than the growing acceptance of enrichment. According to the survey we administered to our members, a fairly large number of UHB children were accelerated more than once, specifically:

> Nearly 85% of this cohort was accelerated (skipped a full year or completed two school years in one year). More than half of students were one year accelerated. According to the surveys, 20% were accelerated two years and approximately 8% were accelerated three or more years.

Although *subject acceleration* is far from commonplace in schools in Flanders, it appeared that a significant percentage of UHB students (35%) were accelerated in one or more subject areas to accommodate their cognitive strength and interest. Of those subject accelerations, 10% were in languages and 19% in mathematics.

Because subject accelerations cannot be officially certified in Flanders, students often follow these courses without formal obligation. At grade transition, the students must retake these courses.

Since 2015, the Flemish education system has made *individual learning pathways* possible for students including gifted pupils. These pathways allow students to follow an adopted educational program through *"individual exemption from following certain parts of the formation of a particular structural component during part or all of the school year and replacement by other components that do not affect the finality of the structural component."*

However, these individual pathways are granted at the discretion of the school and are not guaranteed adaptations for gifted students. The content of such pathway is determined by the school itself and may be modified or even be discontinued during the student's academic career.

Few schools in Flanders cater to the gifted. Separate schools or programs designed for UHB pupils, do not (yet) exist. Within these so-called schools for the gifted, there are many UHB students; sometimes they feel at home and their needs met, but often not enough. These schools are often started by parents whose gifted children got stuck in the regular education system. Some schools are private, others were (after some time) officially recognized by the government. These schools are not officially designated for gifted children, however, through word-of-mouth, tend to attract them.

From the government's point of view, there are no specific schools for the gifted. The government prefers to implement measures outlined in the Prodia Protocol to address the needs of gifted pupils within the existing educational structures:

> *"There are no recognized special schools for the gifted. There are, however, several schools with projects for gifted students or kangaroo classes (k-classes), extra classes where gifted students work together for two to four hours per week on specific projects or are offered extra challenging material. The Flemish Ministry of Education and Training does not have a list of schools with k-classes. These are schools' own initiatives."*

* * * * * * * * * * *

"Uitzonderlijk hoogbegaafd Vlaanderen"
ouders@145plus.net
www.145plus.net

Ireland

Dr. Colm O'Reilly, Director CTY Ireland, Dublin City University

Ireland has an approximate population of 4.7 million people. The Department of Education and Science, operating under the authority of the Minister for Education and Science, oversees both policy and funding related to education. Education is compulsory for all children in Ireland from the ages of 6 to 16, or until students have completed three years of second-level education. The Department currently employs just over 100,000 individuals and manages a significant budget. In 2019, the budget exceeded €9 billion, with approximately €1 billion allocated specifically to special needs education. The budget covers salaries and pensions for teachers, non-teaching staff, and academics, as well as student grants for schools and higher education, adult education initiatives, labor force development, school transport, and the Department's administrative expenses. None of this budget in 2019 was allocated to the education of gifted children.

Gifted education in Ireland is a relatively new concept and was mostly overlooked within the country until the 1990s. For over a century, the education system was dominated by the Catholic Church in a country where over 90% of the population was Catholic. Most of the schools were built on church grounds and were controlled by diocesan representatives. This dominance had a direct impact on how government parties implemented policy relating to education. Traditionally, Ireland was a poor country with limited natural resources, and agriculture was the predominant occupation in many regions. It wasn't until 1967 that secondary school education became free for everyone. Even as late as 1970, fewer than 30% of boys and fewer than 40% of girls completed secondary schooling (Whelan & Hannon, 1999). There were very few employment opportunities and emigration was high during this period. Against this bleak backdrop, little attention was given to gifted students or special education in general.

By the start of the 1990s, a changing attitude towards special needs education was developing. Previously, many students with special needs had been neglected or, in some cases, removed from mainstream school. The change in thinking brought the system towards a more inclusive ethos. The Special Education Review Committee, established by the government in 1993, was tasked with gathering advice and expertise from professionals in the special needs areas and advocating for best practices. The Committee's report (DES 1993) provided the first Irish definition of giftedness, which drew heavily from Marland's (1972) definition. It identified proficiency across several categories: general intellectual ability, specific academic ability, creative thinking, leadership, visual and performance arts, psychomotor ability, and mechanical aptitude. The publication of the Education Act in Ireland in 1998 led to an increased call for this area of special needs to be addressed. While the Education Act recognized that every individual should receive an education suited to their needs, further clarification was required regarding students with special educational needs. Consequently, the Education for Persons with Special Educational Needs Act known as the EPSEN Act was published in 2004. However, while the Act addressed various special needs—such as dyslexia and other learning difficulties—it made no reference to giftedness as a recognized special need in Ireland. As a result, no resource hours were allocated to support gifted students through special needs teachers. This omission was a significant setback for advocates of the gifted movement in Ireland. Although schools were now legally required to support students with special needs, they were not obligated to consider gifted children within this framework.

In 2001, the National Council for Curriculum and Assessment (NCCA) was established as a statutory body to advise the Minister for Education and Skills on matters related to curriculum and assessment for early childhood education, primary, and post-primary schools. The NCCA also aims to carry out, use, and disseminate research for the purposes of advising and debating best practices in education. Importantly, they aim to engage with learners, teachers, and other stakeholders to support innovation in education. In 2007, the NCCA addressed the area of highly able children by publishing a set of draft guidelines for teachers working with students in that category. The term "gifted" was not explicitly used; instead, the phrase "exceptionally able" was adopted to describe students who require enrichment and extension opportunities beyond those offered to the general cohort of students. The following description was used and is the closest in terms of a definition of gifted children that Ireland has published.

With that in mind, approximately 5-10% of the school population may be considered exceptionally able, demonstrating very high levels of attainment in one or more of the following areas:

- general intellectual ability or talent
- specific academic aptitude or talent
- visual and performing arts and sports
- leadership ability
- creative and productive thinking
- mechanical ingenuity
- special abilities in empathy, understanding, and negotiation.

A subsequent review of these guidelines by teachers and school principals found that they were most effective in helping school management and educators audit and review school policy related to gifted children. However, feedback also indicated that the guidelines offered insufficient support for teachers to effectively differentiate curriculum.

The highly–profoundly gifted are really not recognized in Ireland at all. Currently, the only formal program for gifted students in Ireland is the Irish Centre for Talented Youth (CTYI). CTYI was established following negotiations with Dublin City University and the Center for Talented Youth at Johns Hopkins. University personnel were interested in launching an international program modeled on the principles of the CTY program. CTYI was started at Dublin City University in 1992, with the following aims:

- To identify through national and international talent searches pre-college children who reason extremely well mathematically and/or verbally
- To provide talented youth both from Ireland and overseas with challenging and invigorating coursework and related

educational opportunities through an annual summer program, and on Saturday classes during the school year

- To provide teacher training and support services to schools participating in the CTYI prograM
- To assist parents in advancing talented students by providing access to information and resources
- To research and evaluate talent development and the effectiveness of program models and curriculum provision

(www.dcu.ie/ctyi)

To date, over 60,000 Irish students aged 6 to 17 have participated in programs run by CTYI at Dublin City University. CTYI also administers a Talent Search to identify high-ability students. Letters are sent to all schools in the country, requesting that they identify students who have scored at or above the 95th percentile on a standardized test. As of 2016, up to 75% of schools in the country have participated in the Talent Search. After the talent search, qualifying students are invited to attend an awards ceremony at Dublin City University to recognize their achievement.

As part of its mission, CTYI runs Saturday enrichment courses for primary school children at various centers across the country. These courses typically focus on non-curricular subjects, giving students the opportunity to study topics not usually covered in school. Examples include Forensic Science, Medicine, Science of Tomorrow, Engineering, Computer Programming, Journalism, Legal Studies, and Psychology.

Another out-of-school program option for gifted students is summer programs. CTYI offers two and three-week residential summer programs at Dublin City University for high ability secondary school students. Course offerings include Biomedical Diagnostics, Theoretical Physics, Criminology, Corporate Business, Social Psychology, International Relations, and Writing for Life.

CTYI also runs two other programs for gifted students at Dublin City University. Since its establishment in 2006, the Centre for Academic Achievement (CAA) program has allowed over 2,500 primary school students from socio-economically disadvantaged areas of Dublin, Limerick, and Cork to attend after-school enrichment courses in a university setting. The program aims to encourage high-ability students—who might not otherwise have access to university resources and materials—to pursue an academic path and reach their full potential. The other program is an Early University Entrance Program.

The perspective on the classes at CTYI are to benefit the student academically and socially. CTYI courses are typically in subjects offered at third level and are taught by subject-matter experts, often part-time lecturers or postgraduate students from the host institution. In this way CTYI students have access to third level facilities and teachers who have knowledge in their area of interest. In traditional primary school settings, students typically have one teacher for all subject areas and limited or no opportunities to develop deep knowledge in specific academic disciplines.

The variety and depth of subjects offered by CTYI is important because, although Irish second schools have specialist teachers in different subjects, the available course work may not be sufficiently challenging for some students—or in some cases, the subject in which the student excels may not be offered at all.

Summer programs for gifted students may vary in length and focus, but most share several components: an accelerated and enriched curriculum, dedicated staff, interaction with peers of similar ability, and a supportive environment. While these programs typically emphasize academic development, they also include activities designed to foster peer acceptance and social growth. Many high-ability children report feeling different from their peers, so being in a program with like-minded individuals can enhance their sense of belonging. This is quite common on the CTY Ireland program where many students really enjoy the social experience.

Turkey

Dr. Melodi Özyaprak, Ph.D., Gifted Education

The general perception of giftedness in my culture may include parts of various concepts. Practicality, sophistication, wisdom, leadership, humour, and scientific expertise are all commonly associated with giftedness. Practical intelligence is considered a concept related to giftedness for lay people in my culture. Basically, solving problems quickly and developing a solution suitable for the context. Not a long-term solution, but an applicable solution or idea which is going to save the day. Creativity is also a concept related to giftedness in our society. Scientific and technological are generally considered more important than artistic creativity. Individuals who can navigate challenges and impossibilities to produce innovative, timely solutions are often considered talented. Creativity is sometimes used interchangeably with practicality.

A person who excels in math and science—such as physics, chemistry, or computer science—is often considered gifted by both laypeople and teachers. Our society usually values social relationships, but these kinds of people (math and science geeks) are not expected to be social. Their unique ways of communicating are accepted since they are perceived as nerds. They might be perceived as awkward in their communication; this oddness may be considered a sign of their giftedness. In relation to this, people who can memorize a lot of information and share the information fluently and skilfully are also seen as gifted. In our society, possessing a wealth of knowledge and being able to express it fluently is often valued more than the ability to think critically and ask meaningful questions. In fact, the more incomprehensible the transfer of knowledge and the higher the language, the more gifted the person may be considered. Vagueness of the language is a positive phenomenon in this context. There is a saying, "this person is like a book," which refers to someone who knows a great deal of information and carries it with them—though it's not necessarily useful in and of itself.

Humorous people can also be defined as gifted in our culture. Recognizing contradictions and expressing them without causing social tension and conflict is an important skill. I think this preference of speaking through implications can provide a more open dialogue in communication. Finally, leadership is an important concept associated with giftedness. Key concepts commonly associated with leadership include military intelligence, strategic thinking, the ability to manipulation, power dominance, authoritarianism, and holding a prominent position or important title. "There is a firestorm in their eyes" is an affirmative description used to refer to these kinds of people in our culture.

In summary, in our culture, gifted individuals are often seen as those who can solve problems quickly and practically, generate creative ideas, offer clever, in-the-moment solutions, and navigate challenges effectively. People with strong social skills and the ability to influence others—those perceived as dominant and authoritarian—are also considered gifted. However, contrary to this general view, individuals who are entertaining (such as comedians) or those who may appear socially distant or awkward but are highly knowledgeable (typically scientists or mathematicians) are also recognized as gifted.

People define those with such characteristics as "geniuses." These individuals are often described as possessing exceptional military intelligence, being profound leaders (such as Atatürk), or achieving remarkable success in a particular field—typically in quantitative domains like science. They may also hold prestigious positions or title associated with intelligence and accomplishment. Alternatively, some are perceived as eccentric or socially withdrawn, yet known for their "crazy" or unconventional inventions. Such people are described as having a brain that "works like a machine"—able to process information rapidly or calculate with speed and precision—earning them the label of being extraordinarily intelligent.

Different educational interventions are possible for gifted and talented children in our country. There are two basic types of school, private and public school. Within the private school category, some magnet schools offer education exclusively to gifted students, while others have dedicated gifted classes within a broader school setting. Additionally, certain private schools that provide differentiated instruction within mixed ability classrooms. Regardless of whether a school is public or private, the Ministry of Education allows for the possibility of accelerating students by up to two consecutive years at the primary level.

In public schools, there are also pull-out programs. BİLSEMs (Science and Art Centre for gifted students) are also available as out-of-school programs. In BİLSEMs, gifted students can receive after-school training at the primary and secondary school level on the weekend or on weekdays. This training is focused on acceleration and enrichment and is discipline oriented (math, science, music, etc). Universities offer summer and weekend courses with differentiated and enriched content that gifted students may attend. One example is the Education Programs for Talented Students (EPTS) at Eskisehir University, which includes accelerated and differentiated programming specifically designed for gifted learners.

For academically gifted students, there are Anatolian High Schools and Science High Schools. For artistically talented students, there are Anatolian Fine Art High Schools in which students are selected through specific assessments and permitted to enrol in the school. Finally, a curriculum for the first magnet public school for gifted students in secondary level was written via a project coordinated by Uğur Sak in cooperation with TÜBİTAK and the Ministry of Education. The cognitive approach dominates for the education of gifted students.

I believe that in Turkey, a gifted education approach emphasizing acceleration, enrichment (including both general thinking skills and domain specific skills), and depth currently holds the most prominence. However, there are also projects and institutions that incorporate moral and values-based curricula and focus on social-emotional development of gifted students. For example, at Beyazit Ford Otosan Primary School—where I served as both a practitioner and coordinator—social-emotional development lessons were integrated into the regular curriculum as an enrichment class, alongside courses in creativity and thinking skills. I also had colleagues who were available to address the emotional needs and challenges of gifted children. In private schools, students are similarly supported by counsellors when needed. However, meeting the cognitive needs remains the primary focus in gifted education at present.

Slovenia

Dr. Mojca Kukanja Gabrijelčič

In the 21st century, gifted children are probably a more valuable resource in any country than, say, oil or gas. We must, therefore, respect the small group of individuals whose exceptional abilities play a crucial role in driving scientific, industrial, technological, and cultural progress.

In Slovenia, however, the education of gifted students faces both philosophical and practical challenges rooted in the nation's commitment to egalitarianism. An egalitarian society presupposes the complete equality of its members, even if some try to improve their position. In this respect, egalitarianism is unjust in both society and education. The result is a system that skews both the less successful and the gifted. Even more troubling, radical egalitarians argue that individuals do not deserve their naturally acquired gifts and talents, as these are not earned through effort, virtue, or moral merit. They are privileges received for free.

Over the last twenty-five years, researchers in Slovenia have made significant strides in understanding the needs of academically gifted individuals. The goals of public education are to educate all students, promote equity, and achieve minimum competencies for all. As a result, students with high ability, whether general or specific, and those with high levels of motivation have become almost invisible. We need to recognize, openly, that skills are not evenly distributed, and that a single curriculum for all is utterly absurd. Gifted Slovenian students are often unproductive and bored. In the current environment, gifted students see their intelligence as a stigma rather than as a means and measure of success. They often hide their abilities, which is an obvious obstacle to their intellectual development. Therefore, we cannot say with certainty that gifted students in Slovenia are fulfilling their potential.

Although educational reform in Slovenia and abroad has long called for changes in the education of gifted and talented students, very little has actually changed for students themselves. The fundamental problem still lies in teacher education and teacher training. Giftedness and talent development is compulsory or optional for teacher training.

While training is optional, schools in Slovenia are expected to have an active policy for gifted education. The current policy, *Working with Gifted Students in Primary School*, (1999) outlines a process for identification, strategies for provision, and the development of each individual student. However, it has not been properly implemented in practice. The policy as written calls for a process for identification, strategies for provision, and the development of each individual student. In Slovenia, giftedness is not defined solely by IQ but is understood to encompass a wide range of skills and talents—including performing arts, sports, entrepreneurial skills, motivation, problem solving, leadership, teamwork, creativity, and social-emotional competencies.

The Slovenian Ministry of Education provides funding to elementary schools for the identification of gifted students and the delivery of appropriate instruction and enrichment opportunities. Because of a systemic failure in identifying giftedness, we have up to 26% of students recognized as gifted in Slovenia. Society's perception of gifted students and their identity is negative or dismissive. In Slovenia, efforts are underway to modernize the concept of giftedness in response to the evolving demands of contemporary society and the expanding educational needs of gifted students.

Despite the updated gifted programme guidelines, Slovenia still faces a complex problem. The main issue lies in the interdisciplinary inequalities in the terminology of talent, intelligence, creativity, and giftedness. Authors unevenly place different, foreign terminology in the Slovenian research and educational field. However, the conceptualization of giftedness and talent is not fully structured. In some cases, the terms overlap and alternate (for example: talent, giftedness, specific and general giftedness, and high potential).

The Slovenian school system also provides all the necessary conditions for the development of gifted and talented (hereafter referred to as "gifted") students. However, in Slovenian school policy, the idea of "medio tutissimus ibis" according to Ovid is firmly established. The middle way is the best way. In some countries, independent departments have been established within relevant ministries to support the development of gifted students. In our country, interest in formally and informally working with gifted students is only beginning to revive. The greatest obstacle to the development of gifted students is the weak awareness and the lack of competence of those in charge. The less-than-conducive atmosphere stifles the motivation and ambition of highly able and successful individuals. Scientific discussion of this complex situation remains limited and is typically framed in the language of egalitarian rhetoric—terms such as justice, equality of opportunity, inequality, fairness, discrimination, social mobility, and responsibility. As a result, gifted students in Slovenia are the least researched in the educational field, despite the fact that their natural abilities constitute inalienable and non-transferable resources.

In Slovenia, gifted students are defined as children and adolescents who exhibit extremely above average abilities or qualities. In the intellectual field, giftedness is manifested mainly in convergent thinking. Gifted innovation across various fields is primarily characterized by divergent and creative thinking, originality, novel solutions, flexibility, and fluency. Giftedness is also recognized in the artistic fields, in social and leadership skills, and in self-management. Highly gifted individuals are those who are in the top 5% of the distribution, and extremely gifted are those who are in the top 3% of the target population. Traits in these areas may be expressed or perceived—as potential, behavior, outcomes, or performance whether through an idea, action, solution, or product. General or specific giftedness can manifest in characteristic behaviors throughout development and learning processes, particularly when nurtured by appropriate support. This includes both personal and environmental influences which, under favorable conditions, can lead to high levels of achievement.

Unfortunately, we have yet to approach giftedness with a truly holistic approach. When working with such a group of students or individuals, it is essential to ensure that the curriculum, learning models, differentiated content, and learning objectives are adaptable. Teachers must apply higher-level understanding standards and a broad range of didactic methodologies to appropriately address the specific needs of the course. Furthermore, creativity and critical thinking should be actively promoted through concrete examples, supporting materials, and in-service training. A gradual introduction—beginning, for instance, in kindergarten—would be necessary to establish a holistic approach. Therefore, active change and commitment is required.

The greatest challenge in Slovenia is the lack of understanding, recognition, and identification of gifted students, along with the inadequate application of learning modalities and strategies suited to their needs. Teachers consistently report that the most pressing issues in gifted education include the absence of specialized teaching aids and supplementary materials, a lack of specific didactic guidelines, and difficulties related to creating individualized educational plans for gifted students. They also criticised the organizational aspects of working with gifted students.

The system of gifted education in Slovenia has been criticized mainly because giftedness is not addressed in a holistic way. The research findings pointed to the problematic Slovenian school system. Specifically, challenges include issues of professionalism, legal frameworks, and the shortage of adequately trained and highly qualified teachers.

We have an old concept from 1999, which is used by all schools. However, in 2019, an updated concept was published, which has not yet been approved by the Ministry and is "in limbo/pending". The new concept is very well done, but unfortunately, has not been implemented.

In the new proposed concept, support for gifted and talented students in Slovenia is primarily offered through additional instruction across various subjects, special projects, and individualized education programs (INDEPs) tailored to gifted students. Personal enrichment opportunities include clubs, differentiated instruction or curricula within mixed- or homogeneous-ability groups, as well as individual learning and research activities. Additionally, various extracurricular activities—such as music festivals, physical education programs, private courses in music and drama, summer camps and courses, government-funded Zois scholarships, and special scholarships from private and professional associations—are also available.

Adjustments for gifted students in Slovenia are implemented with consideration for each child's needs. They are based on the identified characteristics of each gifted or talented student and are designed to support these students in accordance with the principles and objectives of pedagogical work in primary schools. There are two pedagogical adaptations: organisational and content. These adaptations are planned and documented in an individualized learning program for each identified gifted learner.

We believe that teachers must begin with a student-centered approach, applying tailored knowledge standards and individualized learning methods. The focus should be on promoting and supporting the development of each student. This requires the teacher to design and professionally implement an individualized curriculum using a personalized student profile. The outcome is a differentiated curriculum with higher knowledge standards and additional learning tools. Teachers would then apply this curriculum alongside a diverse range of differentiated teaching strategies, adapted to the student's needs, abilities, and interests. Unfortunately, this concept has not yet been implemented in Slovenia.

In recent years, the Republic of Slovenia has placed increasing emphasis on the need to train educators, teachers, and school counsellors to recognize and support gifted children. In addition to in-service teacher training, several national-level measures should be implemented. First, an external supervisor or inclusive educator should be introduced to assist in planning, implementing, and evaluating instruction for gifted students. Second, teachers across all disciplines should be provided with rich teaching materials, instructional aids, and specific didactic recommendations for working with gifted and talented learners. Third, short in-service training opportunities—such as workshops, training courses, and seminars—should be made available. All teachers should understand the basic characteristics and needs of gifted students, as well as the core principles of instruction for this population. Their expertise and commitment to professional development should be documented through a nationally recognized certificate. Fourth, teacher consultation services should be available at the secondary school level. Finally, an appropriate annual program of in-service training should be established, including opportunities to pursue postgraduate studies in inclusive and gifted education.

In 2019, policies for working with gifted and talented students were modernized. The revision of the *Baselines for Creating a Renewed Definition of Gifted and Talented and Working with Them* was informed by several key legal, programmatic, and conceptual frameworks. These include: (i) *Concept: Discovery of and Work with Gifted Students in Nine-Year Primary School* (1999); (ii) *The Concept of Pedagogical Work with Gifted Students in Secondary School* (2007); (iii) the *White Paper on Education in the Republic of Slovenia* (2011); (iv) contemporary theories of giftedness by selected authors such as Gagné, Heller, Pfeiffer, Renzulli, Robinson, Subotnik, Sternberg, and Ziegler; and (v) the 2013 recommendations of the Economic and Social Council of the European Union, Section for Employment, Social Affairs, and Citizenship, on unlocking the potential of students and young people with high intellectual abilities in the EU.

In Slovenia, the purpose of identifying, nurturing, and supporting gifted students is to promote optimal learning and self-fulfilment in accordance with their natural potential and values, while also fostering a responsible contribution to social development. In doing so, we follow the trends of the humanistic approach. The updated expert platform reflects the commitment of the entire educational system to support intellectual, emotional, social, moral-ethical, and psychomotor development. The holistic development of students across the entire educational continuum.

The updated expert platform (2019) presents school as a stimulating learning environment that values creativity, personal qualities, and developmental growth. It also identifies at-risk groups, including gifted girls, gifted students from lower socio-economic backgrounds, and twice-exceptional learners. Within this framework, fostering talent development is viewed as a means of ensuring equal opportunities—both for individuals and for society as a whole. Notably, the platform places greater emphasis than ever before on the involvement of parents in identifying and nurturing potential and in supporting the creation of appropriate learning tasks.

The current concept (1999) initiated major shifts in understanding the learning needs of gifted students and improving differentiated pedagogy. In particular, theoretical and empirical modernization has been based on several key elements: (i) an updated definition of gifted and talented students; (ii) refined methods for identifying giftedness; (iii) recognition of potential giftedness among all nominated students, for whom schools must provide appropriate differentiation and curriculum strategies; (iv) a discovery process that begins in the first grade of primary school, supported by specific methods and tools for nomination and identification; (v) greater emphasis on inclusive approaches, individualization, and personalization within full-day teaching models, including opportunities for accelerated progression.

Additional focal points include: (vi) the importance of social and cultural capital and the development of autonomous, responsible students equipped with self-management skills in learning; and (vii) the student portfolio as a tool for both self-regulated learning and ongoing monitoring of the gifted student's overall development, with utility extending into secondary education. The updated professional platform (2019) further underscores the importance of teachers' professional development in identifying and educating gifted students across various domains and supporting their holistic personal growth. It also outlines both general and specific guidelines for fostering children's development, starting in kindergarten.

In Slovenia, there remains a significant need for a holistic approach in three key areas: the identification of gifted students, educational practices for working with them, and counseling for the gifted and talented. There is also a pressing need to develop methodologies for individualized programs that extend beyond identification to address the educational needs, lifelong development, and learning trajectories of these students.

Unfortunately, gaps still exist in defining the fundamental concepts of giftedness, particularly around identification. According to the *Expert Platform* (2019), the identification process draws upon a range of data, including results from various psychodiagnostic instruments measuring intelligence and creativity, academic performance across subjects, teacher evaluation scales, extracurricular achievements, and evidence gathered in the student's performance portfolio. A multi-criteria approach has been introduced, requiring that more than one identification standard be met.

Challenges also persist around counseling gifted students. First, traditional concepts of giftedness have primarily emphasized cognitive factors, and in implementing the 1999 concept, Slovenian schools have continued to focus mostly on identified cognitive domains as the basis for creating individualized curricula. However, non-cognitive traits—such as motivation, perseverance, and other personal characteristics that support the development of both talent and personality—are equally important for holistic growth. Second, there is a need for a more substantive conceptual framework to guide counseling practices for gifted and talented students.

It is imperative to raise broader societal awareness in Slovenia regarding the rights of gifted children, particularly their right to appropriate education and treatment. In addition to addressing the limitations of radical egalitarianism in educational programming, there must be a renewed focus on justice. Justice should first be understood as a personal virtue of the teacher and second as an institutional virtue upheld by schools and the educational system. An educational system should not only strive to be high in quality and efficiency but must also be just—ensuring fairness and opportunity for all students.

USA

Dr. Mike Postma, SENG

The general perception of giftedness is that it is an elitist notion. Most folks do not truly understand what it is or what the needs of gifted children are. Many think it is just pushy parents trying to get their way. The majority are not acquainted with the concept outside of famous people like Einstein. Most have never encountered it except in media portrayals that are negative or stereotypical like 'The Big Bang Theory'.

That really depends on the school district or state. There are only a couple of states that mandate gifted education and it is usually part of special ed. services which is not ideal. Most districts have either no programming or a semblance of a program like a once a week pull out in elementary schools. The one bright spot is that many high schools do offer Advanced Placement courses, but that is not gifted programming.

Gifted classes vary. Again, because there is no mandated approach, each varies—some are primarily cognitive-based, while others take a more holistic approach. What is needed is a comprehensive, unified approach to gifted education—one that begins with a foundational understanding of what it means to be gifted, incorporates inclusive identification procedures, and establishes a system that address the social, emotional, and academic needs of gifted children based on their individual starting points and developmental needs.

USA

Dr. Vanessa R. Wood, The International Gifted Consortium (IGC), Research Center for Highly–Profoundly Gifted

Giftedness has not been highly regarded. In the United States (U.S.) the term gifted has been applied to both giftedness and talent development. The concept of talent development focuses more on advanced achievement in one or more domains, such as math or music. Experts in the field often align with one of two perspectives: giftedness as an inborn trait involving natural abilities, or as the result of focused talent development that leads to achievement. In reality, when giftedness is accurately assessed and identified early—and when gifted children are supported by appropriate social and environmental influences—giftedness can be understood as both innate potential and realized achievement.

The Marland Report (1972) provided the first federal definition of giftedness. In the report, giftedness was defined as the expression of specific abilities or aptitudes. Historically, in the U.S. public school system, gifted students are typically first nominated by their teacher—usually in the second or third grade (around ages seven to eight)—and then assessed using a group cognitive abilities test. The CogAT (Cognitive Ability Test) is the most widely administered *group* cognitive ability test. The top scorers of the test, generally scoring in the 95 percentile and above, are placed in gifted programming depending on the number of available spots. Gifted programming typically consists of a part-time, pull-out program for reading and/or math. Identified children may leave the traditional classroom for approximately an hour of enrichment activity once or twice a week. Some school districts offer self-contained gifted programs in which students receive full-time gifted instruction from a credentialed gifted education teacher. If available, self-contained programs are typically offered to those scoring in the 98th percentile or above.

Gifted identification often relies on the child's teacher and their ability to recognize the developmental traits and behaviors associated with giftedness. However, most teachers in the U.S. have not received training in identifying the characteristics, behaviors, and developmental patterns of gifted children. It is typically not part of the education and training of our teachers. As a result, countless gifted students—especially those who are highly–profoundly gifted—go unidentified and do not receive appropriate educational programming.

In addition to the lack of education and training, the U.S. does not have a federal mandate or provide funding for the identification of gifted children. No federal support has been provided for gifted programming for gifted students. The Jacob K. Javits Gifted and Talented Students Act of 1988 is the only federally funded program. This program is specifically designated to support diverse gifted populations and is dependent on annual appropriations by Congress. It also funds a National Research and Development Center for the Education of Gifted and Talented Children and Youth. In the U.S., each state—and often each school district—determines its own process for identifying gifted students, as well as the programming and support those students receive.

Profound giftedness is often associated with genius or unusual intelligence. People find it difficult to understand and take interest in these individuals unless they can personally relate to giftedness themselves. Rarely, programs for highly–profoundly gifted student exist in the U.S. public school system. However, they do exist. Whether the program addresses and fulfills the unique educational and developmental needs of the highly–profoundly gifted requires separate assessment.

The United States has several based organizations dedicated to supporting the educational and social-emotional needs of gifted children. These include the National Association for Gifted Children (NAGC) and its state affiliates, the National Association for the World Council for Gifted and Talented Children (WCGTC), Supporting Emotional Needs of the Gifted (SENG), the Davidson Institute, and the International Gifted Consortium, Research Center for Highly–Profoundly Gifted.

Among these, only two nonprofit organizations—the Davidson Institute and the International Gifted Consortium, Research Center for Highly–Profoundly Gifted—exist specifically to serve the unique needs of highly–profoundly gifted children and adolescents. Established in 2015, the IGC Research Center is the only known international research organization dedicated to advancing and disseminating research focused on better understanding, identifying, and supporting the distinctly different development (social, emotional, physical, cognitive, altruistic-moral) documented in highly–profoundly gifted children, adolescents, young adults, and families; and designing research-based educational programs to meet these distinctly different developmental and educational needs.

Public high school programs for highly–profoundly gifted students are rare. Instead, gifted students are often offered AP (advanced placement) courses, similar programs, or access to college-level courses—typically at the local community college. However, these offerings are not specifically designed to meet the unique educational needs of highly–profoundly gifted students. One public school exception, for middle and high school students, is the Davidson Academy for the profoundly gifted in Reno, Nevada. When provided with no other option, families move from all over the country for their children to attend this rare to find school. Private schools for gifted students exist throughout the country at a high tuition cost to the parents. Grade acceleration is not typical, but more likely accommodated through a private school. Schools—whether public or private— specifically designed to meet the educational and developmental needs of highly–profoundly gifted students are virtually non-existent.

IGC Education-Outreach and state gifted conferences provide training for parents, teachers, school administrators, counselors, and psychologists to address common misconceptions about giftedness. Without education or training, giftedness can be perceived as high academic achievement. Often gifted students are thought to be those students that are in all AP classes or who get all As. Gifted children can be expected to be good at everything. And, because some things do come easily for them, expectations can be unrealistically high. In general, most do not understand the unique social, emotional, physical, cognitive, and altruistic-moral characteristics, behaviors, and developmental patterns associated with giftedness. As a result, the greater-than-typical sensitivity, intensity, and awareness that accompany gifted development are frequently misunderstood.

It is a common myth that gifted children will be fine on their own. The reality is that highly–profoundly gifted individuals, like everyone else, need like-minded peers, mentors, and practitioners with whom they can genuinely connect. To support their unique educational and developmental needs, we must ensure appropriate, early, identification, positive social-environmental influence, and targeted support.

Germany

Andrea Brackmann, Dipl. Psych.

Until 15-20 years ago, gifted people were hardly known in Germany. Through parent associations such as the German Society for the Gifted Child (DGhK) and a study by the Marburg gifted project (2000), greater awareness of the needs of gifted children has been fostered among educators, psychologists, and the general public.

Socially, there are two different ideas in this country. Highly gifted individuals are often perceived in one of two extremes: either as child prodigies, geniuses, and high achievers, or as individuals who struggle with school, social, and emotional challenges. Neither does justice to the reality of gifted people. In the USA, gifted children have routinely been recommended by teachers for IQ tests and support measures, whereas in Germany, giftedness has often only been recognized when school or social problems emerged.

Overall, in the last two decades, there has been more and more literature on giftedness, counseling, and support measures. The assumption that overambitious parents have their children tested for giftedness remains stubbornly persistent, despite no evidence of this in my experience. Usually the opposite is the case, the parents try to slow down their inquisitive offspring so that they don't attract attention at school.

For a long time, in Germany, gifted adults did not appear in psychology or in the public eye at all. That began to change about 10 to 15 years ago, thanks to various publications and guidance from psychologists and coaches specializing in giftedness, including my first two books.

The phenomenon of highly or extremely gifted children (and adults) is still largely unknown in Germany. Some consultants and coaches mention the term "giftedness" on their websites, but it is often neither clearly defined nor grounded in scientific understanding. My book, *Extremely Gifted—The Personality Structure of the Highly Gifted and Geniuses*, is a first step towards raising greater awareness of the topic—much like Els's book *Slapende Leeuwen*. The prevailing belief is that giftedness is too difficult to measure and occurs too rarely to warrant research or broader attention.

We have no special programs for our most gifted. For gifted people in general, there are funding measures in various states, but they are not uniform, and they are not nationwide. Some schools in Hessen have a "seal of approval for gifted students." Gifted children are anchored in their school program. However, implementation in practice is often associated with obstacles for parents and children. Half of the classes at the Brecht School in Hamburg are filled with highly gifted students. Turbo classes or express train classes in high schools in Baden-Württemberg are a way to offer acceleration.

Since 2018, a project initiated by the Ministry of Education and Cultural Affairs has been in place to support the promotion of highly talented students. Approximately 300 schools in Germany participate. Over a ten-year period, various models are being tested to determine how best to support particularly high-performing students. It will take a long time before the results are available, and the uniform measures are implemented.

In Germany, it is often the parents who suggest special support for their children. In my psychological work with gifted individuals, personalized support measures—developed collaboratively with parents, teachers, and psychologists—have proven effective. These individualized accommodations may include early school enrollment, grade skipping, or participation in enrichment or pull-out programs such as the Ford-Förder-Projekt (FFP). Some parents of highly gifted children enroll them into boarding schools or private schools. However, these choices are limited, and attendance comes with a high cost.

Most gifted classes or schools are primarily geared towards high-performing students. The distinctive personality traits of gifted individuals—such as perfectionism, a strong sense of justice, heightened sensitivity, and a tendency to self-doubt—are only gradually gaining recognition. However, these characteristics and behaviors are only partially considered in pedagogy.

Chapter 12
Testimonials from Parents

Parents of Emma and Zoe

We quickly noticed that Emma was different from other children. It seemed as if the other children were behind in development. Every child develops differently, but we began to realize that those differences were great. Emma's interests were different and deeper. She was more articulate than the rest of the children at school. We noticed that she was a completely different child at school than at home.

We had Emma officially tested when she was almost 9. Emma's IQ score was assessed as highly–profoundly gifted. We had our doubts before. With our second daughter, Zoe it became clear much sooner because of our previous experiences with her sister. We knew what to look out for and the psychologist who tested Emma told us that the likelihood of Zoe also being gifted was very high.

If we look back and her development as a baby, there were, in retrospect, clear signs.

For example, despite being born prematurely, she slept very little and only in short intervals, showed advanced development in some areas, was constantly seeking stimulation and attention, and appeared exceptionally alert.

Zoe realized that she was different from other children. She had a very rich vocabulary that she only used at home. Unlike her sister, she needed a lot of sleep, but she was also a very alert baby. Despite her premature birth, she had no delays in development. For example, she intently focused on things at only a few weeks. She developed an interest in English very early and one of her first sentences was "I can't do that." Zoe has a very strong will. Also evident in our children:

- A great sense of justice from a very young age.
- Very intense behavior, needs a lot of attention, asks a lot of questions, talks a lot (even if they should be sleeping).
- A lot of sensitivity to stimuli.
- Very articulate at an early age. She had conversations with children and adults.
- Asynchronous development, especially with Emma, it was clearly noticeable.
- Fear of failure and perfectionism; if something doesn't work right away, they get angry, want to stop immediately, and cry. Sometimes they simply do not want to start something because they already know in advance that it is not going to be quite right or as they have it pictured in their head.

At school, no measures were taken. They didn't even notice that Emma was ahead. I first heard that she was significantly ahead in reading from a friend who volunteered as a reading parent at school. Eventually, by the end of the school year, her teacher mentioned it as well. I only heard from Emma herself, about two years later, that she was a lot further ahead in arithmetic. She told me she and another boy were the only ones who were ahead of the class in arithmetic exercises. We switched to home schooling after the first year. In the third year, I noticed that the regular subject matter was no longer sufficient, and I switched materials for extra challenge. However, this proved to be insufficient.

Zoe never went to school. I have tried to offer her as much challenge as possible at home, but I have noticed that the typical school curriculum never offers what Emma needs. So, I am always looking outside of the school curriculum for learning materials. Zoe indicated that the first year's course material was too easy, so I tried to differentiate as much as possible.

Over the years, we experienced many ups and downs with our children. Emma had not been feeling well for a long time. She has had frequent abdominal pain since the second kindergarten. This improved a lot through homeschooling, but there were still periods when she was bothered by it. This often indicated that there was a need for more challenges, but sometimes there were other causes. We noticed this during the Corona quarantine.

Emma has a lot of hobbies that she enjoys doing. However, during Corona the hobbies were dropped, and she no longer suffered from stomach pain.

It became clear to us that there was also a kind of "social stress" that played a role in her stomach pain complaints. Emma often feels lonely because she has difficulty connecting and children have no interest at all in the things that interest her. Socialization is very difficult for her, although she very much likes to be social.

We noticed that when we found the right challenge and her interest was aroused, she felt better, and we would see her eyes twinkle again. The biggest up for her was her visit to CERN. She radiates completely when she talks about it. It was at CERN that she realized what it felt like to turn her brain on; she was the only child among adults.

We have had a very difficult time with Zoe from the age of one and a half. She went through a "hellish toddler puberty," often hurting us when things didn't turn out the way she wanted, or when we didn't immediately understand what she wanted. In retrospect, it turned out that she experienced a lot of frustration because she couldn't express herself the way she wanted. For example, when she was angry, she wouldn't just say "I'm angry" she would say, "I'm really angry because you don't understand me." She has a very strong personality and an enormous will to get her way. We have long been concerned about her behavior which was sometimes extreme, but we can now say that it is much better.

If we could do it all over again, we would have taken Emma out of school more quickly. Knowing what we know now, we may have never sent her to school and instead opted for homeschooling from the beginning. That would have prevented many problems and damage. What I certainly would have liked to have done differently was not to hesitate and to get her tested or to at least have begun the conversations sooner.

For far too long, I thought that we were the only ones who saw that they were different, and I was afraid of being dismissed as "just another mommy who thinks her child is smarter than the rest."

On the other hand, maybe it was good that we hesitated for so long because Emma and Zoe do not like to show their potential and if we had taken the step earlier, they might not have wanted to show it during the test. At this point, she felt different and was unhappy, but she did not know why. During the test, she realized that she really enjoyed showing what she could do.

For Zoe, we would choose home schooling again. When Zoe was two and a half years, we went to a therapist, but in retrospect, I would never see a therapist who isn't experienced with giftedness. It is a big misconception that these children are all prodigies who fly smoothly through school material and that life happens without problems. People need to realize that these children have a different life. They experience everything so differently and just have a hard time with being different. Often, they would just like to be ordinary, like most people.

A completely different approach is needed for these children. Highly–profoundly children do not fit into our education system. When they are forced into a traditional system or try to fit in on their own, they often become very unhappy or develop psychological problems. In an ideal world, the education system would be completely different. Traditional exams are also not self-evident for these children.

Even though they know the subject matter, they sometimes get bad scores because the question does not match their way of thinking.

Schools must find the courage to deviate from the beaten path. There is too much adherence to coloring between the lines with the idea that every child should be able to do the same things at the same time. An automated school system does not meet the needs of these children.

Parents of Dan

Dan skipped many steps in his development. He never crawled but suddenly learned to walk at 11 months. He was certainly not the fastest in learning to speak. He could dial his grandmother's phone number at a very young age, which came in handy once when I suddenly became unwell in the bathroom. Although he couldn't convey who he was with words, my mother quickly understood who was on the phone.

He was very quick to understand in all areas. He understood everything you said, but he didn't talk. In the first kindergarten, he turned out to be a very social child. He waved to everyone and knew all the names of the older fellow villagers. "Hi Jenny! Everything good?" It was great when you went to pick him up from school.

As a small child, he could not tolerate certain items of clothing. For example, labels in clothes, buttons, or Velcro on shoes irritated him. "Mama, that hurts my head" he said when you opened the Velcro. At the age of seven, he choked on a lollipop. This incident apparently made a strange link with Dan. He didn't want to eat anymore, and Dan visibly lost weight. A visit to a child psychologist was necessary.

After a few sessions, we received the message: congratulations, your child is gifted. And that was that.

I have always been very open to Dan about this. The years that followed were full of ups and downs. At school, Dan achieved very good results, but every time the message came, "He can do better if he wants to." The school offered him extra work, however, this felt more like a punishment to Dan and so he adjusted and made sure that he was in the middle of the pack. He excelled only on themes that really fascinated him.

We were often told that Dan is not social. For us, however, he was extremely social, but only with people he had a connection with. He did not click with peers, and he was more likely to seek contact with older or very young children. Playing together with peers usually resulted in a fight. Dan came across as quite 'dominant' to them.

His hunger for knowledge was apparent early-on. And while some said I was crazy for already teaching my seven-year-old child, I am glad that I was always honest with him. What else do you do if your child has serious questions about life? No subject was taboo for us, and we spent several hours together while he took a bath, for example, talking about many subjects. His transition to the first high school was not too bad.

He had a great connection with a teacher who saw something in him. Looking back on that in retrospect, I think she made sure he kept it going for so long.

After school, he spent time with his teacher in nature. They walked the dogs, or the horses, and she was the one who taught him coping mechanisms.

Over the years, he also often struggled with physical problems such as reflux, stomach discomfort, or headaches. The last year he went to school he often developed panic attacks in the early morning before leaving for school. He also suffered from germaphobia. After several visits to the doctor, he was prescribed antidepressants, but after a few days, Dan himself made the decision that these were not the solution for him. After a few visits to a psychologist, who turned out not to really like him, I ended up with Els De Wit. Since then, we are much better.

Now, it is time to regain the bond he lost with society. Dan has taught himself tactics to protect himself, so as not to get hurt. He is a very sensitive "bird". He never learned that you have to work to achieve anything. He will therefore always choose the easiest way, afraid of failure. He is very much looking for what he wants. It's like we have a teenager times three in the house.

After his school days, Dan would work part time in a sandwich shop. There, it turned out that he has enormous flexibility. His extremely enthusiastic employer thought he did a fantastic job. Yet, at home, he won't even put his socks in the laundry basket. Dan knows exactly what is expected of him. However, he does not always "act" as he calls it. I believe that's why he likes to stay up late.

Parents of Finn

As a baby, our son was very alert. He could keep busy as long as there was enough variety and challenge. He had a rapid acquisition of language and quickly learned the different colors. We grew with him and subconsciously gave him the challenge he needed. We could not compare him with other children because he was our first child and the oldest in our family. He grew up as a very mischievous and funny boy who loved to read books and dress up. He amused himself for hours with role-playing games, animals, Legos, or Playmobil. He was very good at puzzles, and his vocabulary was enormous for his age. He had fun times in the nursery until he was two years old, when he was tired of it. Every day we gave him a backpack with toys from home that the other children were not ready for.

We regularly had to fight against claims from others that we were giving our child things that were too difficult for his age. As his parents, we felt he needed it.

He started in the entry class in January with a very sweet teacher. Our son loved going and was given plenty of new challenges and materials. The following school year he was with the same teacher, in the same class, where he was presented with the same materials, and the same themes. Soon he did not want to go to school anymore, it was "boring."

As a toddler, he found it difficult to say goodbye at the school gate. His teachers told us to keep the goodbye short, but he still cried heart-breakingly and wanted to go home. A few days a week I took him to school myself, the other days he was dropped off by the caretaker. In the latter case, everything went smoothly at the school gate, because he did not have the same relationship with his caretaker as with me, so the teachers thought it was me as a parent. In the end, it turned out that he found school very boring, and the schoolwork made little sense to him. This was seen by his teacher as laziness, but she was also shocked by his interests and his extensive knowledge about themes such as 'Egypt'. Yet it took a while before we came to giftedness.

We experienced many struggles with our son. We were always looking for new challenges, sports, music. He quickly tired of everything. He either thought it was boring, could not learn new things quickly enough, or the way of learning was too childish. We were regularly told that he was adapting to the middle of his class or group and that he only progressed when a different classmate set the example. Because of this, his teachers never got to see what he could really do.

The older he got, the more difficult it was to keep motivating him to start something or to stick with it. He quickly gave up on everything and hardly undertook anything new himself. It was the same with cycling and swimming. If he feared not being able to do something the first time, he preferred to avoid it altogether. He did not learn that you can only master some things by trying and practicing. He was eventually tested, and the result came as a big surprise to us.

The test was done privately because anything related to school was not a good experience. He was understood by the therapist and had pleasant chats. He did not feel pressured, but he did have clear signs of fear of failure. Explaining this to the school turned out to not be easy. There was little understanding; there was simply too little known about this subject. We had many conversations at school, but his teachers felt they wanted to see what he could do before moving on. This collided with our child's great frustration. He couldn't show what he could do, he adapted, and he didn't want to be different. He got extra work for a while when he was finished with the daily assignments.

But he soon found out that he was the only one to get extra work, so he adjusted his work rhythm to that of his classmates.

It is a pity that education does not have enough information about exceptional giftedness and hardly any tools to support gifted children. Every child is different and has different needs, but the lack of support took our son's confidence away. He didn't feel like anything anymore. He lost his playfulness and spontaneous way of life and thought a lot. Every evening, we sat together on the "big" bed and many big life questions came up. Fortunately, he was able to talk about his feelings and about what he was experiencing. Luckily, we have a strong bond with him, and he told us a lot about himself. He explained things in detail and gave his own opinion. He often pointed out to us that what you expect from a child, you have to do yourself to set a good example. Even now, he makes us think, he often offers us a different point of view. He frees us from entrenched patterns in society, even though he does not get the understanding that he deserves. His school career is still going through peaks and valleys. Depending on the teacher, he feels happy or not and he may or may not learn. He is difficult when working with others and must first understand the meaning of something before he wants to cooperate. No one really knows exactly what he needs. We tried many things in vain until he didn't want to try anymore. He has made it clear on several occasions that no one can help him, that we do not understand him. He often can't find the energy to try something new.

He was really looking forward to high school. It would be fun there; he would learn new things there. However, the disappointment soon came. And although he chose his own school and field of study, his disappointment was great when he realized that 'his' expectations were not being met. The learning process went without saying. He achieved good results with little effort, but he was unhappy in the class. He changed schools, back to his group of friends with whom he had graduated from primary school. This was a familiar environment, and it seemed as if we were back on track again. He blossomed, enjoyed the friendships, and his performance remained good. But this soon came to an end. Because of a new study choice, he had to change schools again, finding himself in a new environment with unfamiliar expectations and a new class without any of his friends. Once again, he encountered a lack of understanding from his teachers, high performance demands, and assignments he perceived as meaningless. We met with the school, but we were repeatedly confronted with the fact that the school had no knowledge or understanding of gifted young people. Over the years, we collected a lot of information as parents. We gave the schools tips and opportunities that we knew worked. But for schools this was unprecedented. They were afraid that the approach would be too different from the rest of the class. We were asked to seek extra help outside the school. We believe every student has the right to an adaptive education. It was apparent that they cared only for the students who performed less well, but what about our son who needed a challenge or for his learning to be accelerated? He went to school for one more term daily, even though it was clearly torture for him. He went to see his friends. His performance declined because studying was no longer automatic, and his fear of failure surfaced. He went to school less and less, found little energy, lack of understanding from teachers, and he eventually ended up completely at home, resting and doing nothing. At the time, that was what he needed. He is now homeschooling and is studying for his diploma through the examination committee. A good alternative when you are tired of school, but it is not easy to figure everything out yourself. As a parent, you make certain decisions in the best interest of your child, but even then, you encounter negative reactions from your environment.

As parents, we have looked for all possible solutions to make our son happy again. We did not always succeed in that, until you have no choice but to accept the situation as it is. At that moment, you learn to let go of your expectations. Our son was exhausted; he no longer had the energy. Therefore, we gave him the opportunity to rest, to press the pause button, and to climb up again under his own power, without expectations; to find himself again at his own pace. We are taking small steps forward, but we do see our son becoming himself again. As a parent, we are delighted to see our child happy again.

Listening to your child's needs and responding to them with confidence is the most beautiful gift you can give your child. Our journey had obstacles, and many more will follow, but what turns out to be the most difficult is going against the norms of the environment and society.

We went against the expectations imposed upon us as to which course you must follow to become successful. We instead took a side road as we found necessary, we are happy that we persisted. We hope our children realize that what you believe in can come true. Our children's happiness and well-being are our priority!

Fortunately, our son can see the end of the tunnel. He is gradually starting to see where he wants to go and which direction he wants to take in his professional life. At the same time, he would also like to help children and young people who are going through the same thing as him. We encouraged him to make this happen.

For years, we were on a quest for the right guidance, and we found this at Talentvol. Our children love to attend the Talentvol activities where they can develop into happy young people in their own way. Here they are not different, just themselves!

Parents of Amy, Lynn, and Lucas

We are a gifted family. The oldest is Amy. Our middle is Lynn, and the youngest is Lucas.

Physically, there were big differences between the kids. Amy walked at 18 months. Lynn and Lucas both walked around their first birthday. All three were talking and making sentences by two years. They knew all the colors before they were three and could count to 20 before they were three. They could recognize letters and make short words by their 4th birthday. When Lucas was three years old, he recognized many different car brands just by seeing the logo. Amy achieved all primary school reading skills by the time she was seven years.

All three kids have been depressed. Lucas's depression lasted for over a year. Our intensity as a family often causes misunderstanding, but not in our family. The best thing is how our children understand, support, and complement each other; and how they discuss, philosophize, and think about the world, society, their ideals, and their dreams.

How did we find out that our children were highly–profoundly gifted? Our middle child had many problems at school; she behaved completely differently at school than at home. We did not recognize our daughter in conversations with the school. She turned out to be a major underachiever. She was tested and we were told that she was highly–profoundly gifted. Our oldest was then tested. She is a people pleaser. Above all, she wants to be liked and do well. She did not want to stand out. Her giftedness was discovered from the test. The youngest has not been formally tested but based on what we have learned from our two oldest children, the many books we've read, the guidance we've received from Els, and our recognition of his intensity, we are confident that he is gifted.

For our children, dealing with being different is still a struggle. Especially now that the oldest is entering puberty. In kindergarten, when they realized that they were different, it was tough. But it is also nice and beautiful. Being able to empathize and empathize easily. Being open to other' views. Not always following the beaten path.

We try to explain giftedness to them by giving examples from our own experience and through books and videos. We explain how we experience things. We always communicate openly especially about feelings. This way, they can give their intensity a place in their lives.

We barely explain highly–profoundly giftedness to others. As parents, we feel that we are not understood.

In the beginning, there was often an immediate negative reaction. The prevailing view of giftedness is that you are very smart and do not have to do anything. We received comments such as "that's a luxury problem." We do mention that the children are gifted and if there is genuine interest, we will go into it further.

What do we think is necessary for highly–profoundly children to flourish? Recognition, peers, and most ideally, our dream, a different school system.

Parents of Axelle

Axelle raised her head after one week, rolled at five months, and crawled at eight months. She was a very alert baby who hardly took naps, and she still sleeps very little. She walked at 14 months and never fell. At three years, she was cycling without training wheels with no practice.

She smiled very early and interacted with us. At 9 months, she had very intelligible chats with only two words. She could already use complex words like library, baby, and she performed the emotion "angry" on command. At 15 months, she could use perfect sentences with correct pronunciation, including the letter "r." Very early on, she could use and understand complex humor.

She could do all the preschool skills such as knowing colors, numbers, and recognizing letters, at 18 months. She could draw a child, in detail, at four years. She mainly taught herself how to read in our mother tongue at three and a half years and she read English books at age seven. By the time she was three, she was already contemplating life and death questions.

There was no adjusted education for her, so she dealt with school fatigue and depressive symptoms. At school, she was a happy, normal child, but at home she became unmanageable and had many, many tantrums. She had and still has an incredible hunger for learning. She experienced underachievement and a fixed mindset. She was afraid to fail and showed extremely adaptive behavior.

At the age of two and a half, Axelle started school enthusiastically and came home the first day with asking when she was going to learn how to read and write. The class was very troublesome for her, so we decided to let her go half days. She adapted to the other children so much that she began to doubt things like colors and such and started drawing below her actual ability. Our daughter was looking for all sorts of excuses not to have to go to school. She even pretended that she was sick. Before we even stepped into the car, we had an angry, aggressive, and sad girl. Every single time.

The teacher saw a clever girl who still seemed young from a social and emotional point of view.

She started the first kindergarten class in another school. We requested that she be accelerated to the second year of kindergarten immediately, but during our school tour, the headmistress asked to show us while leaving Axelle with an unfamiliar teacher. She began to cry and clung to me, and based on that reaction, the director concluded that she was not yet emotionally ready for the second-year kindergarten, so the acceleration was denied. The first year was a complete disaster. Axelle had little connection with the teacher and an extreme fear of failure. We asked the teacher for additional tasks and expansion. We got the message that children had to play in kindergarten and do not have to do worksheets. As a result, Axelle did not play and withdrew in her own world. At the parent meeting, it was suggested that she might have autism. The teacher said that she would be surprised if she improved. We then decided to have an IQ-test done immediately. Axelle went only half days.

After the IQ-test we asked her to be accelerated, but we still had to wait until after the Christmas holidays. These weeks were hell. After the Christmas holidays, it was better for three weeks and again, Axelle was depressed, angry, and unhappy. According to the teacher, she made a lot of mistakes in her work, and she was way too slow. I insisted on giving her more difficult tasks, but they didn't. At the end of the year, they gave her assignments from a year up which she did flawlessly and quickly. We asked if our daughter could start primary school, since she could already read. She was allowed to go to first grade in the mornings and then back to kindergarten in the afternoons. Axelle did not like this, because she did not belong anywhere.

At the parent meeting in October, the teacher suggested that she be placed in the primary school full-time. This was still difficult because they did not adapt anything for her, which resulted in many psychosomatic complaints and absences. Second grade went okay, except that Axelle didn't want to read anymore and she hated times tables.

In third grade, there was no rapport between Axelle and the teacher. Axelle was not seen, and was underperforming severely, especially on tests, so the teacher did not see her abilities. We had a depressed child for a whole school year until corona came to rescue us. She no longer had to go to school and could follow her own pace. In fourth grade, everything was repeated until we decided to do a day at home and an extracurricular day program. It helped, but the stress remained high. We continued to have an unhappy, angry girl who developed tics and an extreme fear of failure. By the end of the year, we had to keep her at home. We had no other option but to start homeschooling her, hoping that Axelle would be happy again.

What I've learned throughout the years is that, by deepening your knowledge of the matter, you grow together as a family. You learn to convert negative energy into positive energy. You connect with your true self. We greatly enjoy Axelle's unique personality, her creativity, her ingenuity, her humor, and her energy. We provided challenging extracurricular hobbies, chosen by Axelle and we followed her interests as much as possible. This really helped her.

We found out quickly that Axelle was highly–profoundly gifted. The pediatrician found her early language exceptional. There is also a hereditary factor. Axelle's mom is gifted, and we have our suspicions about her dad. Giftedness occurs in both of our families.

We encounter misunderstandings and attempted misdiagnoses. A kindergarten teacher suggested that our daughter was "autistic" because she preferred to be on her own and withdrew into her own world. She called the other children in kindergarten "babies," and she felt out of place there. She adapted to the others. By accelerating her early, she found more connections among the group of children. It really helped that she was easily accepted by the class. The moment that the teacher acknowledged and accepted her differences, we slowly and quietly saw her blossom. However, Axelle still shows adaptive behavior and is still afraid to truly be herself in school.

When helping Axelle understand her differences, we explain she is a fast thinker and that she thinks differently. We also explain to her the characteristics that come with being gifted, besides thinking differently. We framed all this with some examples from her own life. Family spontaneously noticed that she was very ahead. We are scarce with explaining, unless someone asks or notices something. She skipped two grades, and we simply say that it was necessary for her development.

We do not feel understood as parents. The environment sees giftedness as a luxury problem with the idea that everything will work out on its own. At school they see no problems and we believe they think we are exaggerating or that we are the pushy parent-type, or that we are too occupied with her giftedness. When your child excels, you get jealous reactions from other parents.

Unconditional love is necessary for highly–profoundly gifted children to flourish. You need to be on the same team as them; they need to depend on you for support. Help them to dare to be their authentic self as much as possible. They need psychoeducation and sufficient challenge in all areas. You really need to find peers for your child! Make sure that you notice the pitfalls and obstacles and adjust accordingly.

Highly–profoundly gifted children are so much more than just their cognitive abilities—be mindful not to define your child solely by their giftedness!

Parents of Ava and William

What has always stayed with me is that our children were both able to speak very early and clearly (also for a stranger). They often used "difficult" words perfectly and in the right context. We occasionally received comments or glances about this. My memory sometimes fails me, but I am talking about 1 year or even earlier. They were both very alert from birth and very quickly followed our gaze. They also responded very quickly to us. They barely ever laid in the playpen; they were never content to do so. From the moment they got into the stroller, it was much better. Then they could see what was happening. Naps throughout the day were also quickly non-existent. They wanted to explore; it seemed as if sleeping was a waste of time for them. On the motor level, they were not ahead of their peers, quite the contrary.

William was rather lazy, he was "smart," but he didn't excessively show it. He did what was expected of him and that he did it well. Nothing more, nothing less. Sleeping has always been an issue. His head was always full. He couldn't get to sleep until midnight and often had nightmares. We were sometimes called to school to see if he was getting enough sleep. This lasted until he was about nine years old. Even now, he still does not sleep well.

Ava is very eager to learn. She was already giving herself homework at age four in preparation for the first grade. She watched her brother a lot and wanted to do "homework", just like him. I bought her workbooks so she could work after school if she wanted to. She taught herself the letters and could already read a little when she went to the first grade.

Our dinner conversations are about the universe, black holes, life (and death). Fascinating and nice. We don't know any better, but I don't think we're your average family. Nothing is ever just accepted, there is always an explanation or negotiation.

Our path has not been a smooth one. We encountered so many problems. I certainly do not want to come across as negative, but our path has been anything but easy.

We have had to figure everything out ourselves. The only difference today is that sometimes we get help from people who specialize in giftedness or who can be a sounding board. Unfortunately, we had to find these people ourselves.

Many schools are not open to giftedness simply because there is far too little knowledge about it. Or the wrong assumptions exist, such as a gifted child should always have 10/10 or they need no explanation. It both surprised and frustrated me that we, as parents, always had to take the initiative—teachers and school counselors never informed us, noticed anything, or offered additional challenges unless we explicitly asked. So, what I would like to say above all: keep your eyes open, listen to your instincts, and stand up for your child, even if you get strange looks. You know your child the best; follow your motherly instinct. I am not at all in favor of 'labelling', but I have experienced that unfortunately, it is sometimes necessary to be believed. That is why we, on our own initiative (and it is unfortunately quite expensive but necessary), had our children tested. I am convinced that this has opened some doors—though people still occasionally ask if he scored that high by accident, simply because our son is underperforming. It is still, unfortunately, seen as a luxury problem. If only they knew…

Fortunately, there are some schools that have come a long way and are really trying. The question is, is it enough?

And then there is the gossip, from other parents at the school gate when your child skips a year. I know I must be the bigger person, and I try to be, but I can't deny that it affects me. Besides, our children must feel it too. I really missed contact with parents, mothers who were in the same boat. In all those years, I have subsequently been able to meet a few parents with gifted children and that gives me so much validation. It feels so good that you can talk to another parent who truly understands—someone you don't have explain everything to, and with whom you exchange support and practical tips. All those little things make a world of difference. So often it was a lonely road.

I now try to be that parent for other parents, someone they can talk to. Seek like-minded people, it really makes a difference.

Skipping grades also extends to other domains such as hobbies. Your child is in a classroom with children who are older, and she (understandably) would like to follow dance class with these friends in the same year. So, you must also ask for an exception in dance class. Sometimes it is an issue, other times it isn't. And you have to advocate for your child yet again.

Just as extra effort is required of the teachers, it is also required of us, parents. We had to organize many trips to museums, libraries, cities to learn something. It was (and is) never boring! We have grown enormously as parents; I am the most grateful to my children for that. Your priorities shift. When I hear other people, I hardly ever judge because I realize I don't know the whole story. I would like to ask the same of other parents, be kind and do not immediately judge. It has changed me (for the better), as a mother and as a person.

I wanted to have a career, but I made the conscious decision to work 60% so that I was also available for our children, because they needed it. Even now, with adolescents, it is a privilege to be able to stand next to them as they become young adults. I wouldn't have wanted it any other way. And they are also so much more than gifted. It is easy to forget that they are also funny, beautiful on the inside, cuddly and sweet, children and adolescents.

As new parents, we had no idea they were gifted. I had a lot of experience with young children, in youth movement, as a babysitter, nieces and nephews; I was experienced, but I couldn't figure out the differences in my own children. The meltdowns, not wanting to sleep, seeming dissatisfied. For my husband, this all seemed "normal." It was only when our son was in the first grade that I followed my gut feeling and we went to have him tested. I recognized him in a book I had read on ADHD, autism, highly sensitive, but I couldn't place him anywhere. I had never thought about giftedness at all.

With our daughter, we were much quicker. We already had the knowledge and experience from our son. Neither my son nor my daughter showed problematic behavior so no misdiagnoses. Our daughter was very clever. We had her do the second and third kindergarten in one year and we had her tested at the beginning of primary school.

Only later, did we realize they were both highly–profoundly gifted. At first, it was just a number for us. The identification of giftedness was intense enough. It is a gift, but not always a blessing.

We already knew, as it has been researched over the years, that many very gifted children drop out of school or do not graduate. I am a bit afraid of the future, but you also adjust your thoughts. Every parent wants the best for their child and sometimes I do feel that our son is throwing away his talents. On the other hand, happiness is all that matters and that is what I wish for him!

As for the test results, our children were relaxed with the identification. It was "normal" for them. I don't think they've ever been bullied about it. They found the questions from others about it annoying. We have never communicated their IQ score because we did not consider it important. We have told them they are blessed with a beautiful mind and that is why they sometimes get bored in class. We assured them we will always seek solutions for them.

We explained their giftedness little to none to other people. Of course, we told the people were close to, such as grandparents, my sister, and my best friend, but that was it. And school of course. It's not that we're ashamed of it, but I don't want to deal with all the fuss, the questions, and the jealousy. I'm very much aware that they exist. When our daughter accelerated, we couldn't really "keep it a secret" because the classmates told their parents. People talked about it at the school gates; we live in a small village. The best reactions were those people who came to us to ask for an explanation. But overall, we handled it modestly. Now, I sometimes think too modestly. I never let our daughter write the year in which she was born in friends' books, only

"April 23" to keep a low profile. Now, I think that was bizarre, as if she shouldn't be who she was.

We were never really understood, certainly not in the first years. At the small school in our village, we were the difficult parents. We were the parents who thought their child was an "I-don't-know-what." We were not taken seriously, even after the testing. That's why we changed to a larger school in the area where they already had a little experience with gifted children. There, we were understood, and they really did their best, but it continues to be a challenge. Despite all the efforts, challenges, and projects, the fact remains that our children hardly moved beyond their comfort zone and therefore never really learned to learn. They didn't learn to fail or to persevere, which does not make it easy once they reach high school.

Personally, I think a major overhaul of traditional education is needed. But I don't know if it is even manageable. A change of mindset towards giftedness, education, and training for the people who interact with and teach gifted children is really necessary.

Highly–profoundly gifted children also learn very differently. This year, it became clear that the way things are presented in class does not engage William at all. Nothing is questioned. Just accepted and rehearsed. He gave up completely, and we have had great difficulty keeping him motivated. His average mark is six out of ten along with the occasional failed test. His behavior in class is often annoying, to the point of arrogance. I'm afraid of where this will lead.

Our daughter has had a hard time emotionally. She has little or no connection with the children in her class, which has made it very difficult for her to find her place in high school.

In high school too, we had to fight for an individual program which means that a lot of valuable time was lost. Fortunately, the school is willing to go along. There needs to be more awareness and acceptance. Only then can they respond to their needs.

Fortunately, there are now a few organizations that fight for our children. I try to pass on information nights or webinars, but often nothing is done with this. There are just as many children who drop out from the bottom who drop out from the top. I may sound a bit cynical, but despite all the efforts we as parents have done, I have the feeling that we have only half succeeded.

We are fed up with the endless talks about enrichment. Acceleration is often seen as "the last option" but sometimes it is just necessary. Several times, we did not dare to do so because we received little support.

Peers are also very important. Someone they can be completely themselves with and with whom they feel accepted.

William is lucky enough to have a group of friends where he feels good, although none of his friends are gifted. Ava has no "real" girlfriends, and that's a very sensitive thing. Especially in puberty. She is really looking for depth in her friendships while the conversations at school are mainly about make-up and boys. That is why I like Talentvol. At Talentvol, they meet others who recognize themselves in the things they experience. They don't feel so "different" anymore.

Parents of Joseph

> *"By the way, you don't want to have a highly advanced child, that leads to madness"*
>
> *"No need to worry, that's why your child is uncertain"*
>
> *"He will grow out of it; it's just a phase."*
>
> *"Just stop giving him books at home, then he won't be that way ahead in class"*
>
> *"All parents think that their child is much more intelligent than the rest"*

It's me, a mom of a nine-year-old very gifted boy and I hear it all the time.

Joseph was a very happy, playful, and extremely alert baby. At four months, he started to crawl, and the floodgates opened. Books, toys, blocks, pencils everything was interesting and getting bored was not in his vocabulary.

Joseph had rapid language development and loved to put it into practice. Singing, counting, the alphabet, colors, the solar system.... Joseph absorbed everything like a sponge, and I enjoyed the interaction. When I look back, I really don't know how many letters I wrote, countless, but everything had to be perfect. The letters, numbers, his tower of blocks, imperfection was not accepted.

At two and a half years, Joseph started pre-school. A bit of a difficult start because we were not used to living our lives separated from each other. But the teacher was lovely, the rest of the toddlers were nice so within a few weeks school was accepted, and Joseph enjoyed going. The third week, the teachers wanted to meet with us. Unsuspectingly, we went. The teacher was very nice, but she was struggling with what to do with him. He was not unpleasant in the class and worked with the other toddlers, but he lacked enthusiasm. The spark in his eyes came when he was sitting in the reading corner reading books to the other children. His pre-school career was shortened with the hope primary school would bring more challenge. Looking back on his pre-school time, Joseph had a great time. The teachers were amazing and always looked for challenges for him while also enjoying spending time with peers.

Elementary school was a struggle for Joseph from the beginning. "No exceptions, everybody has to do everything." Within no time, our happy son changed into a huddled bird. When reading, writing, and counting he had to start from the beginning. Joseph became more and more unsettled about school. Every morning, I brought a crying child to school. It broke me to see him suffer.

We consulted with the school and decided to change the strategy; Joseph started half days at school. In the afternoon, he went to an International School; an epiphany, Joseph loved it. The mornings were still a struggle, but he was looking forward to the afternoons. When I saw his enthusiasm and efforts, I knew that at least for the moment, we found a good solution. That's why we decided to switch to the International School; he was back on the bright side of life.

But you just can't change fate. The school changed the headmaster and made a lot of changes to the system. New rules are not always better. We had a lot of meetings and discussions, but the school had little understanding. We were perceived as frantic parents, and we were told that Joseph needed to adapt, but he became very frustrated. He lost his self-confidence, his humor, and he became fearful and suspicious. At six years old, for protection, Joseph built a wall around himself. When a teacher told him, he had a serious psychological disorder, that was the straw that broke the camel's back.

We quit school, and I started homeschooling. The first weeks were a journey, but gradually the puzzle pieces fell into place. We found a system that worked well for both of us, and he made significant progress. Even more important, I saw the glow in his eyes and the excitement for all the new things.

He went to a computer and chess club but that was only for two hours a week. His social skills lagged. We realized that contact with adults was not a problem, but that interacting with children his own age was more difficult. That's why we decided to start with school again.

He wasn't excited, but he started at a new school. And again, he tried to adapt to his classmates, but frustration grew day by day. He really struggled to meet the expectations. And we began meetings again with the teachers. How do you explain that at home he makes the most wonderful things, his humor and jokes are delightful, but at school he won't even solve the easiest math problems?

Once a month, Joseph goes to Shine, an extracurricular day program. A small group with highly advanced children. He looks forward to these sessions because he likes the topics, and he is getting more and more used to the other children.

Joseph feels that the other children think, behave, and act like him, and that's a safe feeling. "It's good to see that I'm not the only one who thinks out-of-the-box, "he stated after only a few sessions.

But how do you cope when the world overwhelms you? Children who have a keen imagination, interest, hunger for more, and perfectionism are labelled as strange, shy, and introverted. And they may perform poorly when being observed even though they are more than competent.

Highly advanced children are very bright and creative, but many suffer from low self-esteem. They are not neurotics as they have often been mislabeled. There is so much misunderstanding that we must deal with.

It will be an eternal quest, but it's worth it. We continue searching, looking, trying to find a way. I hope that one day our little, curious, happy, bright toddler, who talked to everybody because everything he knew was something "the whole world had to know," will lose his distrust of "the bad, dangerous world."

I always tell him: "You have to walk through the rain to reach the rainbow" and I believe this to be true.

Parents of Lauren

My husband and I noticed early on that Lauren was intelligent and that she was overexcitable (see Dabrowski). In her first months of life, we mainly noticed her irritability. She responded enormously to stimuli, mainly stimuli from the environment. Other mothers would walk around with their baby in a stroller until they would fall asleep. At one month, our baby would be clawing upwards out of the stroller. Finally at six months, she would sit in the stroller; she wanted to see the world. It was the same thing in the car seat; she would always cry until she could finally sit up. Finally, we had a quiet car ride because then she could see and absorb everything.

Before Lauren was one year old, we already noticed that she saw the world differently from other children. In kindergarten, she took toys in her hands and turned them over and over. She studied them. When we read books, her concentration and attention span were incredible; she was clearly absorbing everything. She wanted to interact and play before her peers did, but that often frightened other children. While at the same time, their unexpected reaction startled Lauren. She couldn't understand why other children would hit each other and she began to approach children more cautiously.

When Lauren started to talk, everything went fast. She thought so quickly that her words could not keep up with her train of thought. Lauren spoke remarkably fast. Her thoughts were always a few sentences away. Someone once told me I think in 1000 words; this certainly applies to Lauren.

At a young age, we took Lauren to a speech therapist who helped her to pronounce her words more clearly and to slow down a bit so others could understand her. This helped reduce the frustration Lauren was feeling. Lauren enjoyed these sessions because our speech therapist recognized and, more importantly, acknowledged her giftedness and did not hold back when using difficult terms.

In Belgium, most children start kindergarten at two and a half years, but I had Lauren start a little later. Some worried whether Lauren would lag the other children, but she already knew all the colors, including light and dark nuances and how to name her shapes perfectly. She also recognized her name in writing. If I read a page or a long poem, Lauren would know it almost by heart after reading it only twice. She could concentrate on something for a very long time for her age. She enjoyed working in workbooks for hours. Puzzles were easy for her. Counting and counting back to zero was no problem, just like the alphabet. I wasn't worried about her keeping up academically. I was worried because of her "hypersensitivity."

That is why we started school with half mornings. I knew there would be a lot of stimuli coming at her. This turned out to be the right choice; Lauren's behavior at school showed that she was overstimulated. Lauren was really looking forward to going to school, believing she was going to learn there, but it was a big disappointment. Lauren had a hard time with the busyness of school and the behavior of the other children. She became compulsive in her actions. The school did not understand her behaviors, and we received negative feedback.

When she came home from school, I had a child who worked in workbooks obsessively. She clearly needed this structure and peace after a busy and turbulent day at school. She grew exponentially; she taught herself to read and calculate, and her vocabulary was enormous. At bedtime, we did not read the usual bedtime stories. Instead, we went through an entire encyclopedia about dinosaurs, space or other. Latin words didn't hold her back. Her hunger for learning was and still is enormous. I can still remember her at 3.5 years old watching all kinds of videos about volcanoes on YouTube, in foreign languages.

Because it was clear to us that her school had neither knowledge nor understanding of giftedness and was not willing to make adaptations, we wanted to have her tested. Lauren said more often that she found school boring. We were still holding on to the idea of keeping her at this school.

At four and a half years old, we had an IQ test done and it turned out that Lauren was highly–profoundly gifted. During the test, it became clear how Lauren's motivation fluctuated.

The easier and simpler the task, the less likely she was to try. The more difficult the assignments became, the faster her train of thought went, and the faster she made connections.

She demonstrated that she was among other things, an associative thinker. We were advised to find a suitable school for her. At the same time, we contacted Els De Wit from Talentvol. I wanted to see if Lauren would gain more self-confidence by being with like-minded people and possibly experience more peace of mind. The support from the external care providers (speech therapist, occupational therapist, and psychologist) all recognized and acknowledged, separately from each other, Lauren's giftedness was an important aspect and advised us to take further steps.

When Lauren started at Talentvol, we noticed she began to recover. She could show us her authentic self. That was very important to us. Our child was looked at with understanding and that gave us peace of mind. Just like at home, at Talentvol, Lauren showed no compulsive behavior. Because she preferred these enrichment classes, we noticed that Lauren was more reluctant to go back to school. Most of the time, we dropped her off at school crying; and when we picked her up, she was crying or unhappy. It was clear that we could not continue like this. Ultimately, we made the decision to switch Lauren to a gifted school during her third year of kindergarten. This gave her the opportunity to get used to the new school before the first year would start.

Should we have made this choice earlier? I don't think we would have done it any differently. We have a highly sensitive child who is more intense than even the moderately gifted child. Ultimately, we have always held Lauren's health and well-being of paramount importance, and we fought for it (that's how it felt).

Lauren was welcomed to a warm nest at the new school. A kindergarten teacher looked at our child with understanding and love. Lauren could read there as usual. She no longer had to do boring assignments. She still had her fears, and the other children were very busy, but she was able to deal with it better here. When I picked her up, I had a happy child. For the first time, she hugged her teacher; that was a clear sign for us. Lauren had never done that before. But she still needed a challenge. When my husband was perusing English-language scientific articles for his work, she climbed onto his lap and started reading along.

When she went to first grade, our daughter continued to change. She rarely cried when she had to go to school, and she came out of school happy. Lauren was crazy about her teacher. The teacher saw that Lauren needed a lot more than she could offer. On the second school day of the first year, we were invited to a special pathway for highly–profoundly gifted children. We were told that Lauren would probably have to accelerate one or more times. A few weeks later, we were told that the teacher could no longer find a challenge for Lauren and that they would certainly accelerate her, but that their preference was first with Lauren's social and emotional well-being. They wanted to boost her confidence.

After the autumn break, the acceleration no longer worked for Lauren, and we saw her slip away. She didn't want to go to school again. We had a conversation with the school, and they decided to let her accelerate to second grade after the Christmas holidays. Her fears started to dominate again; we chose a hybrid transition. She took the second-grade subjects in the mornings and then she returned to the first grade to relax. There, she felt familiar and safe. She took courses in music, STEM, and foreign languages with her classmates and the teacher she loved. The school has worked great for her so far. She has had no problems with the acceleration.

Lauren seems to have an innate sense of languages. This was also noticed during the enrichment classes at Talentvol where she enjoyed English and Swedish lessons. Els De Wit from Talentvol offered us a mentorship in English lessons for Lauren. The idea was to further challenge her and to serve the purpose of meeting her hunger for learning. It was thought that if she mastered the language, she could learn much more on her own. We presented this to Lauren, and she was wildly enthusiastic. She immediately knew the possibilities this would offer her. She set herself a goal and envisioned following her favorite wildlife biologist. She remarked we wouldn't have to translate for her anymore.

Lauren now receives high-level English lessons on Saturdays. She is taught by Nadine Van den Eynden Morpeth, PhD. She is a Doctor of Arts and Philosophy. Classes focus on British English grammar and correct pronunciation. Lauren's mentor, Nadine does this well, with a lot of passion; she has understanding and love for both the profession and our child. Her enthusiasm is infectious. She treats Lauren as an adult, so they click well together.

At six years old, Lauren can already pronounce tongue twisters which her teacher's university students are still tripping over.

Lauren does not like it when she makes mistakes and she has very high expectations of herself. She really enjoys correcting her parents and grand-parents and showing them the correct spelling rules.

In those moments, she demonstrated her understanding of all the lessons. Her talent for language has not gone unnoticed at school either.

Lauren needs moments to release the tension. She finds these moments with her animals, in nature, making up stories, and drawing. Reading comics and books also allows her to let go of her thoughts for a while. Lauren can draw beautifully for her age. She has a brilliant eye for detail and drawing is a great outlet for her. When she is busy in her head, her drawings often become chaotic. Her thoughts fly back and forth, and her pencil follows across the paper. This is very therapeutic for her. The calmer she is, the more beautiful and realistic her drawings become. Lauren has an enormous imagination and likes to make up many stories. We have many storylines at home, all of which work around a specific theme (current affairs, inventions, jokes, etc.). Recently, Lauren also wrote her first book on the computer, written by a child for children.

The measures we have taken to arrange everything for Lauren have included:

- Hiring a psychologist to administer an IQ test to our daughter.
- Seeking external guidance through enrichment classes for exceptionally gifted children. (Talentvol by Els de Wit)
- Collaboration and follow-up with a psychiatrist who arranged for a medical certificate so that Lauren could calmly get used to her new school by allowing her to go half days.
- Switching to a school for gifted children.
- English lessons.

Whether all these measures will be sufficient, we assume not. In everything we see, Lauren is very mature for her age and therefore finds it more difficult to connect with even her (exceptionally) gifted peers. She thinks more like an adult and always carries a lot of responsibility. That makes it difficult for her to connect and to feel completely good with her peers.

Now, we see Lauren feels best with children who are older than her, for example she seems to do best with 12-13 years old or adults. When we went on a day trip with a gifted 13-year-old boy, they had in-depth conversations together on topics such as the universe and the Mesozoic era. All these measures have led to a better future for Lauren, and we will certainly have to take more measures in the future to guarantee her well-being.

Even though Lauren is only six years old, we have had ups and downs. The ups are her intense way of looking at life, how she enjoys the little things immensely, her personal growth, and her enormous developmental potential. The switch to a school that understands giftedness was worth it. To see Lauren so much happier makes us, as her parents, happier. I am grateful every day that we took these steps. We really enjoy her witty responses, her puns, and her quick, out-of-the-box way of thinking.

The downs have been the overstimulation when she first went to school. Also, her perfectionist and dissatisfaction with her results. Her frustrations with other children's thoughtlessness. Her fears of people she does not know. The downs have also included having to defend your child against teachers or other people due to their lack of knowledge and understanding of giftedness.

We will always try to frame everything for her; situations and learning environments. There are still so many misconceptions about giftedness and highly–profoundly gifted children. So much has already been written about this, but I would like to mention it again:

We (and I think I am speaking on behalf of many parents of gifted children) are not parents who want to boast. We are not patting ourselves on the back, "look how smart my child is." Let's be very honest; it would have been easier if they were "average" and could therefore keep up with the rest. But we are parents who want the best for our children. We want our children to be happy too. They have tremendous development potential which can only manifest itself under the right circumstances.

Gifted children often encounter problems in regular education, but this applies even more to highly–profoundly gifted children. I really think there is a need for schools designed for highly–profoundly children. The government should be committed to this group, however, that is often not seen. By now, it is outdated to say that these children can manage just because they are intelligent.

I think teachers should be taught about giftedness and the extremes of high-profound giftedness during their training. And they should be exposed to a lot more in-service and professional development training. Traditional schools should offer much more enrichment classes. We see this trend in the Netherlands, but not much in Belgium. And within a school, there should always be one or two teachers available with knowledge and understanding of giftedness and highly–profoundly gifted children. Gifted children need this understanding and guidance.

School administrators and counselors working with students and their parents should also receive more training on giftedness with the goal of providing better guidance and support. Equally important is the misunderstanding and misdiagnoses of these children. Due to the hyper-sensitivity of these very gifted children, they are often not seen as "normal" and are labeled with autism, ADHD, Asperger's syndrome, etc. But what's normal? Maybe we should get rid of this thought. I recommend Dabrowski's theory as educational material for experts, training courses, etc. More knowledge and understanding of the greater sensitivity must be viewed and placed in a completely different context.

Parents of Anna

After Anna did the first and second kindergarten in one school year, she ran into a lot of problems in the first year of elementary school as a five-year-old. The headmistress of her international school simply stated that she should adapt to the others and to the program. The depression beckoned and Anna didn't feel like playing anymore. She was completely tired of school and always wanted to spend hours in her own room after school. Our daughter was very angry that the other children were allowed to learn new things, and she wasn't. She thought that was so unrighteous.

The nightmares came back, and Anna used every trick in the book, including hiding the car keys in the play kitchen so she did not have to leave for school. Fortunately, her English teacher provided a ray of hope. She encouraged Anna to persevere and to learn at her own speed and level. However, we decided it couldn't go on and switched her to a Montessori school. There, she could at least learn at her own pace and work independently. Her teacher took care of her tailor-made enrichment, including book reviews and math at her level. We quickly noticed that Anna, among a class of first and second grade (Montessori 6-8), followed the content of the second grade with no problems at the age of five. Among other things, she was also allowed to work on times tables, which she explicitly asked for after discovering the concept of multiplication herself a few months earlier.

After the summer holidays, our six-year-old went to second grade, with the same teacher. The class added the third grade (Montessori 6-9). After the first month, it went downhill.

Anna suffered from her fixed mindset, desperately trying to conform to the way the other second-grade students worked. At one point, she even went back to reading letter-by-letter because that's what the other children did.

A lot of compulsory tasks had to be ticked off in terms of schoolwork that no longer matched her level. It became clear to us that the enrichment was no longer satisfying her need to learn; Anna had been on a learning diet for a while.

As parents, we began to scour all possible scientific literature to find answers. At the age of three, Anna was tested highly-profoundly gifted. We quickly connected the dots. The typical measures for gifted children were not enough. For years now, two to three years, Anna has been ahead of her peers with no real effort. If she really wants to learn something, age or speed limits do not apply.

Anna is like an express train; she is constantly on the move. The only way to sit her down is by giving her a book. It has been this way since she started walking at eight months. But even while reading, positions are changed every few minutes. She also demonstrates speed in her learning. Sometimes it appears that no content can be too difficult, too complex, or come to her quickly enough. Many school assignments are not complex enough. Preparing a talk about a Belgian king is an uphill struggle because of the differences between what she can say in school and all the questions she asks at home –from the Battle of Waterloo and the basis of tax suffrage to the First World War and the Spanish flu– it is enormous. This makes schoolwork very frustrating. Facts do not interest her at all, because facts alone make no sense to her.

She is like a young puppy, full of energy, zest for life, and eagerness to learn, but what is offered at school is -proverbially- only fish food. Perfect for large and small fish in the classroom, but the puppy wants more. She is hungry all the time. Of course, the puppy cannot show what is inside her if she only gets fish food.

At home, we provide as many learning moments and activities as possible so that the puppy feels good. The after-school agenda is packed. Every day there is one activity, and she still wants to add a few more.

Often, we go "down the rabbit hole" like Alice in Wonderland. You may remember that Alice encountered all kinds of objects along the way during her fall. We eat spaghetti Bolognese and Anna starts talking about a French religious cantique, by Saint-Jeanne, that she has been humming for days. We talk about the armies of Sainte Jeanne d'Arc, and she compares it to Alexander the Great's armies. The Hundred Years War and the invasion of the Germans in 14-18 are reviewed, as well as singing in authentic voice, for the cantique. We also talk about Julius Caesar all the way, and about the Roman emperors. At such moments, her hatch is open, and she makes more and more connections between the information that she encounters.

Anna needs little sleep and at home we say a hundred times a day that she should take it a bit easier, for our own peace of mind, and for the preservation of the parquet floor. In learning, we notice she is very intuitive and often only needs half the explanation. Often, she does not read the assignment and just starts, only to get stuck a few sentences later and then her fixed mindset takes over. She learns easily where she feels a clear connection with the teacher, who then helps her acquire a skill as autonomously as possible.

Her profoundly giftedness became even more evident during the first lockdown, when I had to homeschool her. The content of the second and third grade was totally inadequate and far too fragmented. When you start talking about fractions, she makes the link directly. During this time, it became clear to us how poor the lesson content was for highly–profoundly children and how much she had been craving learning at school.

Anna is often a chameleon when interacting with other children. She can read all social cues directly and knows exactly what is expected of her in terms of behavior, especially towards adults. If the adult expects to see a good girl, then she plays that part. However, when adults approach her with certain expectations, she immediately dismisses them as untrustworthy. These adults do not get to see her true nature. Whether it be a teacher or a neighbor, a hint of friendly politeness comes over her, a façade behind which she closes herself off. She immediately knows where and with whom she can be herself and where she cannot. Besides home, there are few to no places where she can truly be herself. School is certainly no longer that place.

It is difficult to deal with children who are not yet at the same point in terms of development, because the playing behavior is very different. For example, a girl from next door might come over to play for an hour, but she will never truly get to know Anna—because Anna won't reveal what she's thinking and feeling; their styles of play are just too different. This leaves Anna feeling angry and frustrated, her need for connection with a playmate is not met.

And that is where the problem lies, because an average ten-year-old has nothing to say about Roman gods. Meanwhile, Anna knows she will be alienated from the group if her true interests come up, so she stays silent and does her best to blend in. After a playdate like that, we're often left with a lot of frustration and anger—because Anna simply isn't interested in the things most ten-or eleven-year-olds care about. Children who are at her developmental level are better playmates. The spheres of interests are more similar.

Finding friends is not easy. Also, because she sets very high standards for friendship, and clearly expects the other party to do the same. If not, she prefers to talk about "acquaintances". It works better with other highly–profoundly children. She also does well with children on the autism spectrum, who regard friendship as an established fact.

Asynchronous development is a peculiar reality. For example, a four-week-old baby who pulls herself forward one meter to get closer to a toy. At six months laughing at slapstick humor. And at just eight months takes her first steps and 24 hours following uses the potty neatly and continues to do so consistently in the following months. The 20-month-old toddler who clearly tells you she doesn't want a diaper anymore at night and that she will not wet the bed. And then, remarkably, she keeps that promise for years to come. Asynchronous development is the child we take with us to Paris and who, at two years, points out all the monuments we pass by in the car, just like in her favorite children's book about Paris. The toddler who, sitting in her pram, a few months later finds that the Cathedral of Cirencester is very similar to the Notre-Dame of Paris. (And she was right, they are two Gothic cathedrals). The three-year-old who perfectly sings along to at least fifty songs in two languages and who can recognize and name all the letters of the alphabet, large and small. The four-year-old who taught herself to read. The five-year-old who devours books and learns English, so well that she can attend camps with peers while on vacation. The six-year-old who thinks that Homer has not thought carefully about the story of Achilles. The seven-year-old who knows a poem by heart after reading it twice, and can repeat it in Dutch, French, English, German, and Mandarin.

But the speed of her brain collides with her body, which causes frustration when drawing because it is not perfect. Or, in cycling, because practicing is far too dangerous, like swimming, because you can drown. However, when she was ready, the day before her sixth birthday, Anna suddenly learned to ride a bicycle. Swimming followed by six and a half, after many hours of private lessons. Other children generally think much less about it. She has a very clear sense of danger and will never take irresponsible risks. As a toddler, she never climbed on chairs and tables. We only had to explain the dangers of sockets and cables once. With an asynchronous six-year-old in the house, you have conversations about the battle of Waterloo and Brexit at the table, but you still must help with knotting pajamas.

Anna is evaluated well below her actual level of thinking when it comes to school. For her, there is no fun in experiencing the result of her "effort". How would you react if someone congratulated you for brushing your teeth? And let ownership be exactly what every student needs to make the learning process run smoothly, namely, to learn the pleasure and satisfaction of learning something new and to master it well afterwards.

In the classroom, the pride of being able to successfully complete a difficult problem is denied to a highly–profoundly child such as Anna.

Anna does not find a suitable learning environment at school, even after acceleration, content breadth, and enrichment. School was a tough ordeal for years: the eternal talks with teachers, staff, and board members, the label "pushing parent" that soon falls into your hands, the disbelief about progress because Anna does not trust the teachers and therefore does not always show what she is really capable of.

The overwhelming feeling of "being different" and to think beyond the field of understanding for the average teacher sometimes frightens her. In Anna's experience, you should not be yourself, because the teacher of the third kindergarten does not want the children to read themselves; she does not think that is normal. As a result, our four-year-old hid to the teacher that she could read for the entire school year.

After the first lockdown, we reluctantly took a different approach, after seeing how our daughter blossom during that period. After allowing Anna to process the period of school trauma, homeschooling brought for the first time the necessary peace and challenges for everyone in the family. The first lockdown came at just the right time. It turned out to be a transition period, in which Anna completed the third year of elementary school.

Homeschooling is only possible because we can count on a team of people where Anna can completely be herself.

As parents, we share the responsibility of many subjects, and the grand-parents help according to their areas of interest. The piano teacher and the supervisors of external classes for highly-profoundly gifted children help to ensure emotional and mental well-being. External teachers broaden Anna's horizons. Her well-filled program includes not only primary school subjects that she completes at a rapid pace, but also native French, English, German and Mandarin, piano and choirs, ancient history, cooking, botany, swimming, athletics, and theater lessons in English. There is also plenty of playing and romping around, and the carefreeness typical of childhood has returned.

There are of course also challenges, because learning something remains a tough one for a girl who rarely allows herself to "learn." She expects herself to master everything immediately. That works very often, and for Mandarin or French grammar, say, the novelties are acquired immediately, but when learning a new piece of music on the piano—although Anna tries to do so—this is not always possible. If Anna has to think about something, she assumes she does not know it, because she has to think about it for a while and so—in her eyes—she has not yet fully acquired it. She also regularly throws in the towel when she has to think about calculations. Because she is so sensitive, this often goes together with an eruption, and the pages sometimes fly around. Hugs and reassurances always help here.

In homeschooling, we have started the fourth grade, but we also work independently of the structure imposed by the grades. We try to find the zone of proximal development (as cited by Vygotsky), with assignments that she is not yet able to solve completely independently.

Anna will take her primary school exams. Afterwards, we look forward to a year (or two) in which she can choose what she wants to learn. The idea of a " gap year " speaks to her mind, and she has a long list of learning interests including Arabic, patisserie, hieroglyphs, reading archeology, going to archeology camp, and helping in an animal shelter; something is added every week!

Resources

GiftedConsortium.org

The International Gifted Consortium (IGC), Research Center for Highly–Profoundly Gifted is a 501c3 not-for-profit organization dedicated to collaboratively better understanding, identifying, and supporting the unique social, emotional, physical, cognitive, and altruistic development of giftedness through the eyes of the highly–profoundly gifted. The IGC accomplishes its mission through: Open-Access Research, Education-Outreach, Professional Development, and Research-Based Educational Programs designed to meet the distinctly different educational and developmental needs of highly–profoundly gifted children, adolescents, young adults, and families.

Talentvol.be

Serving highly–profoundly gifted children, teenagers, their parents and the environment.

Echa-site.eu

The European Council for High Ability (ECHA) aims to advance the study and development of potential excellence in people. The major goal of ECHA is to act as a communications network to promote the exchange of information among people interested in high ability—educators, researchers, psychologists, parents, and the highly able themselves.

Globaltalentmentoring.org

Global Talent Mentoring fosters excellence and innovation in science, technology, engineering, mathematics, and medical sciences worldwide for exceptionally talented youth through evidence-based, long-term online mentoring.

Etsn.eu/category/youth-summit/

At these meetings, the participants can establish life-long friendships and international contacts, and their work in an international environment as well as opportunities to familiarize with other cultures and education systems is often an asset for their future career. In addition to meeting their peers, they also get acquainted with iconic figures of international talent support.

Davidsongifted.org

Our mission is to recognize the nation's profoundly gifted youth and support them holistically so they may reach their highest potential.

Sengifted.org

SENG is a nonprofit network of people who guide gifted, talented, and twice-exceptional individuals to reach their goals intellectually, physically, emotionally, socially, and spiritually.

About the Authors

Doehee Ahn, Chung-Ang University

Dr. Doehee Ahn is a Professor, Department of Education, School of Education, Chung-Ang University, Seoul, Korea. She has received her Ph.D. in educational psychology at the University of Alberta, Canada. She was the Director of the Reasearch Institute of Korean Education at the Chung-Ang University, and the Editor-in-Chief of the Korean Journal of Gifted/Talented Education, and Korean Education Inquiry. She has more than 100 scholary articles published and presented at national and international conferences on motivation, positive psychology, and gifted education. She is currently on the Editorial boards of many education journals in Korea. Her research interests are on motivation, academic engagement, positive psychology, and developmental patterns of gifted.

Andrea Brackmann, Dipl. Psych

Andrea Brackmann, Dipl. Psych, is a licensed clinical psychologist and cognitive behavioral therapist, who has worked with gifted and talented children, adolescents and adults for two decades in Frankfurt/Main in Germany. In her practice she provided evaluations and therapy and offered child and parent groups and consultations for school personnel and other professionals. She is a member of the *Deutsche Gesellschaft für das hochbegabte Kind* (DGhK). Within the last fifteen years she published some of the most known books in the German-speaking region about emotional and social needs, personality traits and multifaceted inner world of gifted children and adults, most recently *Extrem begabt—Die Persönlichkeitsstruktur von Höchstbegabten und Genies*. She raised a gifted son and lives in Jena.

Seokhee Cho, St John's University

Dr. Seokhee Cho is a Professor, Department of Administrative and Instructional Leadership, School of Education, St. John's University, New York. She has received her Ph.D. in educational psychology at the University of Alberta, Canada. She was a Fulbright senior researcher at the University of Connecticut in 1996. She is currently the Director of the Center for Creativity and Gifted Education. She has been the Principal Investigator of Project HOPE, Project TEAMS-New York, and Project BRIDGE funded by the Jacob K. Javits Gifted and Talented Students Education Program of the US Department of Education since 2009. These projects share common goals of recognizing under-represented gifted/talented students, challenging them with high expectation, and providing them with differentiated instruction. She has more than 200 scholarly articles published and books on gifted education and creativity in STEM field. She serves on the Editorial Boards of seven education journals including *Gifted Child Quarterly*. Her research interest lies in nurturing and evaluating creativity in STEM, nurturing talent of under-represented gifted students including English learners, and family processes.

Juah Kim, National Research Center for Gifted and Talented Education (NRCGTE)

Dr. Juah Kim is a Research Fellow, National Research Center for Gifted and Talented Education (NRCGTE), Korean Educational Development Institute. She has received her Ph.D. in Curriculum Studies at Ewha Womans University, South Korea. She served as the Director of the National Research Center for Gifted and Talented Education which is designated by the Ministry of Education from 2016 to 2020. She had been the Principal Investigator of Korea Gifted Education Longitudinal Study, Policy Research on Amendment of Gifted Education Promotion Act and the Corresponding Enforcement Decree and Formulating the 4th Master Plan for Promotion of Gifted and Talented Education funded by MOE. She has more than 90 scholarly articles published and government policy reports on Gifted Education and National Curriculum Framework. Her research interest lies in Longitudinal Studies in Gifted Education, Differentiated Curriculum and Instruction, and Educational Policy.

Hyeseong Lee, Lewis University
(https://orcid.org/0000-0002-7137-8874)

Hyeseong Lee is an assistant professor of Elementary Education at Lewis University. She earned her M.A and Ph.D. in Gifted, Creative, and Talented Studies at Teachers College, Columbia University and Purdue University, respectively. Her research interests include topics related to talent development, young, gifted learners, underserved population in gifted education, and teacher education. Prior to her current position in higher education, she worked as an elementary and preschool teacher both in South Korea and the United States.

Min Jung Lee, Old Dominion University
(https://orcid.org/0000-0002-5488-7626)

Min Jung Lee is a postdoctoral fellow at Old Dominion University. She received her B.S. in chemistry in South Korea and M.S. and Ph.D. in Science Education from Teachers College, Columbia University. Her research interests include formal and informal STEM education and teacher education, specific to their knowledge, belief, and self-efficacy. She is also a certified chemistry teacher in both the United States and South Korea.

Roland S. Persson, Jonkoping University
Roland S Persson, PhD, MFA, FCollT, is professor of Educational Psychology at Jonkoping University, Sweden. A former Western classical pianist and music educator now a research psychologist his research focusses high achievement (talent), giftedness and the macro-social dynamics as well as the sociobiological foundations of human ability. He is Fellow of the College of Teachers, London, England and is affiliated with the International Centre for Innovation in Education (ICIE) in Ulm, Germany. Dr Persson is currently assigned to the Human Resource Progamme in the field of Psychology in the School

of Education and Communication and is a member of its Lifelong Learning Research Group.

Contact: roland.persson@ju.se

Peter Visser, University of Antwerp
https://orcid.org/0000-0002-5488-7626)

Dr. Peter Visser is philosopher, assistant didactics of philosophy, and researcher at the University of Antwerp. He is the coordinator of primary schools at VEFO vzw (https://www.filosofieonderwijs.be/) and teacher and coordinator of Kangaroo project for groups of '(highly– profoundly) gifted': foreign language course—CoPI at AV Edegem https://www.andreasvesalius.net/onze-school

Els De Wit, Talentvol

Els De Wit is the founder of Talentvol, an organization that supports highly–profoundly gifted children starting from toddler age. She is a contributor and a member of the Research Team at the International Gifted Consortium (IGC), Research Center for Highly–Profoundly Gifted. She is a co-author of the international study on the prevalence of overexcitabilities in 88 highly–profoundly gifted children and the author of the book *"Slapende Leeuwen"*, the first Dutch-language book about highly–profoundly gifted children. Els holds a master's degree in Multilingual Communication and has taught in higher secondary education for many years, where she was also involved in gifted education. She has completed a training program in Philosophy with children and adolescents. Talentvol operates across all of Flanders, providing highly–profoundly gifted children with what they need most: a space where they can truly be themselves. The organization offers individual programs, group programs, information sessions, and counseling.

www.Talentvol.be | info@Talentvol.be

Vanessa R. Wood, Psy.D., Clinical Psychology; M.A., Gifted Education

Dr. Vanessa Reineke Wood is Co-Founder and President, The International Gifted Consortium (IGC), Research Center for Highly–Profoundly Gifted and Principal Consultant of Gifted Assessment, Identification, and Development (Gifted AID). Dr. Reineke Wood is the co-principal investigator and corresponding author of the 2024 published study, Prevalence of Emotional, Intellectual, Imaginational, Psychomotor, and Sensual Overexcitabilities in Highly and Profoundly Gifted Children and Adolescents: A Mixed-Methods Study of Development and Developmental Potential. She is also the corresponding author of the 2020 publication, How Can We Better Understand, Identify, and Support Highly Gifted and Profoundly Gifted Students? A Literature Review of the Psychological Development of Highly–Profoundly Gifted Individuals and Overexcitabilities. Dr. Reineke Wood designed programs to fit the educational and developmental needs of highly–profoundly gifted children and adolescents. She is the host of the IGC podcast, Room with a View and she trains parents, teachers, administrators, counselors, and psychologists on the behaviors, development, and developmental potential of highly–profoundly gifted students. Dr. Reineke Wood collaborates with stakeholders and leaders across the globe and across disciplines to better understand, identify, and support the distinct social, emotional, physical, cognitive, and altruistic development of giftedness, highly–profoundly gifted individuals, and families through IGC Open-Access Research, Education-Outreach, Professional Development, and Research-Based Educational Programs. VanessaWood@GiftedConsortium.org GiftedConsortium.org

www.ingramcontent.com/pod-product-compliance
Lightning Source LLC
Chambersburg PA
CBHW070746011225
36114CB00007B/16

* 9 7 8 1 9 5 3 3 6 0 4 7 2 *